Media and Political Engagement

One of the most difficult problems facing Western democracy today is the decline in citizens' political engagement. There are many elements that contribute to this, including fundamental socio-cultural changes. This book summarizes these contexts and situates itself within them, while focusing on the media's key role in shaping the character of civic engagement. In particular, it examines the new interactive electronic media in terms of their civic potential. Looking at the evolution of the media landscape, the book interrogates key notions such as citizenship, public sphere, agency, identity, deliberation, and practice and offers a multidimensional analytic framework called "civic cultures." This framework is then applied to several settings, including television, popular culture, journalism, the EU, and global activism, to illuminate the role of the media in deflecting and enhancing political engagement, as well as in contributing to new forms of political involvement and new understandings of what constitutes the political.

Peter Dahlgren is Professor of Media and Communication Studies at Lund University, Sweden. He has also taught at Stockholm University, as well as at Queens College and Fordham University in New York City, and has been a visiting scholar at several other universities. He is the author of many articles and author or editor of several books, including *Television and the Public Sphere* (1995) and *Young Citizens and New Media: Learning for Democratic Participation* (2007)

COMMUNICATION, SOCIETY AND POLITICS

Editors

W. Lance Bennett, *University of Washington*
Robert M. Entman, *The George Washington University*

Editorial Advisory Board

Scott Althaus, *University of Illinois at Urbana-Champaign*
Larry M. Bartels, *Princeton University*
Jay G. Blumler, *Emeritus, University of Leeds*
Daniel Dayan, *Centre National de la Recherche Scientifique, Paris*
Doris A. Graber, *University of Illinois at Chicago*
Regina Lawrence, *Louisiana State University*
Paolo Mancini, *Universita di Perugia*
Pippa Norris, *Kennedy School of Government, Harvard University*
Barbara Pfetsch, *Wissenschaftszentrum Berlin für Sozialforschung*
Philip Schlesinger, *University of Stirling*
Gadi Wolfsfeld, *Hebrew University of Jerusalem*

Politics and relations among individuals in societies across the world are being transformed by new technologies for targeting individuals and sophisticated methods for shaping personalized messages. The new technologies challenge boundaries of many kinds – between news, information, entertainment, and advertising; between media, with the arrival of the World Wide Web; and even between nations. *Communication, Society and Politics* probes the political and social impacts of these new communication systems in national, comparative, and global perspectives.

Titles in the series

C. Edwin Baker, *Media, Markets, and Democracy*
C. Edwin Baker, *Media Concentration and Democracy: Why Ownership Matters*
W. Lance Bennett and Robert M. Entman, eds., *Mediated Politics: Communication in the Future of Democracy*

Continued after the Index

Media and Political Engagement

CITIZENS, COMMUNICATION, AND DEMOCRACY

Peter Dahlgren
Lund University

CAMBRIDGE
UNIVERSITY PRESS

CAMBRIDGE UNIVERSITY PRESS

Cambridge, New York, Melbourne, Madrid, Cape Town, Singapore, São Paulo, Delhi

Cambridge University Press

32 Avenue of the Americas, New York, NY 10013-2473, USA

www.cambridge.org

Information on this title: www.cambridge.org/9780521527897

First published 2009

Printed in the United States of America

A catalog record for this publication is available from the British Library.

Library of Congress Cataloging in Publication Data

Dahlgren, Peter, 1946–
Media and political engagement : citizens, communication, and democracy / Peter Dahlgren.
p. cm.
Includes bibliographical references.
ISBN 978-0-521-82101-8 (hardback) – ISBN 978-0-521-52789-7 (pbk.)
1. Political participation. 2. Democracy. 3. Mass media – Political aspects.
4. Digital media – Political aspects. 5. Online social networks – Political aspects. I. Title.

JF799.D25 2009
323′.042–dc22   2008012059

ISBN 978-0-521-82101-8 hardback
ISBN 978-0-521-52789-7 paperback

Contents

Preface

I feel privileged to have access to so many generous and inspiring colleagues, and to be able to encounter them in different contexts; this book has received lots of assistance along the way for which I wish to express my gratitude. Some of this help has been in collective settings for which it becomes impossible to name all names, but my appreciation is in no way diminished.

My institutional home base, Media and Communication Studies at Lund University in Sweden, is a small but highly dynamic unit headed by Gunilla Jarlbro, where the atmosphere of collegial support and solidarity is really terrific. I am grateful to our doctoral students for the climate of constructive critique that they help generate, as well as for specific feedback on texts I have put forward.

Two recent experiences as a visiting scholar were particularly rewarding in the writing of the book. First, I want to express my thanks to l'Institute Français de Presse, at l'Université de Paris II, headed by Josiane Jouet. Secondly, the manuscript was finished while I was in the visiting scholars program in Communication and Culture at the Annenberg School for Communication, University of Pennsylvania, organized by Barbie Zelizer; access to that intellectual environment was a tremendous asset, for which I am very grateful.

I was fortunate to participate in the network program "Changing Media, Changing Europe," financed by the European Science Foundation, which afforded many fine opportunities for discussions central to the themes of this book.

Participation in the Euricom colloquia in Piran, hosted by Slavko Splichal, has offered inspiration in a splendid setting.

The European Network for Doctoral Studies in Communication and Media, which has recently become the Young Scholars Network within

the new European Communication Research and Education Association (ECREA), has in its various guises over the past years offered lively
summer encounters. I am most appreciative to the past and present
coordinators and participants of these gatherings.

The institutional exchange program between Lund University and,
first, l'Ecole des Hautes Etudes en Sciences Sociales, and then l'Univér-
sité de Paris III, funded by the Swedish Foundation for International
Cooperation in Research and Higher Education (STINT), has helped
put me in touch with French colleagues and with an environment that
has helped to expand my horizons.

The recently completed research project on Young Citizens and New
Media was funded by the LearnIT research school (part of the Knowledge Foundation of Sweden) in Sweden, under the direction of Roger
Säljö. This funding has greatly facilitated my work. My research associate
in that project, Tobias Olsson, and I have been shuttling ideas and texts
back and forth to the point that it becomes very difficult to specify which
ideas derive from whom; he deserves much thanks. I am currently
involved in an EU sixth frame project, CIVICWEB, headed by David
Buckingham, that offers a new and rewarding context.

I have also benefited from feedback in various forms from the following
colleagues: Maria Bakardjieva, Elizabeth Bird, Kees Brants, Bart Cammaerts,
Nico Carpentier, Daniel Cefaï, Stephen Coleman, John Corner, Nick Coul-
dry, Lincoln Dahlberg, Daniel Dayan, Kristian Feigelsen, Beatrice Fleury,
Jostein Gripsrud, Micheal Gurevitch, Joke Hermes, Klaus Bruhn Jensen,
Sonia Livingstone, Brian Loader, Denis McQuail, Fredrik Miegel, Lars
Nord, Louis Quéré, Phillip Schlesinger, Eugenia Siapera, Katarina Sjöberg,
Jesper Strömbäck, Jacques Walter, Janet Wasko, and Lennart Weibull.

It was W. Lance Bennett, one of this series' editors at Cambridge
University Press, who originally proposed that I write this book. I have
benefited greatly from his encouragement and support.

Karin, Max, and Finn confirm to me that the civic domain is not the
only one for meaningful engagement.

Thank you all; the book's inadequacies are of course all my own
invention.

I gratefully acknowledge the permission to use materials in this book
that have been previously published in different forms (English language
first publications), as follows:

> "Civic identity and net activism: The frame of radical democ-
> racy." In Lincoln Dahlberg and Eugenia Siapera, eds. *Radical*

Democracy and the Internet. London: Palgrave MacMillan, pp. 55–72, 2007.

"Doing citizenship: The cultural origins of civic agency in the public sphere." *European Journal of Cultural Studies* 9(3): 267–286, 2006.

"Internet, public spheres and political communication: Dispersion and deliberation." *Political Communication* 22(2): 147–162, 2005.

"Television, public spheres, and civic cultures." In Janet Wasko, ed. *A Companion to Television.* London: Blackwell, pp. 411–432, 2005.

"The public sphere: Linking the media and civic cultures." In Mihai Coman and Eric Rothebuhler, eds. *Media Anthropology.* London: Sage, pp. 218–327, 2005.

"Political communication in a changing world" (with Michael Gurevitch). In James Curran and Michael Gurevitch, eds. *Mass Media and Society* 4th ed. London: Edward Arnold, pp. 375–393, 2005.

"Theory, boundaries, and political communication: The uses of disparity." *European Journal of Communication* 19(1): 7–19, 2004.

"Reconfiguring civic culture in the new media milieu." In John Corner and Dick Pels, eds. *Media and the Restyling of Politics: Consumerism, Celebrity and Cynicism.* London: Sage, pp. 151–170, 2003.

"In search of the talkative public: Media, deliberative democracy and civic culture." *Javnost/The Public* 9(3): 5–26, 2002.

"Media, citizens and civic culture." In M. Gurevitch and J. Curran, eds. *Mass Media and Society* 3rd ed. London: Edward Arnold, pp. 310–328, 2000.

Introduction

H istory not only has its ups and downs, it also has a capacity to surprise us as to when an "up" or a "down" is coming – scientific prognoses and futurology notwithstanding. Thus, in our recent past, the collapse of the communist regimes of the Soviet Union and Eastern Europe took most observers more or less by surprise. In the Western democracies, following the fall of the Wall, the self-assuredness about the political system was running high; "We won!" was a widespread sentiment. It may therefore seem a bit ironic that only a few short years later, in the early and mid-1990s, there was a growing international awareness that not only is the transition to democracy – in Eastern Europe and elsewhere – a difficult process, but also that the established Western democracies had hit upon disturbing times.

Today, scholars, journalists, politicians, and citizens are asking themselves if and how the democratic quality of their societies can be maintained and enhanced, and in what ways our democratic deficits can be addressed. A core theme in this regard is the question of political engagement: Without a minimal level of involvement from its citizens, democracy loses legitimacy and may cease to function in a genuine way. The decline in citizens' participation in the life of democracy has been continuing over several decades, and the patterns are most pronounced among the young. Often linked to this theme are the character and role of the media in society, both newer, interactive information and communication technologies (ICTs) as well as the mass media. Drawing on extensive literature from several areas, this book addresses political engagement and disengagement – and the media's role in this regard – as situated within the tension between the ideals and present realities of democracy.

PROTEAN DEMOCRACY

Democracy emerges, at best, unevenly across the world, through political struggles; it rarely comes as a gift to the people from the powerful circles. In the effort to develop democracy, different societies have had different circumstances and histories, and even varying conceptions about its ideals. Even among the actually existing Western democracies one finds various models at work: Political traditions and the mechanisms shaping political communication can vary significantly (Hallin and Mancini, 2004). Moreover, democracy is continually at risk from antidemocratic forces, some of which even use the processes of democracy itself to further their cause, as we see in the recent growth of extreme right-wing, racist parties in Europe. And in the struggling democracies, the formal appearances may well conceal deeply undemocratic mechanisms and practices: The health of any particular democracy cannot be assumed simply because, for example, elections are being held.

Adding to the complexity is that within political theory there are competing versions of democracy with corresponding notions about to what extent citizens can and should be engaged in politics, and what this engagement should look like. Such theoretical horizons are of course tied up with even more fundamental normative conceptions and assumptions about people and society. Thus, while the emblem of democracy is often rhetorically invoked as an ideal in order to unite, inspire, and mobilize, government "of, by, and for the people" can be given rather different slants and applied in various ways.

Democracy embodies a necessary and irreducible utopian impulse and can be seen as our summary term for "the good society," remaining always a work "in progress." It follows that any view that suggests that the ultimate arrangements have now been achieved – and are suitable for all societies in all circumstances – risks reducing the vision to a form of what might be termed "democratism" – that is, a rigid ideological construct that can obstruct critical reflection, discussion, and intervention.

THE MEDIA CONNECTION

The media are a prerequisite – though by no means a guarantee – for shaping the democratic character of society; they are the bearers of democracy's political communication beyond face-to-face settings. During the modern era, their role in making politics (and society) visible, in providing information, analysis, forums for debate, and a shared democratic culture, is beyond dispute. The modern world would be unrecognizable without them. Today they are ubiquitous and continue to expand. In Western democracies they have been both praised and vehemently criticized, but however we judge them, the media are an integral part of our contemporary reality, a major historical force.

Many factors shape late modern democracy, and we would be foolish to lapse into media-centrism and reduce everything simply to the workings of the media. How we think about public issues, for example, is not simply a mirror of mediated political communication, but the result of an array of variables. Moreover, the media – both the traditional mass media and the newer ICTs – do not function as a unified societal force but are a complex set of institutions, diverse in the way that they operate and in the representations and communicative opportunities that they provide. They are shaped by internal organizational, economic, and technical features as well as by external societal conditions. And increasingly, their present turbulent situation means that their character and their role in democracy are in transition. Thus, to understand the present circumstances, we have to situate both democracy and the media in the context of larger historical changes.

While the media are important factors of change in the contemporary dynamics of democracy, they also help maintain continuity, providing stability via their established ways of covering politics, the collective frames of reference they foster, and the rather ritualistic elements that characterize their modes of representation. The two positions are not mutually exclusive, and both premises inform this book. In part, it is a question of time frame: From day to day we tend to recognize the stable, recurring features of society. As we increase the temporal span of our perspective, however, the changes come more clearly into view. Not least we come to see how rapidly the media themselves are evolving today – a development that inexorably impacts on political communication specifically, and democracy more generally.

USEFUL THEORIES

This book has its roots in the field of media and communication studies, a sprawling and fragmented area of inquiry – but a very exciting one. This heterogeneous character was apparently more problematic in previous decades than it is now. We have learned our postmodern scientific lessons, we are a bit more at ease with epistemological ambivalence, more tolerant of intellectual difference, and perhaps more appreciative of pluralism. In terms of theory, the field is permeable, resulting in a productive "free flow" across its borders. It is useful to keep in mind Denis McQuail's formulation that theory is not just formal propositions, but also comprises "any systematic set of ideas that can help make sense of a phenomenon, guide action or predict a consequence" (McQuail, 2000:7). Such a view highlights theory's function as the intellectual scaffolding for the research we do. It serves to orient us, to pull together sets of facts and assumptions, and it offers normative dispositions. It helps to provide significance to that which we observe, and to suggest the implications of various types of actions or interventions.

Media theory and the allies that it mobilizes have an obligation to help us better understand not just the institutions of the media or the processes of communication, even if these are central, but also the fundamental features and processes of the modern world (which, I would underscore, are increasingly known to us via the media). This world – our societies, our cultures – is not only in rapid transformation, but also in many ways in a profound malaise, a reality that theory cannot ignore. Thus, useful theories, while they can make no a priori truth claims and must remain dialogically open, should strive to articulate empirical social reality with notions of better possible alternatives. It is thus imperative that in the theories we use we can find helpful normative guides that can prompt question-asking and inspire research that might help reduce our collective distress.

DEMOCRACY AND THE MEDIA: THREE TRADITIONS

While I draw generally in this book from various currents in social theory and media theory, not least with constructionist influences, my attempts to deal with the array of problems that cluster around the key notions of democracy and the media derive largely from three specific traditions. I have not tried, nor would I propose, a synthesis of them. Rather, I have used them in different ways, aware of the contributions and problems of each; they come into play clearly, especially in the framework of civic cultures that I develop in Chapter 5. This trilogy consists of political communication, public sphere theory, and culturalist theory.

Political communication derives from its mother discipline of political science, and much of the research work done still reflects this heritage. Research in political communication has traditionally focused on the communicative interaction between the formal actors within the political communication system: political institutions/actors, the media, and citizens. One problem here is the assumption that politics is played out largely in the interaction between these institutionalized actors, thus ignoring other domains and forms of politics. Also, this tradition, in highlighting citizens' opinions and knowledge of politics, builds for the most part upon a transmission view of communication, ignoring both how meaning is culturally constructed and the subjective aspects of citizenship. This tradition has evoked criticisms over the years for being too formalistic, too bound to the prevailing political/ institutional arrangements, too state-centered, too wedded to narrow methodologies – and too nonresponsive toward its critics. I tend to agree, yet this horizon is indispensable for my purposes, since it addresses the important realm of formal, democratic politics from a media and communications angle. Political communication has since its inception also had the theme of nonparticipation as a part of its research agenda.

The public sphere tradition that derives from Habermas includes a range of interests and approaches that take up not only the public sphere, but also related themes such as communicative rationality, deliberative democracy, and civil society. Habermas's (1989) early work on the public sphere was influenced by the critical theory of the Frankfurt School and emphatically asserts the norms of democracy in the face of the historical and social forces that threaten it. Adding his later work on communicative rationality (Habermas, 1984, 1987) opens the door to emphasizing the deliberative, procedural character of communication in the public sphere. The public sphere tradition often looks critically at institutional arrangements, especially in the media, as well as constellations of power and patterns of communication that can support or hinder democracy. While this tradition resonates well with the critical political economy of the media, it often seem oddly removed from everyday sociological realities. Its strength lies in its historical, analytical, and not least normative scope, yet this might be more productively balanced by a greater attention to the socio-cultural circumstances of citizens.

A third tradition builds on various currents within late modern cultural theory; to label it a "cultural studies" approach may seem convenient but is not necessarily illuminating, given the heterogeneity of that field (see Dahlgren, 1997). I thus settle for "culturalist." First it must be said that there is not as yet that much work amassed in this tradition explicitly concerning politics in the traditional sense, though "the political" is often a topic of concern. What the culturalist approach offers is perspectives on such key themes as meaning, identity, and practices – highlighting the idea of sense-making agents. This can be mobilized in conceptualizing citizenship, as well as in analyzing and assessing features of political communication. The culturalist orientation, for its part, can turn our attention to topics such as the subjective realities of citizenship, their processes of sense making in concrete settings, and how these may impact on participation and the modes of engagement. However, it tends not to address the structural, institutional dynamics of democracy and political communication, and certainly the political science approach is strongest in this regard.

We have to accept and appreciate the differences between these traditions. Each can do things the others cannot, and while they together in a sense manifest a division of labor, each has its own coherence and its limitations. Democracy has entered a disturbing era, and we need open, probing theoretical constructs to guide research as well as to provide a critical stance. These three traditions offer different inflections of key concepts such as politics, citizenship, deliberation, and even democracy itself. While respecting their divergent character, we will still make better progress if we see them all as potential resources to engage with, juxtapose, and compare, rather than doggedly defend one against the others. Traces of each appear throughout this book, most obviously in Chapter 5, where I discuss civic cultures, a framework that builds on elements from all three.

THE CHAPTERS AHEAD

I begin this book in Chapter 1 with an overview of the factors contributing to the contemporary difficulties of democracy, emphasizing the specific problems of declines in political participation. There are many reasons why citizens choose not to engage in politics; while no doubt some have to do with personal character, our sociological understanding is deepened by looking at changes in the political economic structures and dynamics of late modern society, as well as key socio-cultural transformations. In other words, the character of democracy is changing because its basic preconditions are in evolution. In the era of neoliberal global capitalism, the traditional tensions between market logics and democratic principles become more acute. The governments of nation-states have less maneuverability; real societal power drifts increasingly to the private corporate sector and thereby resides beyond democratic accountability. Also, economist modes of rationality permeate many sectors of society, undercutting democratic values and procedures. The formal political arena has in turn become constricted, offering fewer opportunities for meaningful participation, and thereby engendering disengagement.

At the socio-cultural levels, such long-term trends as the loosening of shared cultural frameworks, the weakening of traditional institutions of socialization, the ongoing processes of individualization, and the growth of network modes of social relations have contributed to further alter the conditions of democracy. These developments usher in new frames of references and life horizons, in which the traditional forms of political organization and mobilization hold less appeal. At the same time, we see new forms of political participation arising, in the extra-parliamentarian domain. The newer ITCs figure prominently here, and, as I take up in Chapters 7 and 8, they are contributing to a reconfiguration of political life – though it is still unclear if this will be sufficient to reconstruct democracy. If nothing else, however, these developments signal altered modes of participation and newer notions of what constitutes politics and the political.

A key feature of the socio-cultural evolutions is found in the developments within the media landscape, the theme of Chapter 2. The massive growth in media outlets; the policies of deregulation and the intensifying of conglomerate structures in the media industries; and the increasing globalization of media organizations, practices, and flows are all part of these developments. Not least, digitalization of the media generally, and the Internet revolution in all its ongoing permutations, signals profound alterations for the circumstances of democracy and participation. Journalism as traditionally understood has reached a historical turning point, while even the access to news does not in itself promote participation. This is because many citizens perceive as too remote the possibility of making some meaningful political connection to the prevailing forms of democracy. Concurrently, organized politics itself is undergoing change via the influx of new actors and new strategies of political communication, for example, as manifested by the doctors of spin. In the wake of all of these changes, we see realignments taking place between the major actors of political and economic elites, citizens, and the media, further reconfiguring the terrain of late modern democracy.

With Chapter 3, I enter into a more detailed discussion about democracy from the standpoint of citizenship and civic agency. I conceptually probe the notion of citizenship, underscoring that this has become an arena for new theoretical developments. The notion of achieved citizens, something beyond the received, formal status, is an important opening, and leads us forward to the idea of citizenship as a form of social enactment, that is, as civic agency. I suggest some of civic identity is a precondition for such agency, and I look to the traditions of republicanism and civil society and public spheres to see how we might formulate civic agency as something that has its grounding in everyday horizons. Civic identities emerge through doing, through experiences in both the public and private spheres of life.

Further, in Chapter 4, I delve into the concepts of engagement and participation, underscoring that engagement, as subjective involvement, can be seen as a prerequisite, a starting point, for participation. Participation, in turn, usually takes communicative forms. Further, to understand engagement and participation at the level of identity and agency, we must usher in the affective dimension and admit that politics requires passion, in the sense of intense involvement, even if liberal democratic theory tends to cling to visions of pure rationality. Passion does not exclude rationality but works in tandem with it; it is neither a threat nor a guarantee for making the right political decisions, only a necessary ingredient for engagement.

In looking at the forms of democratic participation normally encouraged, I argue we should take a very broad view. Voting is but one, albeit crucial, mode. There are many others, and many of them make use of a variety of communication skills. Today, deliberation is at times heralded as the fundamental way for citizens to participate in democracy. I suggest that deliberation, in its formal guise, is very suited to specific situations, notably when decisions are about to be made. However, its excessive emphasis on rationality and its problematic assumptions about equal footing in regard to social power and communicative competence put limits on its utility as a model for general civic participation. I propose instead that we treat civic talk in a broader manner, allowing for how political topics may even unexpectedly emerge in everyday conversations, and how initially private topics can move to the public, political realm. Through performative civic practices the nonpolitical can become proto-political, which in turn can develop into the political. The political, in turn, can develop into formal politics.

In Chapter 5, I pull together many of these analytic threads to develop a framework to help analyze and understand civic identities: They require the support of larger, pluralistic civic cultures to flourish. I model civic cultures as comprising six dimensions: knowledge, values, trust, spaces, practices/skills, and identities. Civic cultures, to be viable and serve as resources for participation, must have taken for granted anchoring in everyday life, in the life-world. They are shaped by many social factors, including power relations, economics, schooling, and not least the media. The model is normative in the sense that it suggests that these features need be present for participation to emerge – and for democracy to function. At the same time, each of the dimensions offers a starting point for empirical investigations.

Chapter 6 takes up television and popular culture, which are compelling sites of engagement. With the help of the civic cultures framework, I examine how television's media logics, especially visuals, invite engagement through pleasure, and how this has from the start set up a force-field within television news. While television news has obvious limitations in terms of contributing to a public sphere in Habermas' terms, I suggest that we need to look beyond these strict parameters. Television, through its popular programming, offers many opportunities for audiences to "work through" a vast array of issues in regard to basic values and social visions in many areas. While popular television can hardly be described as a source for progressive social inspiration, and ideological boundaries are seldom clearly ruptured, across time one can see important shifts in popular perceptions taking place. Its significance for politics should therefore not be dismissed.

This line of reasoning leads us into the broader debates regarding politics and popular culture, and I find compelling the arguments that see a porous boundary between these domains. Popular culture offers spaces where other kinds of knowledge can arise and take on political relevance, as well as opportunities to develop trust and versions of civic identities. It invites us to engage in many issues, sometimes very explicitly formulated, at other times in more diffuse ways, often making them personally meaningful. While popular culture adds to the symbolic terrain of politics, it of course cannot simply replace the more established arenas. Yet, a grasp of its important relevance for politics is central for how we make sense of contemporary democracy.

The final two chapters take up the Internet in broad terms, beginning with the debates around its significance for politics. Chapter 7 explores various attributes of the Internet and their potential for facilitating civic agency. While there is much that speaks in favor of the net's positive role in this regard, the media logics of the net also suggest that we retain some reservations: The Internet does not offer a speedy technological cure to the ills of democracy. At the same time, it has contributed dramatically to how political communication gets done, as well as to the ways in which participation can take place. The civic affordances the net makes available are altering traditional party politics, but most impressively they have expanded the potential for alternative forms of political participation. The ever-developing, inexpensive, and easy-to-use tools, together with the network character of the social relations it engenders, open up a new chapter in the history of democracy. The net represents the emergence of a nonmarket, peer-produced alternative to corporate mass media, yet it remains unclear as to what extent its potential can be developed. There are a number of issues and reservations we need to keep in mind, but at present, the net remains an exciting democratic utility.

The final chapter, 8, charts some of the uses and implications of the Internet in three illustrative contexts: journalism, EU NGOs, and the alter-globalization movement. I indicate the importance of these developments for the various dimensions of civic cultures, while at the same time keeping an eye on realistic limits. In each of the three cases, the Internet must be understood within a larger interplay of media, institutional, social, and cultural factors that impact on the character of democracy. The Internet is unquestionably an invigorating asset for political participation, even if it cannot alter the basic factors that currently plague democracy. Analytically, the Internet, and the media generally, not only play a decisive role in shaping participation, but also, from the perspective of civic cultures, offer empirical starting points for illuminating the civic dynamics of democracy.

A NOTE ON TERMINOLOGY

In writing about democracy, I am for the most part referring to Western democracies – and their problems – though I try to situate them in larger, global contexts; most of my references are to the United States and the UK.

The turbulent evolution of the media landscape results in some conceptual issues. The traditional mass media have increasingly gone online, and there is a growing use of interactive technologies between audiences and mass media formats. Thus, the distinction between mass and interactive media is becoming less tenable. Yet it can still be of use in making some general distinctions within media, and I generally adhere to it, with modifications where appropriate: The nonpolitical can become proto-political, moving on to the political and formal politics, through performative civic practices.

Also, I use the terms "Internet," "net," "Web," and "cyberspace" in a manner that is largely interchangeable, which is admittedly imprecise. My discussion is angled such that the technical aspects per se are subordinate to the social and cultural aspects of ICT usage, and therefore I treat these terms as synonyms for stylistic reasons.

CHAPTER 1

Democracy in Difficult Times

D emocracy, in whatever concrete version it manifests itself, is an incredibly complex undertaking that requires many conditions to be met for it to function properly. These conditions include, among other things, a functioning legal system, as well as a judiciary that operates in an optimal balance of power with the legislature and executive branches. There must also be genuine efforts to move toward universalism in the treatment of citizens and their rights. Further, democracy also has social and cultural requirements as well, as I shall discuss in the chapters ahead.

It is, however, the engagement of citizens that gives democracy its legitimacy as well as its vitality, as something propelled by conscious human intentionality, not just habit or ritual. However, for most people most of the time in the West, while the commitment to the principles of democracy remains solid, the realities of how it operates do not successfully beckon enough people to join in. The long-term trends in the Western democracies show declines in voter turnouts, party loyalties, and trust in government (for a recent contribution on the United States situation, see Zukin, Keefer, Andoliona, Jenkins, and Della Carpini, 2006). Even involvement in civil society organizations is declining, as Putnam (2000) reminds us, while Skopcol (2004) sees civic life in the United States increasingly dominated by professionally driven, foundation-funded advocacy groups with paid employees and mailing lists rather than memberships. People increasingly do not feel inspired by what the politicians propose that society collectively could and should be. Likewise, citizens do not embody a sense of popular efficacy that they can, via democracy's institutions and mechanisms, impact on societal development. At best, one can hope for a solid turnout at election time. Certainly in the West today we can find some obvious exceptions to this trend (for example, the unusually politicized atmosphere in the United States in recent years), yet the decline in civic engagement remains a fundamental problem for contemporary democracy.

ELUSIVE ENGAGEMENT

Some observers might wish to see political engagement approach the levels and intensities that characterize popular involvement with, say, sports or various fan subcultures; others claim that sustained intensities of that magnitude would generate dangerous political instabilities. Over the past century there has been an ongoing discussion that has pitted the ideals of citizenship against its realities – with citizens, especially younger ones, consistently being berated for their lack of civic responsibility, inadequate levels of political knowledge, and unwillingness to get involved in current affairs. Low levels of participation are nothing new and have been chronic throughout much of democracy's modern history. In the United States, from the Progressive Era forward, when the ideal of the well-informed citizen emerged (see Schudson, 1998), writers have lamented citizens' tendencies to pursue the trivial over the serious in the media, to focus on personal interests at the expense of community concerns, and to approach political questions in a less-than-rational manner.

No doubt the most famous of analysts in the early part of the twentieth century in this regard were John Dewey (1923) and Walter Lippmann (1922). In their respective positions and in the debates between them, Dewey is usually seen as the civic optimist, and Lippman the elitist and pessimist. Yet even Dewy was troubled by what he perceived as inadequate civic participation. Since then, many factors have been used to explain the low involvement, and we will take up some of them in the first section. To argue that democracy needs to be expanded with more and deeper engagement on the part of citizens (as this book does) is to take a normative position that must be tempered by caution: Enthusiasm for the democratic imaginary can too easily deflect sociological realism. Clearly there is not much chance that a vast majority of people of a Western liberal democracy will become "active citizens," or even well-informed citizens (see, for example, Delli Carpini and Keeter, 1996, on the levels of political knowledge among U.S. citizens), short of an (unlikely) revolutionary situation.

Thus, my own view operates in a force field between, on the one hand, normatively arguing that democracy and its citizens would be well-served by an increase in participation and, on the other hand, understanding sociologically that there will always be less than we might hope for. Yet, as I argue in the chapters ahead, circumstances are by no means locked; the present remains, as always, in a transitory state. There are certainly varying and often competing analyses about democracy's present situation (cf. Dahl, 1998; Mouffe, 2000; Rosanvallon, 2006; Tilly, 2007, for just a sample of the different voices). Diagnoses about the media likewise can go in different directions. The course I steer through these topics is that democracy most certainly has a future, but that this future – getting out of the present difficulties – lies in finding new ways to embody and express democratic values and principles, rather than trying to reconstruct circumstances that have become historically eclipsed. Many of the social, cultural, political, and technological conditions for democracy are in transition, and we have to incorporate these realities into our understanding of what democracy can and should be.

The next section provides an orienting overview of some major themes in regard to democracy's contemporary difficulties, largely from systemic and political economic horizons. The section that follows highlights important socio-cultural changes in late modernity that alter the preconditions for traditional liberal democracy. I conclude the chapter with a short discussion on two current trajectories of the rejuvenation of civic participation, one more encouraging than the other.

STRUCTURAL SNAPSHOTS

DISENGAGEMENT FOR GOOD AND BAD REASONS

At bottom, democracy is for and about its citizens, and therefore requires some minimal level of civic input to function, even if the specifics of this minimum cannot be identified with any great precision. "Democracy" is not a panacea for all human problems, but it offers the most compelling principle for legitimacy – "the consent of the people" – as the basis of political order (Held, 2006:ix). In some elite models of democracy, the fact that most people are not politically engaged can even be seen as a sign of health: Politics in this view is mostly for the politicians. We as citizens vote them in to take care of political matters; we vote them out if we do not like the job they are doing. It is when things are not working as smoothly as they should that larger citizen involvement manifests itself. This reflects a very clear "division of labor" view: Political representatives represent their voters not only because direct popular democracy is unwieldy in our large and complex societies, but also precisely because most people seemingly prefer not to be bothered. Politicians are to take care of political matters, much like plumbers take care of faucets and pipes.

Other models of democracy and citizenship are explicitly predicated on civic engagement. An emphasis on civic engagement and participation is not to be necessarily equated with a model of "direct" or "participatory" democracy, but is central to democracy even in its pervasive representational form. In some versions of the direct democracy model, citizens are to be involved in face-to-face contexts for important decision-making, thereby bypassing the institutions of representative democracy. Such conceptions of democracy may retain relevance for very small-scale settings and organizations of nongovernmental character (e.g., neighborhood associations and civil society associations). They are of course hopelessly romantic and out of synch with the realities of large-scale governance in modern societies. Rather, we have to accept that democracy is to a great extent representative, and clearly so in most governmental contexts; thus, in representative democracy, participation to a large extent must go via elected officials and other institutional mechanisms.

Within representative democracy, however, there is plenty of room for expanded engagement, in regard to elections as well as other settings. This can involve such traditional activities as working with – and against – parties and elected officials by mobilizing around specific issues, supporting proposed legislation, letter-writing, canvassing, and so forth. Along with the act of voting, such engagement signals citizens' political views to their representatives. While this takes us quite far, it does not go far enough, since it ignores the key role that extra-parliamentary initiatives from informal or "new" politics play in maintaining democracy's vitality. Beyond the structures of established political parties lies an extensive political terrain comprising movements, civil society organizations, networks, and activist groups engaged in particular themes or with specific issues.

Often such extra-parliamentarian activity is geared to influencing political decisions and legislation within the established political structures, but there are also efforts toward extending and deepening democracy beyond these arenas. Formal citizenship per se has not always led to equality of resources and opportunities for all groups of citizens: Various mechanisms of social and political exclusion are still very operative – and are also being challenged on many fronts. Moreover, there are many initiatives aimed at democratizing the state itself – making its various bureaucracies and branches more open, more accountable to citizens. Similar efforts are targeting institutions within the economic sector, at work places, and other major institutions, such as social services, schools, and universities.

Despite all the admonishments to participate, we must acknowledge, however, that from the standpoint of citizens themselves there can be many good reasons to not do so. The lack of citizen participation should not be seen simply as a failure of civic virtue, to be rectified by promotional appeals to moral uplift. Rather, it needs to be understood in terms of both social structural features and the landscapes of everyday life, with their psychological and cultural dimensions. Social structures and everyday parameters are of course related; they become intricately interwoven into the fabric of people's daily lives and their personal horizons.

People's feelings of powerlessness, or cynicism about how politics works, are among the oft-cited reasons. Citizens simply feel that the mechanisms of democracy do not allow for their view to have much impact (see, for example, the results of the extensive British study, Power to the People, published in 2006: www.powerinquiry.org/report/index.php). A good deal of nonengagement can be explained by the undemocratic features of modern society: "Inequalities of class, sex, and race substantially hinder the extent to which it can be legitimately claimed that individuals are 'free and equal' " (Held, 2006:210). Thus, specific social, economic, political, and cultural factors that impact on the resources of particular groups can be barriers to democratic participation.

These factors can generate a sense of personal powerlessness and despair over one's life circumstances, or perhaps a bitterness of having been abandoned or betrayed by the political elites. To feel, for example, that the power elite continuously turn a deaf ear to one's efforts to intervene tends to undercut participation in the long run. Such feelings are not ungrounded: In both the established and emerging democracies, the dangers of ruling oligarchies and entrenched power interests are ever-present. Thus, the vision of democracy represents a threat to those whose hegemony is based on anything other than the legitimate consent of the governed (Rancier, 2007). Resistance to its genuine implementation on the part of those who would lose power, privilege, and/or economic benefit will always be with us.

Basic everyday economic realities in their more drastic forms can inhibit democratic participation in direct and material ways. Bennett

(1998) has examined studies of the American work force and concludes that a good deal of the political disinterest we observe today can be attributed to the profoundly stressful circumstances under which large segments of the population live. The major transformations to globalized, post-Fordist economies wreak much havoc on personal, family, social, and civic life (see also Brennan, 2003). This has to do not least with the harsh demands that work life, often coupled with extensive economic insecurities (the threat of unemployment, low wages, and rising costs of social services), place on families. Child-rearing, personal relationships, long-term planning, leisure time – these and other aspects of private life come under severe strain. For the unemployed, of course, the situation is all the more grim. Economic disempowerment, creeping further down into the middle classes in recent decades, is a significant barrier to civic engagement. Thus, the extent to which the economy can provide reasonably secure employment with adequate wages becomes not just an issue for working people in the general sense of quality of life, but also a key issue for civic participation – reminding us of the social prerequisites for citizenship (see Marshall, 1950).

Data on psychological and emotional disorders and the massive use of prescription drugs (not to mention illegal drugs) paint a picture of deep distress within large segments of the population of the industrialized nations, a situation that borders on psycho-social pathology. This line of thought, about the pervasive psychic devastation of late modernity, tends all too often to be absent in contemporary social and cultural theory. Useful introductions to such a critical psychology of modernity, linking mental suffering to contemporary social, economic, and cultural patterns, can be found in Mestrovic (1997), Sloan (1996), and Elliott and Lemert (2006).

The underclass traditionally has tended to participate less than other groups in parliamentarian politics, for reasons having to do with social exclusion, cultural capital, and political disempowerment – sensing, perhaps (often rightly), that election outcomes would have little impact on their life circumstances. Particularly in these strata many people may feel that they lack the communicative competence to participate. In the middle classes, many citizens can experience cultural norms that block political discussion: Such talk is deemed "inappropriate" as a disturbing element and thus is to be avoided. Many people no doubt also lack sites or settings beyond the home, the workplace, and the shopping mall, where politics can easily be aired. And from a very different angle, our characters and personalities give rise to an array of less-than-good reasons for nonengagement, such as laziness, selfishness, and indifference. The citizenry, that is, "we the people," is of course not comprised exclusively of individuals of noble virtue.

WINNERS AND LOSERS

The functioning of democratic systems in Western democracies varies between countries, yet we can distil some general and interrelated trends in the difficulties involved. We can note first, at an overarching level, an altered contract between capital, labor, and the state, that is, a change in the overall balance of power between them. Capitalism has been a precondition for liberal democracy, and yet tensions remain between this "odd couple." Capitalism generates social power that lies largely beyond democratic control; whereas equality is one of the ideal pillars of democracy, inequality is often the societal by-product of capitalism. Yet democracy needs a functioning economic base on which to rest. The "resolution" in traditional liberal politics has been to try to regulate capitalism with the aim of reducing its negative social consequences as well as its own inner instabilities. The welfare state structures and the Keynesian policies associated with them were a progressive strategy in their time for dealing with such societal tensions. In Europe, the various shades of social democratic measures served to extend democracy and citizenship, serving to modify certain features of social inequality.

However, there were always limits as to how far this could go: Deep-rooted class structures and mechanisms tend to entrench power elites who are to a great extent able to resist – despite changes in government – calls for more democratically responsive and economically equitable social arrangements (see, for example, in the U.S. context, Domhoff, 2005, and his Web site www.whorulesamerica.net). By the 1970s this welfare state model was encountering serious difficulties.

Since then, particularly since the 1980s, we have witnessed in Western democracies a political turn – usually called neoliberalism – where, via deregulation, market forces and private enterprise have been given much greater rein to define the societal landscape, with a concomitant decline in democratic accountability of social power. In the realm of politics, market mechanisms and their logic tend to subordinate most other social considerations. Social inequalities have widened, not least in many developing nations, where such policies have been imposed by the World Bank or the International Monetary Fund. Further, transnational

corporations have often been quick to exploit – economically and politically – situations of disaster in these countries (for a recent polemic on
this theme, see Klein, 2007).

Another consequence of this development is that globalized market
imperatives increasingly compete with the vitality of formal national
political systems: The global mobility of finance capital and all the strategies of outsourcing both the industrial and service sectors put political
pressures on governments. This hinders governments' capacities to act
in the interests of all their citizens, while at the same time subordinating
citizenship to the imperatives of market (Hindess, 2002). Not least, the
inability to extract reasonable levels of taxes from transnational corporations has added to the fiscal difficulties of nation-states. Further, the
low level of regulation and control in the global finance system threatens the whole structure with profound instability, to which the global
economic turbulence of recent years attests. If we add to this picture the
dire situation that global oil reserves are diminishing and their deple-
tion looms in the foreseeable future, various kinds of traumatic – and
anti-democratic – scenarios can readily come to mind.

In the face of such circumstances, the sovereignty of the nation-state
itself is being downsized. The magnitude of this trend has been exagger-
ated in some circles, yet it can certainly be argued that the capacity of
nation-states to deal with financially mobile transnational corporations,
many of whom explicitly proclaim no national allegiance, has been
reduced. Further, the intensified global character of many other contemporary issues, such as environmental dangers, migration, and AIDS,
underscores the need to think of democracy and citizenship in terms that
go beyond the traditional context of the nation-state. There is some
regional institution building in this regard, most notably the EU, where
the task of developing a legitimate and well-functioning democracy is a
major challenge, to say the least. However, the institutional framework
for democracy remains quite thin beyond the regional setting at the
global level (e.g., the UN).

Within the advanced industrial countries, these developments have
been leaving an imprint on the class structure over the past few decades.
For the privileged, the global era tends to enhance cultural diversity and
material choices. For many others, the story is different: Increased insecurity and uncertain futures are moving higher and higher up into the
middle classes. This has to do in part with the overall morphology of the
job market: There is a decline in "solid" employment opportunities,
while the number of low-paid insecure jobs in an expanding service

sector is multiplying. Thus, not only is losing one's job becoming more familiar in the middle classes, as outsourcing, downsizing, and automation increase, but the jobs available offer less of both the income and status associated with a middle-class or at least a stable working-class life style. At the lower end of the economic scale, unemployment statistics are kept down in part by the steady growth of such "McJobs," where people are employed yet still living in poverty. Historically, increasing desperation among the middle classes has not been a good recipe for democracy.

UNCIVIC ECONOMISM

In conjunction with these structural developments, we see the intensification of a mode of thought that some authors call economism (Frank, 2000; Hertz, 2001). Economism is understood as a reductionist mode of rationality whose definitive characteristic is to assert the priority of economic criteria over all other values or modes of reasoning (see also Self, 2000; Touraine, 2001). Corporate values such as winning, efficiency, calculability, and profitability are supplanting democratic values in ways that erode civic vitality (Allen, 2005). This has in turn shifted the ideological climate to emphasize the congruence between democracy and capitalism while downplaying the dilemmas.

This development is of course hardly new: Simmel identified such processes more than a century ago. In a parallel way, Habermas (1984, 1987) speaks of the rationality of the present system as "colonizing" the domains of the life-world. In the context of contemporary market mechanisms, coupled with the expansion and significance of the media as carriers and forces of culture, there is a marked acceleration of these trends. Economist thought is a key feature in the new, dynamic – and unstable – global system. Today, economist patterns of thought are spreading into noneconomic areas and institutions, altering cultural values, norms, practices, and social thinking in many domains – and threatening democracy (Bollier, 1995; Self, 2000). This trend manifests itself not only in the formal political arena, but in most major institutions. Thus, for example, the role of school principals has become less one of pedagogic leadership, and more one of managerial efficiency, often with the result of reducing the democratic climate of school environments – while "civics classes" are supposed to instill the ideals of democratic participation in the pupils (see Bennett, 2007a; Llewellyn, Cook, Westheimer, Molina Girón, and Suurtamm, 2007).

Without actually using the term economism, Marquand (2004) demonstrates its impact. He makes the distinction between the public domain and the market domain; the former being the site "of citizenship, equity and service whose integrity is essential to democratic governance and social well-being" (Marquand, 2004:1). Writing about the British experience, he argues that the public domain has its own specific culture and rules. The neoliberal initiatives of the past decades have not simply consisted of political, economic, and legal efforts to enhance the market domain. They have also involved a struggle to eradicate the culture of service, equity, and citizenship, including an undermining of professional autonomy within the civil service, replacing these as far as possible with a mindset based on the performance indicators, assessments, and audits derived from the market logic of private corporations.

Certainly fiscal crises may necessitate public-sector cutbacks, but what is at work here is a more systematic ideological reconfiguration that legitimizes the private at the expense of the public. It becomes increasingly difficult to appeal to a common citizenship, as the notion of the citizen as a social role becomes marginalized by that of the consumer, where people understandably can find more freedom and pleasure (Miles, 1998; see also Couldry, 2004). The familiar logic – repeated endlessly in advertising (which moves into ever new spaces) is that happiness is basically achieved through buying things, and for just about all problems there is a product that offers a solution. The consumer is inexorably situated in a web of market relations, which largely excludes democratic principles such as justice, equality, and solidarity. That the pervasiveness of consumer logic in contemporary culture is detrimental to democracy and civic values has been argued for decades (for a recent treatment, see Barber, 2008). As Lewis, Inthorn, and Wahl-Jorgensen (2005:133) put it, "For citizens to compete against this deluge of consumerism is an uphill battle . . . a cultural environment dominated by advertising is not a level playing field for citizens. . . . "

I wish to clearly emphasize that the particular problem that I am addressing here is economism, not markets per se. Markets are absolutely essential for social and economic development; so too is a domain of free-choice consumption. The extent to which various social sectors should legitimately function according to market logic – and to what extent – is of course controversial, and there is considerable room for debate. However, I see as unambiguous the claim that democracy cannot be reduced to market logic. What is dangerous for democracy here is the view that markets are actually better equipped than states to allocate resources in society. In fact, the argument is even made that markets are "more democratic," since they reside "beyond politics" – a sort of natural-order mechanism of justice – where the alleged "invisible hand" is also supposed to be blind to the interests of economic and political elites. Ideologically, economism is often manifested as "market populism" (Leys, 2003; Frank, 2000), expressed as a growing public deference to market forces in all areas of social life.

The ways in which the "economy" – the perceived "motor" of society – is represented in journalism is also of considerable significance in this regard (Gavin, 2001). While the economy sections in the press are expanding, and the economy as a dominant theme is spreading into news and feature journalism, topics such as unemployment, poverty, and deprivation tend not to get the attention they deserve, as Gans (2003:55–68) argues. Journalism rarely covers the economy in terms of power relations; the social power of large corporations is seldom highlighted in relation to democratic concerns (see Doyle, 2006). Many topics of a social and political character increasingly end up in the economic sections of newspapers and news programs, there framed as technical economic difficulties, not as issues inviting engagement. We can also note that the implied view of democracy found in upscale economic journalism is not always the most encouraging: An analysis of the political imaginary of the *Financial Times* shows a rather cynical view (Kantola, 2007). Loyalty to democratic ideals seems to extend only as far as the citizens and elected decision-makers make unfettered market forces a primary political goal in the global economy.

Political discourse itself takes on economist attributes: Normative visions, emphasizing democratic values and societal goals, become increasingly in short supply as financial calculations marginalize other concerns. (Writing in the Australian context, Watson, 2004, demonstrates how these trends contribute to the deadening of public language and its degeneration into "management-speak"). The position created for the citizen even within the logic of political discourse becomes all the more that of a consumer (Kantola, 2003): Political ideas are to be "bought," and politics itself and its discourses increasingly embody the attributes of market logic.

GLOBAL DEMOCRATIC PROGRESS – IN THE LONG TERM?

Turning to the formal political system of most Western nations, we observe various degrees of stagnation, where parties tend to be reactive rather than proactive, bypassed by developments in the realms of large-scale capitalism and technological innovations, and outpaced by socio-cultural developments. The margins of governmental maneuverability are narrowing. Institutions central to democratic life, in particular political parties, have become inadequately responsive in the face of the major changes of late modernity. In Western Europe, the past decade has seen the emergence of extreme right-wing racist parties in most countries. A variety of factors are at work here, but certainly these parties exploit the difficulties associated with extra-European immigration. They can also be seen as populist responses from citizens who feel abandoned or betrayed by the political elites, and/or who seek security and stability in a defensive nationalism as a buffer against the uncertainties associated with globalization. Given their values and goals, such groups put democracy at risk.

Ideological differences between parties have become less pronounced, as the drift toward consensus politics intensifies. Political parties have become more *voter-oriented* rather than *member-oriented*, as citizens' identification with specific parties has become looser. On the one hand, politics becomes increasingly driven by discourses of technocratic and economic expertise, with the range of political options becoming narrowed. Political leaders thus indirectly depoliticize democracy, relegating more and more decisions to the domains of expertise and administration. Among citizens in the Western democracies, the arena of official politics does not command the degree of support and participation it has in the past. Many people seem to have at best a very rudimentary sense of themselves as citizens, as members and potential participants of political society. They do not feel that they are a part of a larger democratic project. Carl Boggs (2000) calls this erosion of civic engagement "the great retreat," a withdrawal from the arena of common concerns and politics, and a retrenchment into "enclave consciousness," away from larger collective identities and community sensibilities.

Internationally, after the collapse of communism, the United States has emerged as the world's singular superpower. The United States has not only been supporting neoliberal policies at home and abroad in the past decades, it has also developed a revised mode of foreign policy that has generated controversy among its traditional allies and inflamed its relations with many other nations and groups in the world. The very real dangers of terrorism have generated a "war on terrorism," whose efficacy, however, is greatly contested. It has led to severe restrictions on citizens' rights via the Patriot Act and the Homeland Security Act, as well as to a contraction of the realm of public political expression, including the bullying of the mass media. The Bush administration also introduced an element of Christian fundamentalism into political discourse that has put into question the secular premises and foundations of democracy (see Domke, 2004). Abroad, the United States has been pursuing a unilateralism that led to the American rejection of many important treaties and agreements in such realms as the environment and international justice, while revelations about human rights violations and officially sanctioned torture in its military prisons, notably in Iraq and at Guantanamo Bay, have shocked the world.

However one positions oneself on these issues, it is clear that the United States has in recent years lost considerable international moral authority, and its position as a global leading light for democracy has been seriously damaged. In some corners of the world, not least within the Middle East, where one hopes for the emergence of more democratic arrangements, the notion of "democracy" has in consequence taken on new and objectionable associations in the light of the United States' current actions abroad. Even if a decided political turnaround should emerge, it will still take a long time for the United States to regain its democratic leadership in the world. Further, while the power centers in Washington have rehabilitated the notion of "empire" in their vision for a new global order, there are indications that the United States is paradoxically a weakened superpower. Economically it has become more vulnerable to the rest of the world, given its mass trade deficit, the decline of the dollar – and the emergence of a more integrated Europe with a stable Euro, as well as the competition from Japan. China has a significant grip on the United States' financial situation. These factors too will in all likelihood play a role in shaping the United States' position among Western democracies in the years ahead (Todd, 2003).

While progress is being made in some parts of the world against the devastations of poverty and local wars, the growing global gaps between rich and poor, as well as the ongoing armed conflicts, create instabilities that hinder democratic development. Moreover, the rise of militant political fundamentalism within a number of the world's major religions poses new barriers to the development of democracy: The insistence of a theological foundation for politics or for the state itself enacts a frontal collision with democracy's Enlightenment origins. The challenge to develop something that can be called cosmopolitan democracy in the years ahead will continue to grow (see, for example, Beck, 2005).

China remains a firmly authoritarian state, while at the same time basing its economy on market forces, while in Putin's Russia the democratic progress achieved since the end of communism has been eroding steadily. Also, in Russia and several other postcommunistic societies, "democracy" is not always seen as an inspiring vision. It has unfortunately become linked with what can be called "gangster capitalism," in which former party members could get rich by laying their hands on public resources – to the economic detriment of large sectors of society. The lack of democratic development among the major powers of Russia and China is certainly troubling, however, globally we find a mixed picture (see Norris, 2002). There is a rising demand for formal democracy in societies where this tradition has been weak or absent: In the past two decades, in Asia, Africa, and Latin America as well as Eastern Europe, many countries have made the transition from authoritarianism to some form of democracy.

Observing these trends, Todd (2003) offers a somewhat promising picture if we take a long-term view. Based on a large body of comparative statistics of countries in the developing world, his analysis shows very strong correlations between two basic factors among national populations and the emergence of democracy, namely, generalized literacy and the taking control over and reducing the birth rate. Framing these two key variables within a perspective of modernization, he observes that the historical pattern is very clear: As literacy spreads among national populations, especially women, the level of births declines, setting in motion other socio-cultural changes. These developments more often than not lead to a period of mental, social, and political turmoil, as traditional cultures face serious internal upheavals, often with violent consequences. Various forms of traditionalist, purist, and fundamentalist ideologies and religions come to the fore, trying to hold on to the past (Todd even charts similar processes in seventeenth-century England and eighteenth-century France, as their turbulent modernization processes gave rise to democracy). Yet, citing many examples, he makes the case that, most often, such forms of extremism are a manifestation of a transition period lasting only a few decades, and the march toward democracy continues.

The long-term impact of literacy on the emergence of democracy is clear (Milner, 2001, underscores this theme with data from contemporary democracies). A reading – and, thus, reflecting – citizenry is simply in the long run unlikely to accept illegitimate autocratic rule. Todd notes also that the costs of keeping a literate population subjugated under such conditions is costly – to the extent that such a country is unable to compete economically in the global arena. He underscores this point with reference to an earlier work where he predicted very accurately the collapse of the Soviet Union, for precisely such reasons.

While both optimists and pessimists can find evidence for their arguments about the current state of democracy in the world, I would concur with Todd's (2003) observation that while there is considerable positive democratic energy in many of the countries in the developing world, we are seeing erosion in the established Western democracies. The growing structural gaps between organized political life and people's everyday realities reinforce a sense of distance from the political system. Feelings of powerlessness among citizens, as well as at times the much publicized corruption among officials, are also engendering disaffection. There is growing contempt for the political class, with climates of cynicism emerging in some places, while, more generally, the paucity of new political ideas in a situation where "more of the same" seems intuitively inadequate also serves to turn people away from politics. Of course there are always many notable exceptions to these trends, most visibly in the expanding sector of extra-parliamentarian alternative politics (see Chapter 8), yet this growing atmosphere of "anti-politics" among most sectors of the population in Western democracies must be understood as the consequence of the inability of the political system to meet social expectations and an absence of an alternative and compelling political vision. Economic insecurity, unemployment, low wages, declining social services, growing class cleavages, and ecological threats are all part of a picture that is disconcerting for the vitality of democracy in the Western societies.

SOCIO-CULTURAL TURBULENCE

Democracy is about politics, and politics is also shaped by socio-cultural parameters. We have seen in recent decades how a number of these factors that traditionally have served as preconditions for the way in which democracy has functioned in Western societies are in transition. These particular changes are often associated with the perspective of late modernity and they suggest that the newer modes of acculturation that shape individuals and their group relations have a significant impact on the dynamics of democracy, especially in regard to participation. These cultural changes have their counterpart in the more specific contexts of the media, which I take up in the next chapter.

Cultural Dispersions

First, the dispersion, or fragmentation, of shared, unifying cultural frameworks is proceeding. Societies are becoming more pluralistic and differentiated along several lines: class, ethnicity, patterns of media consumption, cultural interests, life styles, and so on. Shared political horizons become harder to integrate into people's everyday lives when such socio-cultural heterogeneity increases. This dispersion has several origins, but for our purposes here, two are most significant. One has to do with the pluralization of horizons and frames of reference promoted by media, advertising, and consumerist life styles in late modernity. Generally, advanced consumer culture fosters increasing "nichification," or even "neo-tribalism" (Melucci, 1989), as some observers put it, as the multiplicity of tastes, interests, and social orientations accelerates. The popular magazine market can serve as a mirror for this development. If one walks into a well-stocked news agent today, one is struck by the vast array of categories among the magazines: computers, gardening, skateboarding, music, travel, tattoos, cigar-smoking, fishing, antiques, skiing, UFOs, boating, science fiction, popular psychology, celebrities, and so on, most of which in some way link lifestyle interests with strategic consumption.

Consumerism has become all-pervasive as a format for living (Corrigan, 1997; Slater, 1997). As markets and private, discretionary consumption expand, more people feel that they have a greater range of choices they can make in this regard. Globalization, not least in its media-borne modes (see, for example, Morely and Robins, 1995; Rantenen, 2005; Tomlinson, 1999; Strelitz, 2005), further extends the impact on people's coordinates of place, meaning, and identity. In particular, travel and tourism are domains that have increasingly helped promote new ways of seeing the world and oneself. In these developments, for those who can participate, the range of choice – and the cultural niche differences – expands.

The other major source of cultural dispersion has to do with multiculturalism, as the ethnic and religious pluralism of many Western countries increases. The deepening difficulties many Western societies are having in developing in a democratic manner to incorporate ethnic and religious minorities constitutes a central theme in the political landscape. These centrifugal forces problematize a democracy predicated on any lingering notions about a nation-state characterized by homogeneity and a unified public culture. Both consumer nichefication and ethnic pluralism also serve to promote frames of reference and engagement beyond the borders of the nation-state (e.g., global youth culture, diasporic communities), further extending the horizons of collective identities and loyalties.

INDIVIDUALIZATION

Secondly, the various processes and manifestations of individualization (e.g., Beck and Beck-Gernsheim, 2002; Vinken, 2007) play a major role. This is a complex development, inscribed in the fundamental character of modernity from the beginning, yet now accelerating. Individualization has profound psycho-ideological roots that can lead in different directions. On a somewhat superficial level, it may contain elements of simple egoism or reflect the erosion of a sense of social belonging, and thus promote active responses to the massive outpouring of consumer choices. Individualization in these contexts connects with consumer culture and identities; encouraging life strategies, large and small, are for the most part individual rather than collective.

On another level, individualization also signals a growing sense (and value) of personal autonomy, a lack of enthusiasm for authority figures, and a disinclination to become a part of large organizations or entities, where one sees little chance of influence. The norm and the need to express oneself in the context of large institutions like political voting seem to be on the decline, making the task of traditional political parties more difficult. The involvement with abstract political "isms" becomes less compelling. Instead, social horizons tend to emphasize personal life and the graspable local milieu. In this regard, it could be argued that individualization in an indirect way contributes to the engagement in the new forms of politics, as many citizens come to make political connections via personal commitments rather than overarching traditional ideologies.

While individualization can be seen as an obvious correlate to both the cultural dispersions and the erosion of traditional socializing institutions that I take up in the next section, we can also connect it with the impact of the globalized economy. In the increasing absence of secure life plans, in a situation where post-Fordist economies demand mobile, flexible labor power, and where one's life narrative repeatedly is forced to undergo modification, people to a great extent are thrown back on themselves: In what Young (2007) ominously calls the "vertigo of late modernity," the individual is all the more compelled to face his or her changing – and often stressful – life circumstances alone (see also Elliott and Lemert, 2006, for a similar viewpoint. Bauman has explored variations on these themes in several books on "liquid modernity"; see, for example, Bauman 2000b, 2005, 2006).

THE EROSION OF TRADITIONAL INSTITUTIONS

Thirdly, I would highlight processes of what sociologists have been claiming has been under way over a period of many decades. Observers have noted a general loosening of the impact that traditional institutions have in the processes of socializing the individual: Families, schools, churches, neighborhoods, unions, and political parties today have less input in shaping the subject than in the past. While we should be careful not to exaggerate these arguments nor ignore the vast variety in patterns even within any one national society, there is strong sociological agreement that the significance of these traditional institutions for the formation of individual has become more muted in recent decades. Many argue that in this context the media are gaining as key agents of socialization for the individual, given the enormous amount of time that we spend with them, not least even preschool children.

This development suggests a number of things in terms of citizens. First of all, more people may have weaker bonds to these institutions, with the consequence that these institutions figure less prominently in their social horizons as potentially important topics or targets for politics – that is, a growing sense of indifference to the institutions themselves, and thereby a lower motivation to politically engage oneself in issues that touch upon them. Secondly, it implies a reciprocal interplay with the processes of individualization: The less major institutions steer the lives of people, the more individuals will be forced or inspired to develop their own life courses. Finally, new challenges for political communication emerge from these developments. For example, they raise such concerns as to what kinds of issues, and what modes of representation and political address, will appeal to diverse groups of citizens who carry less imprint from traditional institutions but whose knowledge, frames of reference, modes of attention, and leisure time activities are deeply shaped by the vicissitudes of media experience.

THE EMERGING NETWORK CHARACTER OF SOCIETY

Finally, the growing network character of society, at the local, national, regional, and global levels, has become highly significant (a key text in this regard is Castells, 2000; see also Benkler, 2006; Friedland, Hove, and Rojas, 2006). While it can be debated if the network form of social relations has become the basic societal organizing principle for the entire globe, the growing prominence of networks in almost all domains of social life, not least economic production and enterprise, politics, and personal life, is beyond dispute. This is of course a sociological horizon with much variation and in need of elaboration; I will return to it in Chapter 8, but for now we should keep in mind that more and more people are using interactive media to establish links with others and engage in a vast variety of specific interests and activities. Moreover, the pessimism of increased anomie deriving from the growth of such loose ties and transitory relationships does not seem warranted. Surveys of the contemporary research (for example, in Benkler, 2006) suggest that even if, for example, the family as an institution has become weaker, people still maintain close personal ties in their personal lives, and these primary relationships do not seem to be eroded by the growth of network contacts: There is no automatic zero-sum game at work. This development of networking is of proceeding in tandem with the spread of digital communication technologies, a theme I introduce in the following section.

CIVIC REGENERATION: TWO FRONTS

Against the backdrop of these evolving late modern structural and socio-cultural patterns, it becomes rather easy to understand the emergence of two political variants that signal a renewal of political engagement in Western democracies. One works largely outside the political party structure and accords a degree of hope for continued democratic development. The latter operates within both parliamentarian and extra-parliamentarian contexts; while it is understandable in many ways, it is also highly troubling in that it embodies values and views that can endanger basic democratic principles.

Beginning with the latter, the growing malaise derived from the structural insecurity of the broad middle and working classes discussed above has been generating political response. Young (2007) notes a rising "ressentiment" – a combination of a sense of bitterness and a sense of powerlessness that promotes tendencies within these social sectors to look for accessible scapegoats. This expresses itself not only as an increased political emphasis on law and order as well as severer punishments, but even as cultural climates of taboos, prohibitions, correctness, and conformity. Still more serious is the marked swing toward xenophobic, anti-immigrant, and racist attitudes, as manifested by the growing prominence of baleful extreme right-wing groups in many Western democracies.

Young (2007) argues further that from these horizons, the liberal/social democratic elites are seen as more concerned or even allied with the underclass, the immigrants, the socially problematic, and thus the working and lower middle classes turn rightward, engaging markedly in what he calls extensive "othering": Stigmatizing certain groups that are perceived in some way to undermine the socio-cultural fabric or drain public resources. Here, in response to appeals to national, traditional, or religious values, ethnic purity or other constructions of narrowly defined unity, expressions and mechanisms of exclusion against various kinds of difference can take on vicious forms.

In this volume I will be giving more attention to the other, more encouraging counterpoint to the general decline in citizen engagement, which is sometimes called "new politics"; I will use the adjectives "alternative" and "informal" as synonymous designations for this vector. Alternative politics is certainly not immune to anti-democratic tendencies, but I will dwell mostly on democratic efforts in this growing political terrain. These initiatives offer some cautious optimism in regard to the ostensible apathy and disaffiliation from the established political system. That is, if we look beyond formal electoral politics, we can see various signs that suggest that many people have not abandoned engagement with the political, but have rather refocused their political attention outside the parliamentary system. For example, many groups are directly targeting large global corporations for their activities in regard to the environment, working conditions, or other issues rather than going via the formal political system (Danaher and Mark, 2003; Amoore, 2005). Or they are in the process of de facto redefining just what constitutes the political (Bauman, 1999), in ways that scramble some traditional conceptions of public and private domains.

We also see frames of reference and engagement beyond the borders of the nation-state, as evidenced by, for example, transnational social movements, such as the alter-globalization movement and diasporic communities. The media publicity generated by such initiatives contribute to maintaining visibility in a democratic society (see Chambers, 2000, who explores this theme in more detail), complementing the more established processes of news generation. Moreover, in the context of this kind of informal politics, the boundaries between politics, cultural values, identity processes, and local self-reliance measures become fluid (Beck, 1998; Bennett, 2003a, 2003b). Politics becomes not only an instrumental activity for achieving concrete goals, but also an expressive and performative activity.

In the Swedish context, these developments are illustrated in the work of Sörbom (2002). Using life course interviews, she finds that political commitments at the personal level have in fact grown in the past decades, while commitments to parties and traditional social movements have declined. She finds that there are two basic and opposing tendencies at work. On the one hand, there is a general increase in political interest, a growth in active political commitment and engagement at the personal level. Indifference is not her major finding. On the other hand, she observes a diminishing commitment to the established institutions of democracy, especially political parties, suggesting distrust and ambivalence.

In simplified terms, the older respondents, born in the 1920s, say they often felt that politics was something that they were simply mobilized into during their youth, by older people around them, and that politics did not always have all that much personal relevance. For those respondents born in the 1950s and especially the 1970s, politics is something that they seemingly expect should have precisely personal relevance. Among these younger generations, politics is something they reflect about, and critically question. At the same time, across generations, she finds an increasing skepticism toward politicians and parliamentary politics. The result is often a perception of what she terms low "political makeability," that is, citizens do not perceive the formal political system as amenable to intervention. This of course presents hinders for participation.

In an ambitious international comparison, Norris (2002) offers a varied account that is calibrated in regard to electoral politics, and hopeful about new politics. She finds that while participation in elections has declined in many established Western democracies, it has remained fairly stable in others. Moreover, it is clearly on the increase in many of the newer democracies. In regard to the growth of new politics, she suggests that we are seeing the emergence of important new patterns of civic engagement:

> [P]olitical activism has been reinvented in recent decades by a diversification in the *agencies* (the collective organizations structuring political activity), the *repertoires* (the actions commonly used for political expression), and the *targets* (the political actors that participants seek to influence). The surge of protest politics, new social movements, and Internet activism exemplify these changes. If the opportunities for political expression and mobilization have fragmented and multiplied over the years ... democratic engagement may have adapted and evolved in accordance with the new structures of opportunities, rather than simply atrophying. (Norris, 2002:215–216, italics in original text)

Alternative politics is typified by personalized rather than collective engagement, and a stronger emphasis on single issues than on overarching platforms or ideologies. Some analysts claim that part of this development can be understood as a move away from politics based on production to one focused on consumption; political attention is geared more toward the needs of clients, customers, and consumers than in the past (Gibbens and Reimer, 1999). Further, political activity within the new politics is more ad hoc, less dependent on traditional organizations and on elites mobilizing their standing cadres of supporters. It is more typified by decentralized networking (Cammaerts and van Audenhove, 2003). Along with social movements, particularly in the areas of alter-globalization, ecology, feminism, peace, and social self-help, we find a large number of nongovernmental organizations (NGOs) that also can mobilize and absorb citizens' engagement, even across national borders.

It is not surprising that much of this alternative politics coincides with the rise of the Internet and other new communication technologies, given the civic communication that these technologies can facilitate (see van de Donk, Loader, Nixon, and Rucht, 2004; de Jong, Shaw, and Stammers, 2005; McCaughey and Ayers, 2003; Jordan and Taylor, 2004; Boler, 2008), a theme I return to in Chapters 7 and 8. Whether or not these developments are genuinely fruitful for the enhancement of democracy is under debate. For example, it can be argued that civic engagement in single issue politics may be profoundly at odds with the kind of democracy needed to deal with complex societies confronted by many different issues simultaneously. In any case, we should keep in mind that these trends vary in strength between countries, and behind all generalizations can be found exceptions. Overall, though, there is nothing to suggest that the trends discussed here will be reversed; they will most likely intensify, and they do open the door for new ways to think about the contemporary political landscape.

I signaled at the outset the importance of having a good grasp of media developments in order to understand what is happening to Western democracy: Significantly, most of the social, cultural, and political processes I have been discussing in this chapter are made visible or even amplified by the media. In the next chapter I turn my attention to the key developments in the media sector.

CHAPTER 2

Media Alterations

There are many factors that shape the character of democracy and of political engagement within it, but one of the key elements is of course the nature and role of the media. Without a firm analytic perspective on the media, our understanding of democracy will always be elusive. As institutions, the media provide the dominant symbolic environment of society, with patterns of communication criss-crossing the social terrain in a complex fashion. Discussions about media and democracy are often framed by the notion of the public sphere, which emphasizes that the media must provide citizens with the information, ideas, and debates about current affairs so as to facilitate informed opinion and participation in democratic politics. To do so, the media must be technically, economically, culturally, and linguistically within reach of society's members. Also, any a priori exclusions of any segment of the population collide with democracy's claim to universalism. Promoting the idea of the public sphere, which builds on the universalist ideal of something common, shared, to which all citizens are entitled, becomes all the more difficult in an era when market forces have such a strong influence in shaping the character of the media.

In the first section I offer overarching glimpses of the turbulent media landscape, noting the key trends. Following that I focus more specifically on the implications of these developments for journalism. The fourth section examines some of the key developments in the broader terrain of political communication, highlighting not least that altered power relations between citizens, elites, and media. I conclude the chapter with a short discussion on how central characteristics of the media system – what I call the late modern media matrix – impact on traditional notions of civic engagement and political communication.

THE EVOLVING MEDIA LANDSCAPE

Regardless of how one evaluates the performance of the media, these institutions have become the major sites, the privileged scenes, of politics in late modern society. As Castells (1998), Meyer (2002), Garnham (2000), and others argue, from a variety of perspectives, the media are transforming democracy because political life itself today has become so extensively situated within the domain of the media, and because the various logics of the media shape what gets taken up in the media and the modes of representation (see also the collections by Bennett and Entman, 2001; Axford and Huggins, 2001). This view does not mean that politics does not exist outside the media, or that politics has been reduced to a mere media spectacle. It does, however, posit that political actors who want to accomplish things requiring public visibility will always turn to the media (Thompson, 1995; Voirol, 2005, theme issue of *Réseaux*). Political and economic elites make use of the media for the daily routines of governing, for opinion- and image-management, as well as for major initiatives or trouble-shooting in times of crises. Seen in this light, media scholarship has an extremely important role to play in the service of democracy (McChesney, 2007).

The media today are in a profoundly turbulent period, and to understand their present role in democracy, as well as to begin to grasp future possibilities (and threats), it is imperative that we have a basic orientation in these processes. The key developments are of course closely woven together; in summary form, they are as follows.

PROLIFERATION

We have a whole lot more channels of communication today than we had forty or even twenty years ago. Cable and satellite television offers packages with ever-growing numbers of channels. If the number of daily newspapers is contracting somewhat, the growth in magazines has been explosive over the past two decades. And the Internet offers not only a seemingly endless supply of information on its own, but is also increasingly relaying and repackaging the output of traditional mass media. We are awash in media, and most of it is obviously not overtly civic-oriented: Even if various forms of journalism have also increased in recent years, the growth in, for example, entertainment and advertising is much larger. Thus a definitive aspect of the contemporary media world is the intensifying competition for attention – between genres (e.g., sports or news) as well as between media forms (e.g., broadcast radio or the Internet).

At the same time, this abundance easily becomes disorienting; Gitlin (2001) speaks of "media torrents" and "supersaturation," and reminds us that under such circumstances, we must devise strategies for navigating the flood, for sorting and selecting from an output infinitely larger than we can meaningfully deal with. Poster (2006) argues that particularly now, with the new digital ICTs, the deluge of information that pours across geographic borders and cultural contexts can paradoxically give rise to a decrease in meaning. People globally can experience the difficulties of making sense of media worlds that bear no obvious relationship to their own established frames of reference. Other critics argue that much of the media abundance lacks diversity and is merely "more of the same." Yet, as our symbolic environments become denser, and the accessibility of information mushrooms, the degree of choice available today is still very large.

CONCENTRATION

The media industries are following the general patterns found in the economy. Massive media empires have emerged on a global scale, concentrating ownership in the hands of a decreasing number of megacorporations. Such giants as AOL Time Warner, Disney, Rupert Murdoch's News Corporation, and Bertelsmann are among the ten or so leading global media corporations, followed by another several dozen somewhat smaller corporate actors (Demers, 2002). Together they dominate the media landscape of the modern world. The holdings of these corporations encompass all phases of media activity, from production to distribution, hardware and software, across virtually all media forms and technologies. Significantly, via mergers and cooperative ventures, the media industries in the past decade have begun integrating with telecommunications (e.g., AT&T with DirecTV) and the computer industry (e.g., Microsoft and NBC, Time Warner and AOL).

These trends and their implications for democracy are analyzed in a growing critical literature that affirms that democracy is in danger and the need for reform is dire (Herman and McChesney, 1997; Sussman, 1997; Schiller, 1999; Bagdikian, 2005; Hackett and Carroll, 2006; Chester, 2007; Klinenberg, 2007). The work of McChesney represents a sustained effort to illuminate these problems and points to policy options to alter them; see, for example, McChesney (1999, 2004, 2007) and Nichols and McChesney (2005). As the commercial imperatives of the media have hardened over the past few decades, the balance between public responsibility and private profit has been steadily tipping in favor of the latter. Normative goals are increasingly giving way to economic calculation, not least in journalism (McManus, 1994; Underwood, 1995; Franklin, 1997; Croteau and Hoynes, 2001; Henry, 2007). If we look more broadly toward information in the digital era, the processes of commodification continue to intensify, cementing the dynamics of privatization in telecommunication and the cultural industries, and shaping in the transition from mass media to the new ICT landscape (Schiller, 2007).

The drive to maximize profits continues to shape the social relations between technical innovators, corporate owners, government, and citizens in ways that are detrimental to democratic ideals. Journalism and the functions of information distribution end up in the hands of business people and managers who have little exposure to or engagement with the traditions and ethics of journalism. The critical watchdog function and the protection of freedom of expression are not part of the cultural traditions of these institutions. This media concentration not only reduces diversity, it contracts the potential domain of critical journalism. Journalists employed by a large megaconglomerate will generally avoid topics that might damage its wide-ranging interests. When they don't, the consequences can be devastating for their careers (see the collection of accounts of the dire personal experiences among journalists in Borjesson, 2002).

DEREGULATION

Deregulation can be seen as midwife of concentration. Deregulation is the policy process whereby the various laws, rules, and codes that governments use to shape media ownership, financing, and ongoing activities are withdrawn or weakened, opening up the doors to more market mechanisms. Regulation and deregulation can be understood as policy outcomes reflecting the power and interests of various constellations of actors, including transnational corporations, political parties, public officials, interest associations, and advocacy organizations (Bennett, 2004a, 2004b). In a period of extensive institutional and technological restructuring of the media landscape, media policy is of course an area of intense concern, since it is a decisive agency and site for the processes of transformation (McQuail and Siune, 1998). Government regulation can be an easy target for "antigovernment" rhetoric, yet it is the only way that public interests can be asserted in realms controlled by private interests. Baker (2002, 2006) argues that relying on market forces in the media industries is turning into a disaster for journalism and democracy. Moreover, such policies do not even "give the people what they want": People's tastes are not primordial, and can be gradually habituated to what is being offered.

Deregulation has been most strongly manifested in the area of broadcasting, and this has had significant impact on the public service tradition of Western Europe. Public service broadcasting was in need of institutional renewal in the 1970s and 1980s: Virtually all such broadcasting organizations were facing financial difficulties, and charges of paternalism and stagnation, as well as in some countries a too close relationship with the state, were not without validity. However, as many have argued (see, for example, Tracey, 1998) in the new media environment, excessive deregulation has contributed to the erosion of the public service mission. While public service in most countries has restructured and streamlined itself, it is often torn between competing with popular commercial channels on their own terms while yet maintaining a specific identity and profile.

GLOBALIZATION

Globalization has many dimensions, and certainly its neoliberal economic side raises fundamental issues about democracy, not least in regard to the media industries themselves (see, for example, the collection by Artz and Kamalipour, 2003). It has generated a vast literature of both support and concern (Giddens, 2002, offers an optimistic view; Bauman, 2000a, provides darker counterpoint. For a handy introduction to the debates, see Held and McGrew, 2002). The media can be understood as both an expression of globalization and as forces that drive it forward. They are inexorably connected to the globalization of culture in the modern world, even linking it to the level of personal experience (see, for instance, Tomlinson, 1999; Morely, 2000; Rantenen 2005; Strelitz, 2005).

While the implications of globalization are complex and at times ambivalent, we should emphatically not ignore their positive sides, such as enlarging citizens' global frames of reference and social engagement. Thus, political issues increasingly take on a transnational character, and global media in turn can impact on the political agenda of specific nation-states (see, for example, Thussu, 2006a, 2006b). With news journalism at the global level we find a reciprocal interplay between institutions, technology, and political developments (see Hatchen and Scotton, 2007). For instance, public engagement with many international issues – political repression, environmental disasters, famine, and so on – has been made possible by globalized media coverage, especially on television. This remains true even while much criticism is justifiably aimed at the nature of the coverage (e.g., the Gulf War) and the vast black holes of noncoverage of much of the world. Moreover, if we look at the extra-parliamentarian arena, many of the actors – social movements, nongovernmental organizations, activist groups, and so on – work explicitly in transnational contexts, a development enormously facilitated by the Internet.

DIGITALIZATION

Digitalization is unquestionably the major technological trend in the media today; the last two decades have seen a profound technological transformation of the media that continues to accelerate. In simple terms, a common electronic language, based on the "bits" of the computer, is emerging for all mediated communication. Thus, text, sound, voice, as well as still and moving images are taking on a common digital form, with analog formats rapidly disappearing. The traditional mass media are all using digital technologies in various phases of their activities, and we see now in Europe, for example, the ongoing transition from analogue to digital terrestrial television transmission. Digital formats have been firmly entrenched in other media; for example, the CD put an end to vinyl music records in the late 1980s and in most corners of the world films in DVD formats are rapidly replacing VCR. Across the media and cultural industries there are many signs of a "convergence of convergence," as professionals in various media branches interact with each other and with creative nonprofessionals (see Deuze, 2007).

The Internet has been leading a media revolution since the mid-1990s, first as a phenomenon in itself, then as the terrain into which the traditional mass media moved. The advent of online versions of print newspapers had by the end of the 1990s changed the way newspapers operated (e.g., enhanced interactivity with readers, altered periodicity of production, emergence of multimedia formats), even if many of the online versions are still not making much profit. Then broadcasting began to move online in various forms, while other services and communicative forms specific to the net were also rapidly developing.

Today many assert that we are in the age of Web 2.0, with the large array of new and relatively inexpensive multimedia platforms and applications available for many kinds of social interaction. That many applications within the realm of new media – such as portable and even handheld computers, as well as mobile phones – readily link up to the

Internet suggests that we should understand the term "Internet" as a broader phenomenon that emerges precisely through these convergences (see Chadwick, 2006:9). In fact, in this emerging phase in the history of communications technology, we might (albeit awkwardly) refer to the "internetization" of the media, and see that as a structural, architectural development with its own significance beyond the technical aspects of digitalization.

Building on current research, Chadwick (2006:8) underscores several trends relevant to our concerns here: As broadband becomes increasingly available, the issue of bandwidth scarcity recedes, thereby making the multimedia character of the net accessible to more users; this in turn anchors the "expanded" net as a permanent, user-friendly utility in everyday life, for a vast array of communication activities. The classic distinction between "mass" and "interactive" media thereby becomes problematic.

Digitalization of the media in turn gives rise to a trend that could prove to be of unprecedented importance. A number of legal scholars, especially Benkler (2006), argue that in the long-term perspective, the growth of the Internet – despite the obvious commercial colonization – is offering an enhanced environment for individual and collective creation ("peer production"), and dissemination of information and culture. While this view is quite common in many circles these days, Benkler makes the further argument that the global information economy itself, given such factors as the dispersal of capital investment via individual ownership of computers – is drifting further and further toward a "network model." It is thereby eroding the industrial information economy based on private proprietary and profit. This directs our vision to an increasingly robust nonmarket sector for information and culture via digital networks, undermining the traditional model of industrial mass media and opening up the cyberworld for all the more civic activity.

We can note that the first wave of optimism in regard to the democratic potential of the Internet that appeared in the mid-1990s was often built more on enthusiasm than evidence. Today a new ground is emerging for that optimism: One could argue that the social affordances of the new digital media counteract in part the strong structural tendencies toward media conglomeration. Yet, the troubling features in the overall emerging picture remain. Some authors such as Strangelove (2005) are encouraged by the growing inability of the corporate sector to maintain firm control over digital property rights in the face of massive illegal downloading. Further, his optimism is especially nourished by the growth in open source software sharing (e.g., the Linux system), which is predicated on collaboration rather than profits – and can thus be seen as a growing ideological threat to capitalist values and ethics. However, others, such as Lessig (2006), are more troubled by what they see as the shrinking domain of the shared, public commons via private, corporate copyrights. At present we cannot predict how these issues around the democratic character of cyberspace will unfold in the future, but we will have to hope that suitable compromises can be reached that will serve the interests of both democracy and the major industries – as well as the innovators, creators, and artists working within them.

THE TWILIGHT OF JOURNALISM?

The Press in Distress

As an institutionalized set of practices located within the media, journalism of course evolves with the transformation of not only audiences, but also society, culture, and media institutions. Almost two decades ago researchers were already asserting that the "high modern" or "classical" paradigm of journalism is waning (e.g., Altheide and Snow, 1991; Hallin, 1992). This historical mode took shape early in the previous century and based itself on traditional liberal ideals of democracy and citizenship. In this framework, mass media journalism is seen as providing reports and analyses of real events and processes, and contributing to defining the public agenda (McCombs, 2004).

Through its narratives, classical journalism lays claim to accurate and impartial renderings of a reality that exists independently of its telling, and which is external to the institutions of journalism. It is aimed at a heterogeneous citizenry that basically shares the same public culture, and citizens use journalism as a resource for participation in the politics and culture of society. Journalism in this mode serves as an integrative force and as a common forum for debate. Even if journalism in the real world has never operated quite in this way, this paradigmatic model of how it should be has guided our understanding and expectations of it (see Allan, 2004, for a discussion of the professional culture of journalism).

The changes within journalism are usually discussed either under the heading of tabloidization and its issues of quality, economics, and audience attraction, or political tendency, where issues of bias, too close relationships with political and economic elites, or lack of political nerve define the topics of discussion. However, today, other disturbing factors add to the dilemmas, not least the fact that, today, journalism's position within people's ensemble of information sources has been downsized. What the public knows is to a declining degree a result of traditional journalism; this is trend of global proportions (see Thussu, 2007). From these developments, its role in democracy is thus being altered, reduced. Journalism has always had its (necessary) critics, but in these changing circumstances, it appears demoralized and powerless, as expressed by journalists themselves (Fallows, 1997; Downie and Kaiser, 2003, Fenton, 2005). Academic critics further chart these problems (Croiteau and Hoynes, 2001; Zelizer, 2004; Hatchen, 2005; McChesney 2007).

Gans (2003) sees the disempowerment of citizens in the face of political and economic elites as a result of a failed journalism. He also sees the news audience as contributing to the disempowerment of mass media news by abandoning serious journalism. Bennett (2006) scrutinizes news journalism as a complex system that is increasingly detrimental to the needs of democracy, while Carpentier (2007) focuses on a particular aspect of the problem, namely, the reluctance of mainstream journalists to promote participation and discussion among their audiences. To these overviews has been added critical analyses of the impact that the events of September 11, the subsequent "War on Terrorism," and the war in Iraq have had on journalism (cf. Miller, 2004; Kellner, 2003, 2005; Thussu and Freedman, 2003; Zelizer and Allan, 2002; Bennett, Lawrence, and Livingstone, 2007). These developments have not enhanced journalism's democratic role, to say the least.

In this crisis, many journalists and editors themselves feel a profound professional frustration, and there have been a variety of responses in recent decades. In the United States, the Committee of Concerned Journalists formed in 1997 and published a major study asserting the importance of normative professional frameworks (Kovach and Rosentiel, 2001). Another ambitious call to reconstruct journalism is found in Meyer (2004), who looks at the current media situation from the standpoint of the interplay between the profession and the new economic parameters.

No doubt the robust public (also called civic) journalism movement constitutes the most visible effort to redirect journalism's contemporary trajectory. This movement was launched in the United States in the late 1980s, and was also picked up in some other countries as well. Beginning at grassroots levels in a few local newspapers, and then increasingly systematized by a number of academic activists (the most influential being Jay Rosen; see Rosen, 2001), the movement quickly galvanized many adherents during the 1990s. It manifested itself in particular journalistic projects, where newspapers attempted to apply the basic principles to concrete issues. These principles include listening to and taking into account the ideas of citizens in planning stories; exploring new ways to frame stories that would help engage citizens; striving to convey useful knowledge and air alternative courses of action; and keeping track of how well they are actually communicating with the public.

Like most reform movements, public journalism evoked a good deal of hard criticism, especitally from the more established bastions of journalism. Controversies raged (see Glasser, 1999, for an overview of the key issues). The movement was helped considerably by funding from the Pew Center for Civic Journalism; that funding ceased in 2003, and even if a core of enthusiasts formed a professional society thereafter – the Public Journalism Network – many felt that the movement had run its course (useful overviews can be found in Voakes, 2004; Haas and Steiner, 2006). However, one can also argue, as does Witt (2004), that the spirit of the movement lives on, and in fact now, in the age of Web 2.0, the possibilities for public journalism have been all the more enhanced. I will return to this theme in Chapter 8.

Another extensive response to the crisis of journalism is found in the Project of Excellence in Journalism (2004, 2005, 2006, 2007, 2008), affiliated with the Columbia University Graduate School of Journalism and funded by the Pew Charitable Trusts. It offers a detailed annual online report: "The State of the News Media"; the current one, for 2008, is its fifth (www.stateofthemedia.org). The seriousness of the situation is reflected on the first page of the first report: "Journalism finds itself in the middle of 'an epochal transformation,' as momentous as the invention of the telegraph or television" (www.stateofthemedia.org/2004/narrative_overview_intro.asp?media=1). While these reports offer detailed accounts and statistics of not least the decline in traditional journalism and the difficult transitions to a new media alignment, this is no exercise in alarmist rhetoric: The reports constitute a sustained, probing analysis, looking at the different media outlets of journalism, their audiences, economics, and technologies while identifying trends and offering measures in both the long- and short-term perspectives to facilitate the transitions in ways that will be as fruitful as possible.

What is at stake in journalism is not only the immediate information that it does or does not offer. Correct, relevant, and accessible information is of course necessary, but not sufficient. There is also a socialization process, or educational dimension, here. Schudson (2003) writes about journalists as a first-line defense against commercialism. This may seem a bit romantic, but I think we certainly have to take the long view. He argues that "journalists can educate audiences to the benefits and pleasures of reliable, in-depth news reporting, analysis and commentary" (Schudson, 2003:126). He adds that this is a long path, and a slow one, but also the most enduring one.

HETEROGENEOUS AUDIENCES

A central element in the changing conditions of journalism is the evolution of its audiences. Media audiences today parallel the major tendencies at work within the overall socio-cultural changes outlined in Chapter 1. The concept of the "audience" has been evolving along with the media and with researchers' shifting theoretical and empirical orientations (McQuail, 1997; Alasuutari, 1999; Ross and Nightingale, 2003); in the age of interactive media it becomes especially challenged (e.g., Livingstone, 2005b). Increasingly, audiences are becoming more fragmented, and they are expecting more choices in media consumption. Also, the relationship that people have with the media – both the traditional mass media and the newer digital media – is becoming more multidimensional, as media encounters become contextualized in new ways within people's lives. In particular, the new technologies give people much more control over what kind of information they receive, and when and how they receive it.

Among media audiences we can also note a decline in "reading publics" in most Western countries, especially among the young, as image-based media take on stronger positions within news and current affairs. Also, while citizens are becoming increasingly socially fragmented amongst themselves (i.e., seen horizontally), specific market niches emerge from continuing societal segmentation, thus making a hierarchical (i.e., vertical) differentiation more pronounced. The distinction between "informed elites" and "entertained majorities" is on the increase in many countries, supported not least by media economics, as access to deeper information and knowledge beyond the popular media becomes more of a significant economic factor. Overall, the strong concept of "the public" as the voice of the inclusive citizenry moves more toward a weak version of media spectatorship, complemented by a plethora of smaller, more exclusive, and often inter-active, online publics.

Audiences become more "nomadic" and mobile, make more indi-vidual choices, and have more technological capacities at their disposal to avoid being the traditional "sitting ducks" of mass media communi-cation. As the media in their various forms saturate daily life, it becomes increasingly difficult to identify the specific attention a specific group of people accord a specific media output. The situation becomes fluid, as audiences "are everywhere and nowhere" (Bird, 2003). Difficulties measuring audiences multiply: The 2007 report on The State of the News Media (www.staeofthemedia.org) on page 1 of the Overview formulates it this way: "With audiences splintering across ever more platforms, nearly every metric for measuring audience is now under challenge as either flawed or obsolete . . . ."

For journalism, the trends of audience decline are troublesome. The situation in the United States is perhaps the most turbulent, though similar patterns are found throughout the industrialized world. For example, in 1964, four out five Americans read a daily paper; today it is one out of two. The ratings of the three nightly network news broadcasts have dropped by 44 percent since 1980. Regarding the Internet, only 11 percent of young people say that it is a major source of news for them. In 1966, 60 percent of first-year university students believed that following news is important. By 2003 that figure had dropped to 34 percent – one out of three (figures from Cornog, 2005). What is compelling in these developments is the generational perspective: The young are not replac-ing the old as steady news consumers, which drives home the premise that there is no going back to earlier socio-cultural conditions for democracy. We can only look ahead – and the picture is very troubling (see Mindich, 2005, for a detailed investigation into these patterns).

POPULARIZATION/TABLOIDIZATION

Still, the media industries' economic response to journalism's diffi-culties has to a considerable extent taken the form of increased tabloid-ization. The term has several connotations, and in the Introduction to a milestone anthology on tabloidization (Sparks and Tulloch, 2000), Sparks delineates three basic aspects, in both the printed press and television news. The first is the pattern in which news values lead to a focus on scandals, entertainment, and sports, and little on tradition-ally important areas such as society, politics, and economics. The emphasis is often on personal lives, of celebrities as well as ordinary people. The second aspect is broader, and refers to the tendency for media institutions to give less attention to serious news in the context of the overall output. Here, news is given a reduced position within an overall media mix. The third aspect has more to do with issues of taste, and here the debates zero in especially on television talk shows and reality television, where critics castigate what they see as inappropriate and even vulgar displays.

All three aspects of course lead to problems for the standards associated with traditional quality journalism, but the second one, where serious news is reduced, is arguably the most damaging. Even if much of journalism consists of sensationalism, scandal, personification, excessive dramatization, and the derailing of civic-oriented news values, democracy can still be nourished if the mix continues to contain relevant information that is useful to citizens, regardless of what forms it may take. But if this core element continues to evaporate, however, the warning signals should rightly go off.

The media have always wanted to reach large audiences, and it can be argued that tabloidization is but an extreme form of popularization, that is, simply strategies to gain larger audiences. This is intrinsically neither good nor bad – popularization in practice need not be negative per se (see, for example, Dahlgren and Sparks, 1992), even if the distinctions between acceptable popularization and deplorable tabloidization will remain contentious. Popularization can mean making the public sphere available to larger numbers of people via more accessible formats and styles of presentation, helping people to feel incorporated into society as citizens. It can involve taking up topics and experiences from the realm of private experience and introducing them as important and contestable topics within the public sphere (see Livingstone and Lunt, 1994; Meijer, 2001, 2007). In a diverse media landscape, popular forms of journalism can address those segments of the population who may feel excluded by more highbrow formats and discursive registers; such forms can engage, evoke, and provoke, serving as catalysts for discussion and debate (see Temple, 2006).

There are, in other words, versions of popularization. Thus, while popularization can lead directly to the obvious pitfalls and becomes, simply, tabloidization in the negative sense, especially if the bedrock of relevant civic information vanishes, it is not always certain that merely clinging to traditional journalistic formats per se is the best way to defend democracy in a time of dramatic socio-cultural change. It is certainly true that media output must be "opportunistic" in regard to audiences – be tuned in to their tastes, expectations, and so forth. Yet it is also the case that the media themselves bear a responsibility in structuring the horizons of expectation: Offering more fun and placing less demands on the audiences leads to expectations of, well, more fun and less demands. Such developments are at the heart of much of the controversy within journalism today, and they will continue to evoke debate. The big challenge, it would seem, is to develop new popular forms that will both resonate with large audiences and also communicate in meaningful ways about important matters.

WEAK "CONNECTIONS": BAD NEWS FOR DEMOCRACY

It remains true, according to international comparisons (see Milner, 2001), that those nations where quality journalism is available, where public service broadcasting is still viable, and where citizens attend extensively to these media tend to have higher participation in elections. What Milner (2001) calls "civic literacy" does make a difference. However, it may well be that in the case of the Nordic countries, for example, which rank highly in terms of voter turnout, one cannot simply specify the news media per se as the decisive factor. One must take into account the larger picture of media, the political culture, and the relative responsiveness of governments in these small and still relatively homogenous societies.

There is strong indication that it is precisely this ensemble of factors that in the long term is critical: It is not just a question of media performance alone, but also of how democracy is actually working and how citizens experience the political process that will determine the character and extent of civic engagement. A recent ambitious study (Couldry, Livingstone, and Markham, 2007) in the UK took as its point of departure the concept of "mediated public connection," that is, that citizens share an orientation to the public world beyond their private concerns, and that this orientation is maintained chiefly by a convergence in the media that they consume. The significance of this specific rendering of the general notion of the public sphere is that the authors stress that this "connection" is not the same as genuine attention.

Most people, most of the time, are not following news and current affairs. But when something develops that does call for their attention, they can and generally will pay attention – if they are "connected." Those who are "disconnected" generally will not. In this way, mediated public connection can be seen as a resource to be drawn upon when circumstances call for it; one might say that a shared public culture necessary for democracy is thus sustained by people being "civically prepared." Such a connection of course cannot simply be assumed: "It must be sustained by individuals and facilitated by the wider, social, cultural, and governmental context" (Couldry, Livingstone, and Markham, 2007:181).

To be viable, such a connection must be an integrated habit, a part of everyday life. The authors found that most UK citizens have some kind of public connection, that the media play a central role in this, and that there is a variety of patterns of connection. Also, the authors identify some key factors that help sustain it. One important factor is people's particular social circumstances; many said, for example, that discussions at work help motivate them to follow the news. Among younger citizens, reading the newspaper was (not surprisingly) low, yet only a small minority (one in ten) said that they regularly followed the news and current affairs on the Internet.

However, the major problem they identified is that, for a majority of the respondents, there is no clear link between having a mediated public connection and any opportunities for any civic action – deliberation or participation. The authors found "little evidence of UK citizens having had access to 'communities of practice' . . . through which they could act together in the public world; the result must be to make it more difficult to build . . . 'plausible narratives of the self' that link citizenship to the rest of everyday life" (p. 188). Here we hit a sort of bottom line: The fundamental role of journalism in democracy is to link citizens to political life. If citizens are at least linked to the media – if they are thus "connected" – this is an important precondition for engagement. Yet, if they see little possibility to actually participate, if they have little chance to see themselves as engaged citizens, then the problems run deep. (This is a persistent, base-line dilemma for democracy; Yankelovitch, 1991, addresses this problem from the horizons of public opinion research.) And the problems derive basically from the character of the political life and power relations that in a variety of ways hinders participation. Under such circumstances, journalism cannot compensate for "the system"; it has difficulties helping people to see themselves as citizens and facilitating engagement.

POLITICAL COMMUNICATION IN FLUX

COMMUNICATING POLITICS: PLURALIZATION

Turning to the broader domain of political communication, the first thing to observe is the deepening patterns of pluralization and specialization. Compared to just two decades ago, there are now more kinds of actors and forces making themselves felt. Today, a lot of journalism originates with nonjournalists: An emerging stratum of professional communication mediators is altering the way journalism gets done and the way political communication takes place. Spin doctors, public relations experts, media advisors, and political consultants using the techniques of advertising, market research, public relations, and opinion analysis have entered the fray to help political actors and economic elites shape their communication strategies (McNair, 2000, Chapter 7; Cottle, 2003; Davis, 2002; Franklin, 2004; Louw, 2005). Public relations as such has a long history (see Ewen, 1996), but in recent decades it has become more entwined with political communication, thereby further blurring the distinctions between journalism and nonjournalism. We encounter on a daily basis a variety of media and genre that contain political messages or information of one kind or another: Political communication is no longer neatly bounded.

These spin specialists take seriously the fact that the communication of politics in today's world involves different media and encompasses many different actors, contexts, cultural frameworks, power relationships, and communicative styles. It can be argued that strategic forms of news management should be understood as one of innumerable examples of modernization and rationalization (see the collection by Negrine, Mancini, Holtz-Bacha, and Papathananassopoulos, 2007). Moreover, they can also be used by the less powerful, opening the doors for progressive movements to get their messages onto the media agenda. However, in the long run there is the question of the impact of superior resources and influence in determining whose messages get across. Also, while the professionalization of political communication often helps various power holders and special interest groups to pursue their goals, it tends not to augment the position of citizens and the development of a strong, participatory democracy.

In many cases, particularly during campaigns, political communication is being geared to smaller and smaller specific target groups (e.g., Gandy, 2001), based on specialized and often quite narrow sociocultural parameters. This can certainly result in political messages being formulated in a more strategic manner, yet it may also contribute to the diminution of a shared public culture, as the communicative environment of politics for different groups separate from each other. Yet wider audiences of course still remain important targets; not least, the executive branches of some Western democracies have been making increased use of news management and direct communication to the general public. The Blair administration's "New Labour" government in the UK engaged in a "permanent campaign" in the media to manage and steer opinion (Franklin, 2004). In Italy, the economic dominance of Berlusconi in the media landscape has given him unprecedented power to influence the political climate when he was prime minister (Ginsbourg, 2004). In times of war governments of course tend to engage in news management and spin, including outright lies, as exemplified during the war in Iraq.

ELITES, MEDIA, CITIZENS: REALIGNMENTS

While political communication research's tendency to emphasize the interplay between media, citizens, and political actors may at times leave important features of contemporary democracy out of the searchlight, this focus certainly does illuminate key elements in the dynamics of democracy. One of the challenges becomes to map the evolving relations of power between the media, citizens, and other institutions of society; these are always evolving and specific to contexts (see Curran, 2002). Some observers are quick to point to the power *of* the media, in shaping political agendas, in conveying and reproducing certain world-views. Others will underscore the power *over* the media, for example, how politicians, private interests, and audiences influence how the media operate and the kinds of representations of reality they provide. Still others highlight how various power vectors can generate ambivalent force-fields in and around the media. All of these perspectives are of course valid, if not always simultaneously. (The theme of media and power is a fundamental one, and the literature is vast; see Couldry, 2004, for a recent contribution.)

Schematically, we can conceptualize a bounded configuration of four sets of political communication actors: political elites, economic elites, citizens, and the mass media. Looking at the overall developments I have outlined in this and the previous chapter, the first conclusion to be gleaned in regard to power alignments is that the power of the economic elites has expanded at the expense of the other actors. Citizens are situated further from the centres of economic decision-making, not just because the economy has become increasingly globalized, but also because the political elites, who ostensibly represent the citizens, have been losing some power relative to the economic elites, as real power drifts away from representative and accountable democratic systems to the conglomerate corporate sector. Moreover, citizens' relative power has declined, particularly as it has become increasingly fragmented by various social divisions and cultural pluralization, as I noted in the previous chapter. (In passing, it is interesting to note – and a sign of the ideological climate – that the Gallup Poll of October 8, 2007, found that nearly half of all Americans, and three-quarters of all Republicans – perceive the media as too liberal.)

If the economic elite has witnessed a rise in its power relative to the media, the political elite's situation vis-à-vis the media is more ambivalent. It is still the case of two sly foxes trying to maximize their advantage; "symbiosis," a form of mutual dependence, still prevails between journalism and the political class. Political elites need easy access – and preferably favorable coverage – while journalists need good source contacts to get their stories. However, the rules themselves have been evolving, and a different kind of journalism is emerging. With the growth of infotainment genres on television, often hosted by journalists, politicians can obtain more exposure and market their personalities than on traditional news formats (see Bolin, 2007). This development can have a long-term impact on the relative power of political elites.

The imperatives of commercialization are serving to escalate the general level of drama associated with politics. With heightened tabloidization, an intensified dramaturgical framework for journalistic coverage of politics emerges. In highlighting conflict, personification journalism, with its emphasis on emotions and psychology, and especially scandal, puts more pressures on politicians (see Lull and Hinerman, 1997; Thompson, 2000). Politicians, of course, try to make use of these kinds of framing for their own purposes – for example, appearing on popular programs to demonstrate their personal charm – but they are often on the defensive. However, drama not infrequently involves journalists going on the hunt for individual politicians. The media present themselves as guardians of the public interest and the political elites are framed with suspicion, while the economic elites basically get edited out of journalistic discourses about power.

Political elites at times complain that the media are fostering a popular contempt against them. While this popular view of political elites may not be completely undeserved in all cases, there is still some justification to the claim. The media, in their watch-dog role, have also been barking at many shadows, too many trivial and personal details that do not necessarily relate to politics and the public interest. Journalists have at times taken advantage of the political elites' relative decline in power, but at the same time they have not focused their critical eyes on the economic elites. It can also be argued that the media have gained a notch in power over political elites in that contemporary media logics steer the modes of representation; television cameras, sound bites, and so on, compel the political elites to some extent to dance to a tune composed by the media. Yet we should be careful in not exaggerating this shift in power: The political establishment has also become more sophisticated in dealing with the media, and spin is accelerating.

THE LATE MODERN MEDIA: LOGICS OF THE MATRIX

It should be evident that democracy has been thrust into a new era, where the societal and cultural landscapes, and the character of communication, are all contributing to its transformation. The power of the media, and the power over the media, have long been debated, but it is clear that the media themselves constitute an increasingly important factor in the evolving dynamics of democracy. They thus offer an important handle for both understanding and participating in the unfolding of democracy.

MEDIA LOGICS

The mediation of reality always inevitably involves modes of representation, shaped by the characteristics and imperatives of communication technologies and institutions. All accounts of reality are socially situated and constructed; they derive from some perspective, involving particular social optics and value premises. There can be no narratives about the social world that are not also a part of that world, and in some ways shaped by it. While this may signal the impossibility of "objectivity" in some deeper philosophical sense, it of course does not preclude the possibility of doing good journalism. It is, however, useful for journalism to on occasion reflect on the frames that it uses, and on how its production circumstances shape its output. Some years ago, Altheide and Snow (see Altheide and Snow, 1991, for their most extensive treatment) developed the notion of media logic, to illuminate the imperatives that shape the particular attributes and ways of doing things within given media and even within specific genres. This pertains to the procedures of selection, form, tempo, informational density, aesthetics, contents, modes of address, and production schedules. The notion of media logic helps us to understand how different forms of representation can be linked to the specific conditions and attributes of media work, how the imperatives of a specific media impact on what gets represented, and in what manner.

Thus, television as a medium, for instance, is visual and exists in time; the press is a textual medium that takes up space. They have different communicative forms and time frames of production. Hence political actors using these media will have to use different approaches. Also, within any given medium there are important genre differences: A local radio talk show is not the same as a national news broadcast, and a popular television magazine operates differently from a highbrow debate program. Further, with the advent of the Internet and its various communicative forms (e.g., weblogs, discussion forums, wikis) as well as net-based versions of the mass media, we have a whole new realm with its own media logics now developing rapidly within political communication.

The strategies and tactics of political communication are therefore constantly adapting and readapting themselves to the specific media – not least with the help of the new kinds of media consultants. This is manifested in everything from the targeting of messages for specific audience niches to the rhetoric of press conferences and to the conscious adaptation of public discourse to sound bites of suitable length and visuals with dramatic impact. Established elites as well as alternative or oppositional groups trying to shape public opinion must all follow the same path – if they want any chance of attracting media coverage. Thus, politics does not exist as a completely separate reality taking place independently of and outside the media, to then be "covered" by journalists. Rather, politics is increasingly organized as a media phenomenon, planned and executed for and with the cooperation of the media, and in these processes becomes unavoidably altered (Meyer, 2002; Louw, 2005).

Note that this perspective does not claim that there is no real world outside the media, or that everything we see in the media is merely a form of simulation. Rather, it suggests that in the modern world, many institutions, including religion and sports, but especially politics, have adapted their activities to media logics, and in the process have transformed themselves. And the newer interactive media have introduced new media logics into the political domain, not least whereby "placeless" communicative spaces and user mobility stand in stark contrast to the rather fixed locational character of traditional politics.

If the media have become the prime scene of politics, this does not deny that politics takes place in other settings as well, but it does signal a relative marginality of the other forums. This resonates with what was said above about the general political disengagement we are witnessing. In everyday life, in civil society, people are of course still discussing public affairs – and this is of great importance for the democratic development of opinion – but these contexts tend normally to have relatively less bearing on politics when compared to the massive presence of the media. This is not a question of the extent to which people accept or reject the views they encounter in the media, but rather where we find the center of gravity for political dynamics in late modern society. What is at stake here is the overall character of the political communication environment – both mediated and face-to-face – as well as its role in facilitating democratic participation.

THE MEDIA MATRIX

My dictionary offers several definitions of the word "matrix," including "an arrangement of numbers, figures, or signs ... made up of ordered lines"; "a mould into which melted metal, plastic, etc. is poured to form it into a shape"; and "a living part in which something is formed or developed. . . ." Taken together, these definitions seem applicable to the media, in the metaphorical sense that via their various logics the media constitute certain ordered arrangements, they mold and form, and they are "living" in the sense of being nonstatic and ever-evolving. Such was no doubt also the thought behind the successful Hollywood film series with that name, yet we must not therefore ally ourselves with dystopian cyberpunk visions (cf. Taylor and Harris, 2005, who, in also distancing themselves from social pessimism, black leather garb, and gravity-defying combat, use the term to refer to specifically the developments in digital technology and their socio-cultural impact). With the ongoing technical developments of multimedia ICTs with enhanced mobile capacity, contemporary communication technologies are progressing toward a convoluted and dynamic media matrix, an ensemble of simultaneously operative media logics.

The ever-complex logics of the media matrix in the digital age impact on how politics is represented in – and gets done via – the media. The codes, conventions, and discursive frameworks of political communication adapt and evolve, while new communicative practices and strategies emerge. This adaptation is going in many directions at the same time; the media matrix today comprises a number of force-fields that inject more uncertainty into the situation.

Pundits point out, for example, that in the U.S. Democratic presidential primary race in the spring of 2008, Barack Obama made decisively better strategic use of the Internet than his rival, Hillary Clinton, to reach voters at the grassroots level. We could say that in the current media matrix, there is a dispersion of political communication through a variety of modes: Traditional news is now but one form whereby political communication is conveyed. And further, given the growing multivalent notion of what constitutes politics, I would also contend that the definition of what should be classified as political communication is expanding. Thus, pinning down what is actually experienced as political communication may be becoming more difficult, as politics "leaks" into new social and cultural domains.

New media technologies can promote civic empowerment, while at the same time they render citizens more vulnerable to surveillance and control. Marginalized groups can enter the political mainstream more easily – yet also more readily become still more politically isolated. Media representations may serve to promote a sense of powerlessness, foster cynicism, and hinder democratic engagement (Meyer, 2002, offers a recent analysis of this kind). Yet, as McNair (2005) argues, today the various elites are faced with considerable "chaos" in regard to the mediation of politics, and they exercise less ideological control over the political environment. To the extent that this is true – and even allowing for possible overstatement – this can mean that alternative political opinions, actors, and movements have more options, more space in which to maneuver. This of course holds true for antidemocratic as well as progressive forces, however.

Today, many people can share the same information, the same experiences, simultaneously. In one sense, time becomes factored out – yet also it speeds up, as the instantaneous character of the media accelerates the rhythm of communication. Distance can be experienced without physically moving, place no longer necessarily defines the "where" of experience – or of politics. Space in a sense becomes compressed, yet also multiplied endlessly, and public and private spaces become repositioned. And with the rise of mobile media they add a further element of fluidity to the mix.

Yet the swiftness built into modern media technologies can also be seen in the long run as a threat to democracy, according to the theorist Paul Virilio (e.g., Virilio, 2000, 2002; see also Armitage, 2000). From the perspective of the public sphere, such high-speed political communication can be deemed out of sync with the pace of human reflection and discussion, generating stress and unreason, notably in situations of decision-making.

The media matrix impacts on group communication, interpersonal relations, identity processes, work, leisure, and the way we organize our everyday lives, and does so in contradictory ways. It would be odd if the world of politics remained an exception.

It is small wonder that, for democracy, business as usual is not an option. These transformations erode some traditional forms of political communication, while facilitating new ones. All societies, all people, do not of course share equally in these developments, and even for the most ultramediated cosmopolitans, neither place nor face-to-face relations have become totally irrelevant. Still, these developments are so pervasive that they have come to define much of the contemporary historical setting. To see the world through the media's analytic lenses provides a certain perspective, yet we have to also bring other elements into our field of vision. To grapple with questions of civic engagement pushes us also to critically probe some of the prevailing assumptions regarding the nature of citizenship, agency, and politics, as well as to delve deeper into the character of engagement and civic discussion. These are the topics of the following two chapters.

CHAPTER 3

Citizens and Agency

Notions of citizenship have varied widely across time, cultures, and political philosophies. I chart, in this chapter, some key ideas from contemporary strands that will help to illuminate and anchor the basic perspective that I am developing here. This view not only sees citizenship as a formal, legal set of rights and obligations, but also treats it as a mode of social agency. Further, citizenship can analytically be seen to have subjective identities that resonate (or not) with people's other elements of identity. While the advancement of neoliberalism has been undercutting certain areas of democracy in recent decades, we witness at the same time from other corners an energetic renewal of the concept of citizenship. The first section thus discusses citizenship as a growing area of research interest, taking up a number of developments that underscore the importance of its dimensions of agency and subjectivity. The second section explores the idea of how people *become* citizens. Liberal theory in its classic mode tends to assume a fully formed civic subject who enters the political scene (usually at the age of eighteen), but has little to say about the socio-cultural factors that can impact on this development. Moreover, participation in liberal theory is most often cast as an individual activity, ignoring its collective dimension. I therefore underscore the importance of prepolitical socio-cultural experience and the interactional character of participation. The final section explores knowledge as a particular problem in regard to civic agency, focusing first on opinion processes and then on the dilemmas of expert knowledge.

CITIZENSHIP: AN EXPANSIVE TERRAIN

CIVIC AND POLITICAL

Thus far I have largely been using the terms "civic" and "political" interchangeably, but at this point it would be helpful to introduce some distinctions. The term "civic" derives from *civitas*, the Greek city-states, and the Latin *civcus*, indicating citizen. The civic resonates with the notion of public, in the sense of being visible, relevant for, and in some way accessible to many people, that is, situated outside the private, intimate domain. "Civic" then carries the implication of engagement in public life – a cornerstone of democracy. Interestingly, in some contexts, civic also signifies the public good. It conveys a sense of the altruistic, a kind of "service," doing good for others, such as volunteer work. In fact, in political science and political communication research, "civic engagement" is often defined precisely as forms of voluntary activity aimed toward solving problems in the community and helping others (see, for example, Adler, 2005; Zukin et al., 2006), while "political engagement" is reserved for activity oriented toward influencing governmental action in some way.

What falls inside the terrain of the civic, and what remains outside, are questions that cannot be answered unequivocally, because the terrain shifts – we see differences both historically and between contemporary political cultures. Thus, in the UK and the United States, charity work is often emblematic of a type of civic engagement. Yet in modern-day Sweden, where the welfare state has been very strong, such activity (and organizations) have not had a pronounced profile, and charity measures are often seen as personal, individual actions. Similarly, religion in most Western societies has been treated as a private matter, even if religious organizations may be involved at times in social or charity work. Yet, as theological elements enter into political life in various ways, this begins to change, and certain religious organizations take on civic – and political – characters. So while I would certainly retain the key quality of publicness in the concept of "civic," full conceptual closure will continue to elude us.

The notions of politics and the political inevitably encompass some dimension of conflict. We can shed more light on the notions of civic and political by emphasizing how they flow together, rather than trying to keep them separate. If we map the two concepts, we can say that the notion of civic is broader, encompassing the terrain of the public, while it is on this terrain that politics and the political arise. The civic is thus a precondition for the political, in the sense that it situates us in the realm of the public. I thus use the term "civic agency" as a fundamental notion to conceptually anchor people's enactment of citizenship. Thus, if democracy is about the civic in the general sense of the public and the public good, it is *also* about the political, that is, when issues arise in the civic realm that have to do with conflicts over interests, resources, and power. There is no need to beat about the bush on this point: Democracy is no less noble because it addresses political conflicts. On the contrary, collective antagonisms arise in all societies, and it is precisely democracy's vision of offering the best – or least, worst – ways of dealing with them that makes it so valuable.

Another definitional issue has to do with explicitly anti-democratic groups: They are public, but should they then be treated as de facto civic? I would reiterate the definitional foundation: the civic pertains to the democratic character of society, and I would thus not attribute the quality of "civic" to groups that espouse, for example, neofascism, racism, terrorism, or hate. Here the "civic" takes the high road and parts company from that which is merely "public." That said, I would also reiterate that "democracy" can never be reduced to a mantra, and must be continually discussed and debated; we have to live with the fact that there will always be varying models and visions as to what constitutes the "best" or "real" democracy. At least one nonnegotiable criterion in this regard must precisely be that such debates may continue.

Democratic rhetoric often encourages people to "be civic," that is, to engage in public matters and to offer service. Interestingly, people are rarely encouraged to "be political," even in regard to elections. Voting is rhetorically framed as a civic duty or responsibility, not an act of taking a political stand. "Politics" tends to have a negative aura about it. It is often assumed to be self-serving; it is seen as characterized by questionable motives as well as ethics. Yet democracy is not least about how we resolve collective conflicts of interest that arise in society – how we can live together and work out antagonisms in safe and civilized ways, as citizens.

New Directions

A common and convenient starting point in discussions about citizenship as such is to say that at one level it is relatively simple: It builds upon a set of rights and obligations, historically evolved in society, and underscores universalism and equality. In the modern world it has almost always been linked to the nation-state. In this sense, citizenship can be treated as a legal framework that underpins democracy. From this general view, the much-cited postwar writing of T. H. Marshall (1950) in Britain provided a major reorientation in contemporary thinking about citizenship. In the context of welfare societies struggling with class inequalities, he underscored three by now familiar dimensions of citizenship that have defined much of the contemporary discussion: the *civil*, which aims to guarantee the basic legal integrity of society's members; the *political*, which serves to ensure the rights associated with democratic participation; and the *social*, which addresses the general life circumstances of individuals.

In the case of social citizenship, Marshall's thought was that if people fall below certain levels of well-being, they are unable to function in their role as citizens, a theme that takes on new relevance in the light of the decline of the welfare state. A number of commentators today, in the context of multicultural and multiethnic societies in a global context, argue that *cultural* citizenship must also be added to the list (e.g., Stevenson, 2003). This category would include, for example, the rights to have one's own traditions and language, as well as a series of rights that particularly link up with both the common good and minority needs in relation to the modern media.

One can say that the formal status of citizenship conceptually frames political life in modern democracies, by defining rights and obligations, and making distinctions between citizens and noncitizens. Also, the historical evolution of citizenship varies according to the histories of democracy in different societies. For example, the United States, with its emphasis on liberal individual rights and an active civil society (e.g., Schudson, 1998), has had different dominant currents compared to that of France (e.g., Rosanvallon, 2004), where the state has generally had a stronger role in the dynamics of democracy even at the local level, or Sweden, with its legacy of corporatist arrangements. Democracy has witnessed many struggles, as various groups and cultures have made claims for inclusion, recognition, and redistribution. Today, many voices are making claims in regard to citizen rights. As democracy has come to face various challenges in recent decades, so too has this process of trying to attain the espoused ideals been accelerating (see, for example, Kymlicka, 1995; Taylor, 1994; Spinner, 1994). Citizenship, it would seem, has become an increasingly problematic concept.

New concepts come to the fore: For example, the notion of universality as a foundational element of citizenship is being problematized by the themes of difference and identity; some argue (e.g., Young, 1990, 2000) that marginalized groups may require specialized legal treatment by the state in order to help them achieve full citizenship. In a similar vein, recognition as a central element of citizenship has also become prominent. It points to the importance of citizens to develop as autonomous individuals with self-esteem and self-confidence. This concept has been receiving increased attention within philosophy and social theory (see, for example, Honneth, 1995; Fraser and Honneth, 2003). Authors such as Taylor (1994) address the need for a politics of recognition in the context of cultural differences among the citizens of democracy. Especially in the context of struggles of marginalized groups, what is sometimes called the politics of belonging becomes inexorably tied to issues of citizenship and identity (see the collection of case studies by Yuval-Davis, Kannabiran, and Vieten, 2006).

Moreover, in the wake of globalization and the relative decline of the nation-state, we see the themes of global citizenship, postnational citizenship, cosmopolitanism, and global civil society increasingly appearing in the debates (Benhabib, 2004; Held, 2006, Chapter 11; Miller, 2000; Delanty, 2000; Sassen, 2002; Beck, 2007). Kivisto and Faist (2007), in exploring an array of emerging notions of citizenship, note that there is both an erosion of citizenship taking place – for example, as traditional domains of civic activity are marginalized by uncontrolled market forces – as well as an expansion, in such contexts as the EU, globalization, and multiple citizenship. The phenomenon of the World Social Forum, for example, while geographically situated by its meetings in Pôrto Alegre, is transnational in scope, giving rise to a new kind of public space for new kinds of subaltern civic practices (Conway, 2004). Citizenship "unbounded" by the institutional frameworks of nation-states that can specify rights, obligations, and accountability, however, is still at a serious disadvantage. The moral force, intensity of opinion, or political optimism that such trajectories may galvanize must still confront the thinness of institutionalized democracy beyond the borders of the nation-state.

As an effort to bring some order in the many debates about citizenship, Isin and Turner (2002:2) identify three axes of contention over citizenship: *extent*, having to do with rules and norms pertaining to inclusion and exclusion; *content*, addressing rights and responsibilities; and *depth*, the "thickness" or "thinness" of citizenship in terms of how the identities of members should be understood and accommodated. We see struggles based on identity and difference – for example, in regard to gender (including medical and sexual control over the body), sexual preference, ethnicity, and diasporas – that demand not just legal or formal status, but political and social recognition, and even economic redistribution.

CITIZENSHIP: RECEIVED AND ACHIEVED

I would like to introduce at this point another distinction: between those notions of citizenship that are universalist and state-centered and those that are differentiated and based on agency. In this rendering, I follow Angus Stewart's (2001) discussion, though I take some liberty with his terminology to better integrate the perspective into my discussion.

State-centered understandings of citizenship are abstract and formal, defined within the legal parameters of state power. Certainly in terms of the history of democracy, the definitions and guarantees of such citizenship have been major accomplishments. The claim is usually put forth that formal citizenship thus secures universalism and equality. At the same time, however, history has shown that there remain exclusions, inequities, and suppressions of various kinds and to various degrees within democratic societies. The social realities of inequality do not necessarily just disappear via the formal status of citizenship – a critical view long prevalent on the left. In fact, it could be argued that just about all major gains toward a more just and inclusive citizenship have been the result of political struggles – for example, the labor movement, the women's movement, and the civil rights movement.

Thus, we have the second notion of citizenship, that which is based on political agency. It emphasizes that democratic universalism and genuine civic equality remain an unfinished project, and asserts also that there are key differences among citizens that must be recognized and politically addressed. There remain conditions such as marginalization, powerlessness, and exploitation among certain groups, related to status in regard to, for example, gender, ethnicity, and sexual orientation. This opens the door to a politics of difference, a starting point for political agency and a "constitutive" citizenship. Differences as such are not seen as insoluble problems, but rather as a point of departure for civic participation. Political communities that thus arise in the process can be seen as the result of concrete civic practices (Stewart, 2001:208). If the first, state-centered version can be seen as a *received* citizenship, the second, agency-based notion can be viewed as an *achieved* citizenship.

To the extent that received citizenship is found wanting, citizens can make strategic use of their formal rights and guarantees to further expand the democratic character of citizenship. In other words, the framework of state-based citizenship can be seen as an important pre-condition for the agency-based achieved dimension. For example, members of immigrant populations may find that cultural and economic mechanisms operate to hinder their full participation in the new society. Yet, if their freedoms of expression, assembly, and so forth are reasonably secure, this enhances their possibilities for productive political confrontation. Those rights and entitlements that do exist should be valued, defended, and expanded.

There is a growing literature that casts citizenship in terms of social agency, that emphasizes the achieved dimension as sets of practices, using approaches from social theory (cf. van Steenberger, 1994; Beiner, 1995; Janoski, 1998). Not least are contributions from feminist horizons, underscoring the obstacles to women achieving equality and universalism (among this large literature are Pateman, 1989; Lister, 2003; Voet, 1998; Phillips, 1993; Lloyd, 2005). Indeed, we see the emergence, since the 1990s, of citizenship studies (see, notably, the collection by Isin and Turner, 2003, and the journals *Citizenship Studies* and *Education, Citizenship and Social Justice*), as a multidisciplinary effort in the social sciences and humanities. What emerges here is the understanding that the dramatic changes in the late modern social landscape – at the national, subnational, and global levels – make imperative the effort to rethink and update our understanding of citizenship. Stevenson (2003), for example, connects citizenship particularly with alterations in cultural patterns and the media, in ways that parallel my discussion here. How we define citizenship is inseparable from how we define democracy and the good society; notions of citizenship thus remain ultimately contentious.

IDENTITY AND AGENCY

There is a complementary strand of recent work on citizenship that is based in cultural theory (e.g., Preston, 1997; Isin and Wood, 1999) as well as political philosophy (e.g., Clarke, 1996; Mouffe, 1993, 2000, 2005). These contributions highlight the dimension of identity as a key to understanding citizenship as civic agency. In essence, the argument is that in order to be able to act as a citizen, to participate in achieved citizenship, it is necessary that one can see oneself as a citizen, as subjectively encompassing the attributes of agency that this social category may involve.

One of the hallmarks of late modern society is the emergence of the self as a reflexive project, an ongoing process of the shaping and reshaping of identity, in response to the pluralized social forces, cultural currents, and personal contexts encountered by individuals. Moreover, identity is understood as plural: In our daily lives we operate in a multitude of different "worlds" or realities; as subjects, we are positioned differently in different circumstances, making use of different sets of knowledge, assumptions, rules, roles, and modes of discourse (among the large literature that addresses this theme, useful points of entry can be found in Fornäs, 1995; Hetherington, 1998; Taylor and Spencer, 2004). While certain elements of our identity reside more to the core of our sense of self, all of us are to varying degrees composite people, activating different sides of our selves in different contexts.

The idea of composite identities also pertains to citizenship, which can thus be understood as a significant dimension of our multiple selves, though interlaced with other dimensions. Gellner (1994) uses the metaphor "modular man" (sic) to capture this idea. In short, people's identities as citizens (however defined), with their sense of belonging to political collectivities – and perceived possibilities for participating in politics – become crucial elements in the life of democracy. Our identities as citizens involve some form of publicly positioned subjectivity, though we must allow that the boundaries between public and private are constantly being renegotiated. To the extent that citizenship relates to identity, it must resonate in some way with emotionality, with affect; our identities are never merely the product of our rational thought.

In practical terms, citizenship is central to the fundamental issues of social belonging and participation. Identities of membership are not just subjectively produced by individuals, but evolve collectively and in relation to institutional mechanisms in society. Citizenship thus serves as an analytic entry into the study of the dynamics and of social inclusion and exclusion. It invites us to consider democracy's ideals of universalism and equality, and to confront the discrepancies between these ideals and prevailing social realities. Yet the concept embodies force fields: The tensions between the principles of universalist inclusion and the recognition of difference have to be continuously thrashed out in concrete situations. The emphasis on difference can foster separatism and exclusion; tolerance can teeter over to indifference.

If citizenship is a dimension of the self, however, this does not mean that the word "citizen" per se necessarily vibrates with meaning for people. In fact, many people, even those who are civically engaged, can find "citizenship" and its associated terminology uninspiring, to say the least. Different political cultures use different vocabularies, and from the standpoint of research one has to be sensitive to people's own discursive strategies for making sense of their participation in democracy. Civic identity would seemingly be most likely to take on meaning in the concrete activities of engagement, in particular political communities, to achieve particular political goals – rather than hovering at the abstract level.

THE REPUBLICAN IMAGINARY

In the political theory literature, mention is often made of three main theoretic traditions of citizenship: liberalism, communitarianism, and republicanism, the latter two being seen as "challengers" to the dominant liberal paradigm. It is certainly not the case that all political theorists can be neatly slotted into one of these categories, but it is useful to understand the basic distinctions. I will be tilting toward republicanism in the discussion that follows, since this version of citizenship most obviously asserts the role of civic agency and engagement, However, I share Beiner's (1995) perspective that any contemporary theory of democracy must acknowledge some productive interplay between the three.

The classic liberal model of democracy and citizenship underscores individual rights (for the classic nineteenth-century statement, see Mill, 1998/1861). Rawls (1972) is often cited as a major contemporary milepost, even if his focus is on justice. In the liberal vision, the state's role is seen in minimalist terms; the state exists to protect the freedom of citizens, allowing them to pursue their own lives and happiness, without causing injury to others. The citizen pursues his or her interests via making rational choices. With the advent of the neoliberal hegemony, this interpretation of the state becomes further sharpened: The state can promote individual liberty and happiness not least by reducing the obstacles to free exchange in the marketplace. There is an odd absence of sociological perspective in liberal theories of citizenship. The individual is implicitly seen as emerging as a fully formed citizen, devoid of social bonds, out of some socio-cultural black box, ready to play his or her role in democracy. Citizenship becomes an activity where "no experience is necessary"; there is a sense in which the citizen is just "acting naturally" in pursuing his or her own interests.

Communitarianism, on the other hand, can be seen as one sort of response to liberalism's extreme individualism (see, for example, Walzer, 1983; Taylor, 1994; Etzioni, 1993). While its origins are anchored deeply in the history of political philosophy, communitarianism has gained momentum since the early 1980s. Its milder versions make the reasonable sociological claim that shared values and cultural cohesion are important for the functioning of political community. Stronger versions argue that a deeper community is necessary if democracy is to function properly. Community has been a key theme within sociology since the late nineteenth century – often because of its perceived weakness or absence. Communitarianism, in its more ambitious modes, appears to be striving for community at an implausible breadth and depth. In the late modern world there is something mythic about achieving such stable community among groups where it has not already been in existence for a very long time.

Republicanism also generally puts an emphasis on the rights of individuals and groups, and the role of conflict in acquiring and defending those rights is often asserted (for some contemporary presentations, see Barber, 1984; Sandel, 1996; Petit, 1997; van Gunsteren, 1998). Most writers in this tradition acknowledge elements from the liberal tradition (e.g., the emphasis on individual rights) and communitarianism (civic bonds need to be shaped by some sense of community). This view meshes well with the idea of citizenship as a dimension of identity grounded in agency, within the context of pluralistic interests. Moreover, as in liberalism and communitarianism, the rule of law is central for republicanism. But for republicans, the law is seen as a collective mechanism for setting limits in the interest of all, rather than being simply geared to maximizing the freedom of the individual; the notion of the common good plays an important role, indicating the sense of shared, collective interests.

The most characteristic element of republicanism, however, is its insistence on the active participation of citizens in democratic self-governance. As Tocqueville (2004) observed in his study of the United States in the 1830s, involvement in public life is seen not just as a duty, but as something offering its own personal rewards. In participating in democracy, republicanism sees people becoming connected to each other, and developing as individuals. Thus, republicanism underscores not just the formal, legal dimension, as does liberalism, but also an ethical one. Republicanism asserts that democracy requires civic virtues from its citizens, and cultivating these virtues turns citizens into better people by developing abilities that would otherwise remain unfulfilled. In terms of the three axes of tension around the concept of citizenship (Isin and Turner, 2002:2), republicanism can be said to reside on the strong side of all three: *extent* (republicanism strive for inclusion), *content* (responsibilities and virtues as well as rights are emphasized), and *depth* (republicanism leans toward "thickness" concerning the identities of citizens).

As with communitarianism, there has been an upsurge in interest in republicanism in the past two decades, a growing assertion that democracy's problems are to a large extent to be understood precisely as consisting of too little civic engagement and concern for the common good. At the same time, we can see a tension between those who advocate that democracy must do a better job in recognizing and addressing differences and those who emphasize the well-being of all citizens, of the common good. Clearly, the ideal of the common good, linked to the principle of universalism, must not undermine the recognition of difference. The vision of an integrated citizenry and the principle of equality need to be tempered by respect for heterogeneity. Easy? Hardly. Does democracy have any alternative to dealing with such dialectical tensions? The republican answer would be, not if it wants to remain true to its ideals.

At the outer edges of republicanism we find what is termed "radical democracy." Informed by poststructural theory, it combines notions about the contextual nature of identity and subject positions with a view of political struggle as shaped by ever-shifting contingencies. There is no end point for conflict (or for democracy). We-they boundaries are continuously being redrawn as new issues and conflicts (and, thus, publics) arise. It accentuates the centrality of difference and heterogeneity, and the importance of progressive groups building alliances. Even one individual can at a particular point in time encompass several (even contradictory) political positions by virtue of multiple group identities or memberships. Yet, radical democracy retains a republican quality in its emphasis on agency and in its view of the common good: It also affirms a strong commitment to democratic values and procedures. (Key texts here are Laclau and Mouffe, 1985; Laclau, 1993; Mouffe, 1992, 1993, 2000, 2005. For a short overview, see Rasmussen and Brown, 2002; for an extended treatment, see Smith, 1998.)

While republicanism puts on the agenda the sociological theme of how citizens become engaged, the obvious question that arises, however, is to what extent is it realistic to expect that more citizens will participate more in public life? As I mentioned in Chapter 1, ever since the ideal of the responsible and engaged citizen became entrenched in the early twentieth century, its proponents have been shaking their finger at ordinary people for not sufficiently shouldering their civic obligations. Should we merely just join in with such complaints, the logical conclusion being that democracy is a great idea, it just needs a different breed of citizen to run it? Or do we suppress this history and opt for an easy, but unfounded, optimism? Or do we rethink the notion of citizenship itself?

Answers to such questions must of course be equivocal. Simply jumping on the bandwagon of lament would be a dead-end; at the same time, we would be ill-served by just relinquishing a critical view of low engagement and abandoning the normative ideal. Facile optimism can quickly usher us into irrelevance, yet to be locked into a bleak view that nothing in this regard can change invites paralysis. Putting our energies into reconsidering the parameters of citizenship and their ongoing socio-cultural evolution – which is precisely what the sprawling field of citizenship studies is doing – at least holds out the possibility of some conceptual progress.

While nobody anticipates that all citizens will become embodiments of republican virtue, there are no doubt different levels of anticipation, as well as different notions as to what portion of the citizenry needs to manifest such virtues in order to constitute a critical mass – in different societies and at various points in history. There are certainly also conflicting views as to how to attain such goals. Like the democratic ideal in general, republicanism can be seen as containing a certain mythic dimension: It provides a normative vision that serves to mobilize and direct concerns for civic renewal. There is perhaps also the pitfall of nostalgia for a past that never was. At the same time, in terms of our discussion here, this republican imaginary links up with both the notion of citizenship as agency, as achievement, as well as the importance of identity and virtue in regard to citizenship. And it also resonates well together with another conceptual partner, that of civil society.

BECOMING CITIZENS, DOING CITIZENSHIP

CIVIL SOCIETY: AN OPTIMISTIC VIEW

In the literature on civil society, the republican imaginary links up with the notion of citizenship as agency, as achievement. Civil society is a concept lodged within several different intellectual traditions whose premises and vocabularies are not always commensurable. Edwards (2004:vi) remarks in his handy overview that the concept is "notoriously slippery" (for an array of different conceptual versions, see Chambers and Kynlicka, 2002). I'll sidestep most of the issues here, as well as the history of the concept (see, for example, Ehrenberg, 1999). I would note, however, the obvious etymological link between the notion of "civil society" and the concept of "civic," with its links to publicness and the public good, that I discussed at the beginning of this chapter. In loose terms, civil society can be treated as the domain of the civic, the public sites of civic agency, where political participation has its origins. Again, I am avoiding a dichotomization of "civic" and "political," underscoring instead that the political can only emerge in a preexisting civic domain, that is, what we call civil society.

Theories of civil society have been much on the upswing through the 1990s (see Keane, 1998), not in small part inspired by the political developments of dissent in Eastern Europe in the 1980s, but also encouraged by the growth in social movements and new forms of political participation. In some theoretical renderings, it begins to merge with the notion of the public sphere (Cohen and Arato, 1992; Habermas, 1996). At the general level, however, civil society is seen by many writers as the societal terrain between the state and the economy, the realm of free association, where citizens can interact to pursue their shared interests – including political ones, I would emphasize. Even if it may at times be difficult to classify which of the many forms of collective activity and organization should be considered part of civil society, there is a dominant trajectory in civil society thinking that signals a degree of optimism: A healthy democracy needs a robust, public domain of associational interaction.

Such interaction helps individuals to develop socially, to shape their identities, to foster values suitable for democracy, and to learn to deal with conflict in productive ways. Conceptually, a realm of practice, self-creation, and meaning-making comes to situate and anchor the notion of civic agency. On the one hand, civil society can serve as a training ground that "grooms" citizens, with involvement in nonpolitical associations and networks preparing people for civic political engagement and participation (even if mere membership in associations does not automatically lead to involvement with real political situations and conflicts). On the other hand, civil society is also the socio-cultural terrain in which political participation is played out, where people as civic agents are continually developing their skills and sense of self as citizens. The processes of "becoming citizens," of socially and culturally developing civic identities, adds important analytic dimensions to the sociology of democracy.

The civil society horizon places on our analytic screen perspectives on democracy's socio-cultural requirements. Putnam (2000) illustrates this forcefully; his "bowling alone" metaphor captures the lack of communicative interaction among citizens in a time when civic involvement is in decline. This results in a reduced "social capital" among citizens – seen specifically as diminished networks of social contacts – which also implies a reduction in communicative competencies. (For debates around this thesis, see the contributions in Edwards, Foley, and Diani, 2001.) With increased fragmentation and atomization follows a decline in social trust, which further inhibits participation. Alexander (2006), in his recent major effort to rethink civil society in terms of a normative social theory, underscores in a communitarian fashion the shared values and ideals that must minimally bond citizens together. He suggests that democracy has fundamental dimensions that reside outside systemic mechanisms and can only be understood in terms of a community in everyday life and the institutions and networks that foster them. He posits that civil society is a kind of "solidarity sphere," where the values and visions that support the project of democracy can – and must – flourish.

The civil society perspective is, then, along with republicanism, another major tradition within political theory that affirms civic agency and the need for specific civic competences and virtues. Further, there is the important constructionist perspective that tries to take into account *how* people actually become such civic agents – how they self-create themselves into citizens. Even if there are ambiguities here, the civil society perspective suggests the importance of what we might call "suitable acculturation." The message is that to understand how democracy works, we must look beyond its institutional structures and dynamics. While the structures are essential, if they are not filled by real flesh-and-blood people with relevant values, virtues, and competencies, democracy will become merely a hollow formalism.

EXPERIENCE AND SKILLS

The diagnoses as to why civil society is not working as it should do vary – Putnam's view (2000) includes along with much sound sociological reasoning also the somewhat simplistic scapegoating of television culture's monopolization of our time and its general dumbing-down effects; Cohen and Arato (1992) and Chambers (2002), from the angle of critical theory, anchor their analyses in the tensions and complexities of late capitalism. Sennett's (1977) analysis of the historical decline of public character of American culture also pursues a range of socio-cultural factors, including elements of narcissism and the demand for authentic self-revelation.

Stewart's (2001) perspective on achieved citizenship and civic agency underscores that such activity is ultimately grounded in experience. He cites Wolin (1996), who posits that genuine democratic participation is something that on occasion "breaks out" among citizens, something that alters the normal modes of interaction. For democracy to be viable, however, such outbursts of intense affective engagement and motivated participation are in themselves not sufficient. Echoing the republican/civil society notions about virtues and skills, Blaug (1999) argues for the necessity of communicative civic competencies that will enable citizens to make use of such sudden appearances of democratic activity, and empower them. Stewart (2001) also refers to the importance of being able to recognize and interpret different kinds of political situations, and being able to judge what kinds of actions are suitable and necessary. This is a learning process, in which one can gradually, not least through one's mistakes, acquire civic expertise.

Agre (2004) follows a similar line of reasoning, underscoring citizenship's need for social skills that are anchored in everyday life. He takes many of the proponents of republicanism to task for largely ignoring the character and substance of social skills that civic agents must actually apply. For example, he is critical of social capital theory (associated with Putnam, 2000, and others), which builds on the notions of networks and trust, for ignoring that both networks and trust are predicated on concrete competencies of interaction. These skills have to do, among other things, with social interaction; communication; rhetoric; the capacity to define issues; and the capacity to recognize, define, and exploit the relevant political situations for dealing with them. And while we are reflecting on contemporary civil society, let us be sure that our imagery is up to date: While much civil society interaction is still classically face-to-face, within associations, at meetings and get-togethers, and so on, much of it is also mediated, building upon the ever-expanding technologies and opportunities for networking.

There is here a sense of the agonistic, performative quality of politics that we associate with the theorists such as Arendt (1958) and Mouffe (2000, 2005). Agre (2004) argues that citizens must be able to function strategically in their "public personae," and while civic values are essential, agency in political contexts depends on skills. There are many differentiated versions of citizenship in the late modern world, yet they all require various kinds of skills, that are developed through practices in the context of one's lived realities. To achieve – to enact – citizenship, to develop the requisite virtues, skills, and identities for effective civic competence, thus requires practices that provide experience, in the sense of the dynamic development of the subject.

This suggests not only the obvious point that citizenship is in part a question of learning by doing, but also that such civic competence cannot derive exclusively from political society. Here we have to open the gate for crossing the boundary between politics and nonpolitics. I want to carry forward these thoughts on civic agency in the next section, where I address the classic notion of the public sphere, a concept – and a tradition – that has obvious links to civil society theory. A brief interrogation of this tradition may highlight some of its shortcomings, but these in turn can offer some insights about civic engagement and agency.

PUBLIC SPHERES AS INTERACTIONAL PRACTICES

By now, the early Habermasian floor plan (Habermas, 1989) of the public sphere hardly needs much reiteration. He has updated his scheme a few times, notably in Habermas (1996, 2006; see also Friedland, Hove, and Rojas, 2006), taking into account both critical responses and the evolution of society, politics, and the media. Fundamentally, the basic parameters remain: The political public sphere is normatively seen as comprised of the institutional communicative spaces, universally accessible, that facilitate the formation of discussion and public opinion, via the unfettered flow of relevant information and ideas. Also familiar is the critical understanding of the many mechanisms that inhibit the full realization of these ideals, not least in regard to the media. He points to the class biases of the bourgeois public sphere, and feminist critics (e.g., Fraser, 1992; Meehan, 1995) have highlighted the exclusionary mechanisms based on gender.

Habermas and others have come to see that the public sphere is far from unitary; empirically, it consists of vast numbers of sprawling communicative spaces of immense variety. At the same time, these multiple spheres are by no means equal in terms of access or political impact. Some are socially and politically more "mainstream," and situated closer to the powers of decision-making. Others are more geared toward the interests and needs of specific groups, emphasizing, for example, either the need for collective group identity formation or the ambition to offer alternative political orientations, that is, subaltern, counterpublic spheres (Asen and Brouwer, 2001; Fraser, 1992; Fenton and Downey, 2003; Warner, 2002).

In fact, Habermas (1996) develops a two-track conception of political deliberation. On the one hand there are "strong" public spheres that are linked to formal decision-making – legislative and judicial assemblies – and on the other there are all those innumerable "weak" informal settings that allow not only for the circulation of ideas and the development of political will and public opinion, but also for the emergence of collective identities. These have no formalized, institutionalized coupling to decision-making, but the health of democracy rests on the successful mediation between the formal and the informal tracks, which decision-making bodies take into serious account (but not necessarily just slavishly follow) – the views manifested in public opinion.

As I have developed in another context (Dahlgren, 1995), we can specify several dimensions of the public sphere, but for the discussion here it is what I call the interactional dimension that is crucial. The dimension of interaction consists of two aspects. First, it has to do with the citizens' encounters with the media – the communicative processes of making sense, of interpretation. The second aspect of interaction is that between citizens (and between citizens and power holders of various kinds). While this interaction perspective was prominent in the older sociology of the media (I am thinking here of the "two-step flow" tradition; see, e.g., Lazarsfeld and Katz, 1955), it is sometimes ignored in discussions about the contemporary public sphere (and very often in regard to public opinion), even if such a focus is now returning in the context of the increasingly mediated civic interaction taking place via the Internet and other forms of interactive digital communication.

Further, "publics" should be conceptualized as something other than just media audiences; at the same time it is not the case that the distinction is always so clear. Livingstone (2005a) probes the interconnections between the two in a fruitful manner. Audiences, she reminds us, evolve in relation to media forms and thus the concept has to do with forms of communication between people. The notion of public points to people engaged in activities (and in spaces) that are in some way socially visible, that is, not private. As Livingstone argues, generally "audiences" are growing in the modern media world, while "publics" are seemingly facing harder times. Yet, there are many ways of "audiencing," and we should not a priori say that exposure to media output makes one a participant in the public sphere: We may see audiencing as necessary but not sufficient in this regard (the study by Couldry, Livingstone, and Markham, 2007, affirms this in no uncertain terms). Democracy resides, ultimately, with citizens who interact with each other – and who also interact with power holders of various kinds. Further, civic interaction is a social activity, and it thus has its sites and spaces, its discursive practices, and its contextual aspects. These can be explored empirically; political talk always takes place in concrete settings. The public sphere does not begin and end when media content reaches an audience; this is but one step in larger communication and cultural chains that include how the media output is received, discussed, made sense of, re-interpreted, circulated among, and utilized by publics, that is, citizens.

The public sphere thus can be seen as comprised of a vast array of interactional constellations, some relatively more permanent, others more fleeting. While it can be useful to think in terms of a "standing," always-potentially-ready general public, or at least publics with fairly stable ideological orientations, this can be fruitfully complemented with a more dynamic picture of specific issue-publics, that emerge, exist for varying durations, and then eventually dissolve. To the extent that the mass media catalyze the formation of audiences, these audiences coalesce into real publics only through the processes of engagement with issues and discursive interactions among themselves, either via face-to-face settings or various mediated ones. Dayan (2005) argues that publics not only manifest a performative dimension – by doing communicative practices – but also that they constitute themselves as "imagined communities." That is, they take form by defining themselves in terms of a collective "we." Media audiences that coalesce into publics who talk about political issues – and begin to enact their civic identities and make use of their civic competencies – thus manifest a transition from the private realm into the public one, making use of and further developing their cultures of citizenship.

THE PRIVATE PREPARATION OF PUBLIC SPHERES

The traditional perspectives on the public sphere do not help us understand how publics "come alive," as it were, what their sociocultural dynamic look like. Instead, as has often been pointed out, there is a strong normative perspective, where the concepts of public and private encompass an ensemble of notions that readily align themselves into sets of polarities. The idea of "public" is implacably associated with reason, rationality, objectivity, argument, work, text, information, and knowledge (and, one might add, discursively dominant, masculine, and Caucasian). The private resonates with the personal, with emotion, intimacy, subjectivity, identity, consumption, aesthetics, style, entertainment, popular culture, and pleasure. Maintaining this bifurcation in practice and conceptually, however, becomes increasingly difficult.

One of the theoretical quandaries of public sphere theory has precisely been that social and cultural evolution continues to scramble, blur, and reconfigure the distinctions between public and private. This porous character is a development that is abundantly visible in the late modern media milieu (see the analyses by Livingstone, 2005b; also Scheller and Urry, 2003), not least in the blending of politics and entertainment and other forms of popular culture (a theme I will return to in Chapter 6). Identities as citizens are entwined with other identities that we mobilize in other contexts; the boundaries between them are fluid. For example, even our identities in the intimate domain – family life, gender, choices about sexual preferences, birthing, abortion, and medical technologies having to do with the body – can quickly take on political relevance and set in motion varieties of civic engagement (Plummer, 2003, nicely highlights this domain of "intimate citizenship").

The conceptual stumbling block still seems to be that while it appears that we must retain the two categories, the ingrained bifurcation of public and private tends to occlude the obvious socio-cultural connections between them. As Livingstone (2005a) puts it, we need to see how private activities, framed by cultural practice, can indeed have consequences for how the public sphere functions. Moreover, in our everyday lives we always make sense of our experiences, ourselves, and the world around us using a combination of our head and our heart. There is no reason why the public sphere should – or even could – be any different. We should recall that Negt and Kluge (1993), in the context of the debates at the time in Germany around Habermas' theses, argued for the importance of the category of "experience" in understanding participation, that is, reflections on lived personal occurrences and circumstances.

In short, to understand the origins of civic agency and competence, we need to look beyond the public sphere itself, into the terrain of the private – or, expressed alternatively, into the experiential domain of everyday life. It is not a question of collapsing the public into the private (or vice versa), but rather of elucidating the gates between them, and understanding the experiences and subjectivities that people derive in this interplay, and the relevance of these experiences for political participation. While participation in the public sphere depends on skills

that at least partially can derive from nonpublic contexts, such participation obviously further hones these skills. Viable public spheres are a
kind of democratic accomplishment of civic agency, yet they have cultural origins that can be probed and illuminated.

THE KNOWLEDGE PROBLEM: OPINIONS AND EXPERTS

KNOWLEDGE AND THE FORMATION OF OPINION

Civic agency involves stepping into the public sphere, making sense
of media representations of relevant developments, and discussing current events with others; from that other actions may be taken. In all of
these contexts, some degree of knowledge is required. One cannot act
successfully as a citizen in the absence of knowledge, even if the exact
kind and extent of knowledge deemed necessary for civic engagement
has long been debated – not least in the famous exchanges between
Walter Lippmann and John Dewey in the 1920s (see Lippmann, 1922;
Dewey, 1923). Knowledge thus plays a central role in the formation of
opinion, yet this is often ignored or dealt with in a cursory way.

Without rehearsing all the methodological and conceptual issues that
still today hover around opinion research, one can concur with Splichal
(1999), who observes that in the course of the twentieth century, interest
in the social theoretic side of opinion formation tends to decline as the
techniques of measurement grow in sophistication. Opinion research
has tended to work with a downsized epistemological toolkit, clinging,
for instance, to the problematic dualism of facts and values, and thereby
ignoring the intricate ways in which knowledge and values are complexly
integrated in discursive structures (cf. Splichal, 1999, 2001; Glasser and
Salmon, 1995; Lewis, 2001). Opinion becomes operationalized as the
views of individuals, atomized utterances to be statistically aggregated;
the knowledge base on which opinions build is usually ignored. In fact,
the actual empirical charting of political knowledge has been steadily
diminishing from the practices of opinion research, replaced at best with
questions about what respondents *think* they know (Lewis, 2001:109).

The "uninformed citizen," the low level of civic competence, is a
conceptual problem that has long been difficult for democracy and
democratic theory to deal with (see Delli Carpini and Keeter, 1996,
for an empirical study of this in the United States). It is also a practical
problem, since the unease that may be created during interviews by
focusing on knowledge may put at risk the smooth completion of the

interviews. Even when political knowledge is empirically studied in opinion research, it is mostly approached as simple, factual awareness. That opinion and beliefs, as well as knowledge, its frameworks, and assumptions, are discursively interrelated, socially constructed, context-bound, and potentially ideological, is something that has largely not been confronted by opinion research.

This is not to say that traditional opinion research cannot tell us interesting things; it can, even if the political and journalistic uses of such research tend to ignore the scientific reservations that normally should accompany the results. My purpose here is not to critique opinion research per se, but rather to underscore that the ways that it invites us to think about the processes of opinion deflect our attention from two important aspects. First, that opinion formation is a "joint production," one that emerges from citizens interacting with one another. Secondly, that knowledge about political issues likewise emerges to a great extent socially, in conjunction with opinion formation.

Civic agency thus involves generating knowledge (and opinion) together. Fraser (2007) argues that the key critical task of public sphere theory is to reflect on the legitimacy and efficacy of public opinion – to ensure that opinion formation proceeds democratically and that it has a suitable democratic impact. The ethnographic, interactionist legacy of the Chicago School traced such themes, yet was eradicated from the emerging practices of opinion polling fairly early on. Even the relatively late contribution to interactional perspectives offered by the two-step flow model in the mid-1950s by Lazarsfeld and Katz (1955) seems to have lost its analytic relevance in the ongoing development of opinion measurement techniques. At this point in intellectual history, this link between opinion and knowledge, and their relationship to civic practices, could well be brought back into the spotlight by contemporary culturalist efforts to analyze the microdynamics of democracy.

EXPERTS AND DEMOCRACY

Also troubling from the standpoint of civic agency is the fundamental fact that the distribution of knowledge in society can never be "equal"; there are always discrepancies, and as we move ever further into a technologically advanced and highly specialized society, the disparities between expert knowledge and that of the layperson continue to grow. Thinkers as diverse as Plato and Foucault have asserted the inexorable link between knowledge and power. Given the prominent position of science and technology in modern societies, it can be seen as quite surprising that contemporary theories of democracies have little to say about the problem of expertise and its role in politics.

Stephen Turner (2003) is struck by how so few twentieth-century thinkers seriously grapple with the dilemmas that expert knowledge poses for both the functioning of democracy as well as for its theoretical foundations; he sees this as profound "silence" in political theory. He formulates the problem acutely: "In the face of expertise, something has to give: either the idea of government by generally intelligible discussion, or the idea that there is a genuine knowledge that is known to a few, but not generally intelligible. This is a fundamental problem that is not reducible to interests" (Turner, 2003:5). He argues that the evolution in Western democracies – accelerating since the end of World War II – whereby more and more issues require the use of expert knowledge, is undermining popular sovereignty and "government by discussion."

Turner says we just need to open a daily newspaper to observe the long list of questions facing decision-makers that require expert knowledge. We are confronted with problems ranging from economic policy to global warming, from demands for the regulation of a particular pharmaceutical drug to the need for a new urban highway bypass. One obvious dilemma is that citizens usually cannot know if the expert knowledge itself is disinterested; we have seen cases of research that has been "bought and paid for" by, for example, the tobacco industry or those who deny the human impact on climate change. Yet more fundamental is the general problem that expertise inevitably generates exclusionary discourses and closed circles of deliberation, which become barriers to citizen participation. Open political discussion becomes de facto limited to those domains not delegated to the power of expertise.

Expertise is used not least when laws are to be passed. We should be aware that the textbook understanding that "the legislature makes the law of the land" is not accurate: A good part of the law-making originates with specialized state agencies that regulate specific sectors of society: in the United States, for example, the Federal Trade Commission, the Federal Communications Commission, the Environmental Protective Agency, and so on. Other democracies have their equivalent bodies. While regulating these sectors, the agencies are also often cooperating with the vested interests that dominate them. These agencies routinely make use of expertise, specialists who are essentially only accountable to their scientific peers; this places them beyond the knowledge range of the government bureaucrats and lawmakers, as well as of citizens. On what grounds do citizens thus form opinions in the many major issues that confront society? And when experts disagree, when scientific controversies arise, how are citizens to decide between the competing views?

Turner does not pretend to have any solution to this particular dilemma of democracy; he sees himself rather as sounding an alarm. In terms of civic agency, expert knowledge is something toward which citizens will simply have to maintain a position of "critical trust": One cannot reject all expertise as false or biased, yet there is a dire need for increased civic awareness, education, and, where appropriate, what we might call civic counterknowledge, deriving from experts who can participate in and extend "scientific public spheres" to broader audiences. This is all the more important in the modern world, where both governments and private corporations will at times in controversial issues, for example, health and environment, mobilize "experts" whose first commitments are to their sponsors rather than to scientific truth.

Bohman (2000), a leading theorist of deliberative democracy, tackles this issue head-on. He, too, is adamant that what he calls the cognitive division of labor that produces scientific knowledge beyond the grasp of the layperson generates "epistemic dependence," and that this has obvious negative import on power relations and deliberative democracy. To deal with these cognitive and communicative asymmetries, he proposes "creating deliberative situations and institutions in which those affected by experts can evaluate the political credibility of experts and acquire influence over the terms of cooperation with them" (Bohman, 2000:48–49). Further, the cognitive division can be rendered democratic if we can "discover ways of resolving recurrent cooperative conflicts about the nature and distribution of social knowledge and opportunities to communicate. It can only do so if citizens are well informed, particularly with regard to the conditions of social inquiry and public communication" (Bohman, 2000:49). This is a suggestive blueprint, but Bohman understands that its realization is dependent on massive institutional reform, and he in fact invokes a new Progressivism to set it in motion. The reader will understand that, to the extent he is correct, we are in for a long haul on this front.

These reflections on the emergence of civic identity and agency prepare the way for interrogation of democratic involvement as it becomes realized in terms of engagement, participation, and motivation. Moreover, there are various kinds of communicative actions associated with participation; deliberation is often seen as the key mode, yet it is not without its problems. These are the topics for the following chapter.

CHAPTER 4

Engagement, Deliberation, and Performance

To discuss democracy and engagement requires some conceptual ground-clearing. This chapter aims to clarify the general view of citizenship as civic agency; in the next chapter I pull together these thoughts into a framework for analyzing civic cultures. I begin here with a probe of the notions of engagement and participation. From there I explore the problem of motivation, by looking at a classic tension in democratic theory, namely, that between the perceived virtues of rationality and the alleged dangers of emotionality.

Increasingly, contemporary versions of democratic theory render political participation as deliberation; the notion of deliberative democracy has become pervasive. I engage with this development in the second section, arguing that while this ideal, and the model it makes use of, is central for democracy, it also has its limitations. There other modes of participation that should not be overlooked, and there are also a number of issues with the model itself that need to be aired. The final section of the chapter concludes with a discussion that links these threads to offer a performative view of agency, politics, and "the political."

DEMOCRACY, ENGAGEMENT, AND PASSION

ENGAGEMENT, PARTICIPATION, INDIFFERENCE

We often use the concepts of political engagement and participation as synonyms, but there can be a payoff in distinguishing between them. I would formulate it as follows: Engagement refers to subjective states, that is, a mobilized, focused attention on some object. It is in a sense a prerequisite for participation: To "participate" in politics, presuppose some degree of engagement. For engagement to become embodied in participation and thereby give rise to civic agency there must be some connection to practical, do-able activities, where citizens can feel empowered. Obviously not all forms of engagement will enhance democracy; some forms of engagement are directed at nonpolitical areas (e.g., private leisure), while other kinds of engagement may foster anti-democratic developments (e.g., ethnic discrimination).

We live in highly mediated societies, and much of our civic knowledge derives from the media. In a sense, the media bear some responsibility for our political involvement: good journalism must at some level engage us in the world it presents to us. Yet we as citizens also have a democratic responsibility to become engaged and to participate. Some-times the media can facilitate not just engagement, but even participa-tion, as when the Internet is used by citizens for political purposes. However, while engagement catalyzed by media representations can serve as a stepping-stone for participation, engagement in media output per se should not be confused with political participation (except, of course, where media performance itself has been made a political issue in the life of a democracy). Following the news daily only makes one a potentially better citizen.

Engagement must at some point become realized as participation if it is not to dissipate. Political participation is more than simply a feeling one has, it involves some "activity," which can take many forms but often involves acts of communication. It is fully possible to participate with a minimum of engagement – to simply play one's civic role in a routine, nonreflexive way – as a dutiful rather than a self-actualized citizen, to use Bennet's (2007a) distinction. Also, while both engage-ment and participation can be seen as anchored in the individual, I would underscore that the political realm requires collectivities; the engagement and participation of the citizen are predicated on him/her being connected to others, by civic bonds.

Coleman (2007a) makes the point that we should not simply turn "engagement" into a banner word, but need to maintain a critical eye on it. Not least there always remains the question (never fully answer-able) as to what extent any given instance is not just the expression of free will, as we tend to assume, but also derives from a sort of manipu-lation. While this line of inquiry may risk leading us into a philosoph-ical morass, we can at least be alert for empirical evidence of overt instrumental ideological mobilization in relatively closed communica-tion environments, or instances where "engagement" is claimed from forced behavioral participation (e.g., the "cheering crowds" organized by some authoritarian regimes). On the flipside, Coleman (2006) also reminds us that lack of engagement may not just be the manifestation of an absence of something, but can also be interpreted as a political act: One is not simply in a disengaged mindset; one may well have actively, as a political step, chosen to disengage.

In the domain of the civic, the absence of engagement and participation can be expressed in several ways. Certainly the rubric *resignation* captures much of the sentiment held by many who feel that the political system offers them no point of entry for meaningful participation. Resignation deflects engagement in circumstances where power elites seem nonresponsive and one's sense of powerlessness is overwhelming. Swedish researchers Bennulf and Hedberg (1999) suggest three further attitudinal alternatives. The lack of engagement can be understood as an expression of *distrust*, which signals a critical distancing, an active dimension of disengagement that rests on a clear negative evaluation of the political system or at least the alternatives that it offers (which resonates closely with Coleman's disengagement as an active choice). *Ambivalence*, on the other hand, suggests some degree of involvement, but that the motivation for participation is simply not strong enough to overcome the inertia of noninvolvement, or, alternatively, that motivation exists, yet is mitigated by a sense that the efforts required for engagement are simply too great. With ambivalence about, for example, which party to vote for, nonvoting becomes the easiest resolution to the dilemma.

Indifference, however, is of another order. It implies a disinterest in politics and the political altogether, an "alienation" that can psychologically treat politics as irrelevant, at least in its representations in the media. It becomes a topic or an activity on par with, say, "sports," "music," or other forms of free-time pursuit, with nothing that gives it any more compelling quality; that is, citizenship implicitly becomes reduced to one of many possible lifestyle choices. Bennulf and Hedberg (1999) find that among the politically disengaged, distrust and ambivalence, while certainly present, are not the dominant sentiments. Rather, indifference seems to be the psychological condition that best describes most of those who are disengaged (see also Hiley, 2006, on this point).

We can further fine-hone this notion by proposing that indifference can be understood as the consequence of experiencing either a sense of simple remoteness, or a sense of having some superior insight that thereby renders politics as personally insignificant. This latter mode veers toward the stance of what many see as a key structure of feeling promoted by late modern media culture, namely, irony. This aesthetic stance can encompass playfulness as well as cynicism, but in either case, I would suggest that irony may be the foundation for the indifference circulating within some of today's more urbane disengaged citizens. We should keep in mind, however, that indifference – even in its ironic form – is not an ontological state: It can be transformed into engagement via experience. And engagement keeps the door open for participation.

These perspectives on the subjective dimensions of citizens should not be diminished to mere psychologism: They of course relate, in complex ways, to social situations, notably to the widespread difficult material circumstances and consequent stress that I discussed in the first chapter. Yet, despite the difficult situations in which many people find themselves, and despite growing distrust toward government and electoral politics in many countries of the world, the contemporary political malaise does not appear to have shaken people's commitment to democratic values. Large-scale transnational studies suggest that what is happening in the industrialized nations is that the value orientations prevalent among citizens increasingly tend to reject hierarchical authority, but not democracy. This tends to correlate strongly with socioeconomic development, and is interpreted as an important cultural resource for the future of democracy (Inglehart, 1997). Researchers see the emergence of "critical citizens" (Norris, 1999), who are dissatisfied and disillusioned with their leaders and with conventional politics. However, they tend not to have relinquished the basic premises of how a democratic society should function, suggesting that even indifference has its limits.

MOTIVATION: POLITICS AND PASSION

We still need to take one more conceptual step in our understanding of civic agency. This step entails confronting a paradox in regard to agency that is prominent in dominant theories of democracy – from traditional liberal to Habermasian versions. At bottom the paradox is this: Democratic theory (and rhetoric) both postulates and admonishes engaged citizenship; participation is the guiding vision. At the same time, these traditions seem to recognize no motivational grounding for such engagement. They put a strong emphasis on rationality and formal reason, but ignore or even explicitly disparage anything that smacks of the affective, the emotional, or the passionate.

To be engaged in something signals not just cognitive attention and some normative stance, but also an affective investment. Engagement in politics involves some kind of passion. Given all the obstacles that exist to the realization of achieved citizenship, given all the barriers to be overcome before people enter into political discussion or take political action, we would be foolish to deny the indispensable role of the affective side of civic engagement. Motivation without affect would be hard to comprehend. The view that sets rationality against passion is not only unproductive but unnecessary, as Hall (2005) argues.

Hall (2005:13) examines the prevailing arguments within liberal theory in regard to passion and politics, and with the help of Plato, Rousseau, and feminist theory charts a productive path out of this outmoded cul-de-sac. She notes that, traditionally, passion is conceptualized as distinct from reason, and viewed as functioning in opposition to self-control. Political theorists have claimed that it is good for citizens to develop their capacity for reason – but not for passion. Passion is seen as subverting agency, in that it undermines self-possession. She uses the notion of a "crime of passion" to indicate this perception: A person goes out of his or her head and does something both terrible and "crazy." Reason, on the other hand, is seen as the foundation of agency.

She specifies two basic problems with this set of assumptions. The first is that it views passion as a sort of "alien force" that functions somehow independently of the psyche. One can well ask why feelings should be seen as any more of an external imposition than rational thought. We can, in fact, be just as "possessed" by thoughts: We can get stuck in a particular train of thought that we want to avoid, or our mind/attention may wander. Reason can thus also be at odds with our own self-mastery and agency, yet we do not claim that it is a strange power that has taken over our psyche. In short, reason and passion are both a part of the psyche; neither is a foreign power poised to take over the self.

Secondly, Hall points out (2005:15) that democratic theory neglects the interconnectedness of reason and passion; in simple terms, passions have *reasons*: There is some object or vision that is valued, cherished. Passion is not blind; it involves a vision of the good, something to be attained, something to strive for, and often also involves some notion as to how to achieve this good. The strong feeling toward the object or vision that we are passionate about may have derived from careful, rational analysis or from an unreflective assumption, yet there is always a rational element involved. In this sense, reasons incorporate *passions*: Not least in societal and political matters, we find that values, arguments, ideologies, and so on, are often very strongly held. Thus, in the same way that a passion for something suggests a reason for valuing it, a reason for choosing it over other things implies at least some passion for the choice. Likewise, undesirable behavior such as violence and aggression is never exclusively the result of "pure" passion – there are always reasons as well.

To argue that passion and reason are intertwined is not to suggest that the content, or objects in question, are inherently good or bad. The objects – values, visions, and so on – do not have an a priori status of good or evil, but must continuously be debated. Let us be clear: Reasons may be misguided or inadequate. To be passionate about something means that one is devoted to it, enthusiastic about it; one invests time and energy. Yet the object of the passion can always be challenged and debated. Hall sees passion as "intense enthusiasm"; in this sense, it is hard to see why passion should seem so threatening for democratic theory. Would democracy be better served by less intensity? That all depends on the issue at hand; for example, being "mildly" in favor of justice or "moderately" against genocide hardly seem like positive attributes. Indeed, the word "apathy" etymologically suggests "without pathos," that is, without emotion (I am grateful to Stephen Coleman for pointing this out to me). The category "apathetic citizens," then, signals an absence of political passion.

Civic agency – and all agency, for that matter – requires motivation; engagement and participation must have an affective drive. Yet to feel an intense political enthusiasm does not mean that one thereby becomes incapable of rational discussion or loses the capacity for compromise. Passion is crucial for making political choices, creating political community, and motivating political action. No passion, no participation:

> [W]ithout passion people lack energy and commitment to take action, because they lack the sense that their actions will have any meaning or effect .... In order to become politically involved, then, people must *care* about an issue, they must have some *vision* of how things ought to be done, and they must have *hope* that at least some progress can be made toward realizing this vision.... Resignation and disaffection make people docile and obedient to the dominant political order. The motivating power of a desire for a better world is thus crucial to the ability to challenge existing political arrangements and politics. (Hall, 2005:215–216)

We should of course distinguish between passion as a motivating force and as a mode of expression. I would say, for example, that Jürgen Habermas is passionate about democracy – he carries an intense enthusiasm for this ideal and it is seemingly a strong motivational force behind much of his writing. However, his mode of expression is highly rational. Passionate modes of political expression may or may not be suitable or strategic in a given specific context, but my point here is that passion as a motivating force is of analytic interest precisely because it can help us to better understand engagement and participation; it can be probed as a subjective component of civic agency.

While I have been largely discussing individual psychological states here for heuristic purposes, political participation, again, is largely a collective endeavor, a product of shared horizons. Passion not only motivates, it links people together. A shared passion for democratic values can generate civic bonds and affinity, and trust among strangers, and lay the foundation for larger civic identities and practices, thereby maintaining and strengthening civic cultures, as I take up in the next chapter.

DELIBERATIVE DEMOCRACY – AND ITS LIMITS

Interactional public spheres are mainly about discussion, yet how are we to understand such civic communication? What does it look (or sound) like, and what *should* it look/sound like? How can we best envision the interactivity of citizens? A certain idealized view of citizen interaction has come into prominence in the past two decades, galvanizing much of the ongoing reflection on democracy and political participation. Habermas' notions about communicative rationality are among the foundations, but there have been contributions and developments from others as well. This view goes under the label of deliberative democracy, and it melds elements of political theory with perspectives on communication. While it obviously has much to recommend it, there is also a risk that this prevailing understanding of what civic interaction is about can delimit the range of practices that should characterize civic agency in the public sphere, pushing to the margins certain kinds of communicative competencies that are important for a robust democracy.

THE DELIBERATIVE TURN

Talk is seen as constitutive of publics, and it is thus both normatively and functionally vital for democracy. In that sense, the basic idea of deliberative democracy – or, political deliberation, as its central activity – is as old as democracy itself. However, this recent theoretic turn adds new ingredients. The model of deliberative democracy follows the traditional notions of the public sphere and becomes extended via Habermas' investigations into communicative rationality (Habermas, 1984, 1987), where he began developing his ambitious project to reconstruct the legacy of historical materialism, shifting the emphasis from labor to communication as the key to understanding societal self-creation. Building on work from a number of sources, including theories of speech acts and of psychological ego development, he accentuates autonomy, agency, self-reflection, critical judgment, a competence for rational discussion, and, significantly, moral capacity.

Many have discussed and further developed these ideas, relating them to theories of democracy, the practice of politics, subjectivity, and identity, while at times still acknowledging problems inherent in them (cf. Bohman, 1996; Dryzek, 1990, 2000; Fishkin, 1991; Guttman and Thompson, 1996, 2004; see also the collection by Benhabib, 1996). Other contributions have been considerably stronger in their critique of the topic (cf. Agre, 2004; Fraser, 1992; Gardiner, 2004; Kohn, 2000; Mouffe, 2000, Chapter 4; Sanders, 1997). In the debates, some theorists claim that deliberative democracy is only relevant within the framework of actual decision-making, by representatives of the citizens – that is, within "strong" public spheres. Others argue, in an overtly republican manner, that broader, more popular forms of deliberation are needed, and should be spread out as far as possible within the citizenry, beyond the formal decision-making centers, into the public sphere and into as many associations and networks of civil society as is feasible.

As its point of departure, deliberative democracy underscores the importance of providing reasons for decisions taken (here I build on Gutmann and Thompson's [2004] lucid overview). This is a moral principle common to most theoretical versions of democracy, since it lays the foundation for reciprocity. Reciprocity means that decision-makers owe it to those who must live under the decisions or policies that they enact, to provide their constituents with the justifications of the decisions. The dynamics of deliberative democracy are characterized by the norms of equality and symmetry; everyone is to have an equal chance of participation. Also, both the rules of discussion and topics to be discussed can in principle be challenged; the agenda itself is to be mutually agreed upon. Another important principle is that the reasons should be made accessible to all concerned; this means not only that they should in some manner be made public, but also be comprehensible.

Deliberative democracy serves to support the legitimacy of decisions that are taken, thereby enhancing the vitality of democratic institutions.

Also, it seeks to foster public-spirited perspectives in politics, by encouraging the development of clear justifications for one's choices and decisions, as well of a more generalized sense of the collective good. In the process, it thus further develops civic skills. Deliberation strives to generate mutual respect, not least in situations where fundamental moral views are in conflict, thereby promoting understanding and practical rationality in politics. In the give and take of argumentation, it is assumed that opponents will learn from each other, and expand each others' horizons. Deliberative democracy is seen to be especially significant in situations where differences exist, where consensus is not likely, and compromise is the best one can hope for – where partners can arrive at acceptable solutions via dialogue without having to give up on core moral values. Indeed, the capacity to subject one's own views to critical discussion, and the ability to balance strong convictions with at least a small window of self-doubt, are fundamental qualities of ideal citizenship, as Hiley (2006) argues.

This is a very attractive and important vision, one that can contribute to the quality of democracy. However, I wish to highlight some issues with it, and to encourage that we see its limitations and not overload the role we expect deliberation to play in the public sphere. My discussion here will center around three themes: the issue of defining what kinds of talk should count as political deliberation, the issue of excessive rationality, and the problem of discursive power.

WHAT KIND OF TALK?

Contemporary views about citizen talk tends to make a basic distinction between genuine deliberation, that which takes place in political contexts, and other kinds of talk, which can of course vary immensely. Schudson (1997) makes the case that "conversation is not the soul of democracy." His unassailable point is that conversation is basically about sociability, while political discussion is about solving problems. Political talk strives to find solutions to conflicts; it is purposive, goal-oriented. Democratic deliberation is not "spontaneous"; rather it is civil, public, and opens up the door for social discomfort, seemingly the opposite of what is usually intended with conversation. Warren (1996) makes a similar argument, challenging the general idea that political engagement is at bottom attractive, something that most people would freely choose if only given the opportunity. He sees this as romantic dogma, or at best wishful thinking, given the uncertainties and anxieties involved.

Noelle-Neumann's (1993) theory about the spiral of silence – while aiming to explain some of the dynamics of opinion process – also has relevance here: She underscores the awkwardness and fear of social isolation that people can experience around political talk. These authors have a view of deliberative democracy that is not so rosy but realistic: It is a tough undertaking and demands respect. Schudson, Warren, and their allies certainly score points for sociological realism: Political discussion can be uncomfortable, and it is perfectly reasonable that people will often shy away from it.

Yet, zeroing in too tightly on strict political deliberation risks losing sight of everyday talk and its potential relevance for democracy. Their "strong" view of deliberation excludes an awful lot of discussion that can have political relevance, but has no status in a formal deliberative perspective. This becomes apparent if we look at a different point of departure in regard to civic talk, as found in Barber (1984) and other theorists, who attribute potential political relevance to other, informal kinds of interactions. In their perspective, while acknowledging the importance of formal deliberation and its settings, they look beyond it to better understand the processes by which the political emerges in speech, to become civic talk, in particular via the stimulation of interaction with the media.

They emphasize the permeability of contexts, the messiness and unpredictability of everyday talk, in order to put forth the view that politics, and thus the individual's role as citizen, is never an a priori given, but can materialize in various ways within informal everyday speech. "Conversation," then, may not be the "soul of democracy," but it always contains the potential to tilt toward some kind of political engagement. Even if such talk may not fulfill the strict requirements of deliberation, it may still be of relevance for promoting civic agency. When most people talk about politics, they tend do so with people they know and with whom they share basic political assumptions and values, that is, with like-minded social contacts, which avoids conflict. Such talk is not deliberation in the formal sense – since political conflict is absent – yet may still be experienced as politically edifying. Certainly it has its limitations; it may serve to cement, rather than challenge, individuals' views. Yet, the fact that it is experienced as sociable does not mean that it is irrelevant for the political life of democracy.

Unconstrained, meandering, and unpredictable talk always embodies the potential of becoming civic, of generating the political, and establishing links between the personal and the societal. The private sphere can be said to transmute into the public sphere in those microsituations when discussion turns to politics; the position of the participants switches from private persons to citizens. The looseness, open-endedness of everyday talk, its creativity, its potential for empathy and affective elements, are indispensable resources and preconditions for the vitality of democratic politics.

Barber (1984) asserts that even if citizens' interaction may be wanting in terms of deep knowledge and well-thought-out opinions, it is crucial for maintaining a sense of a shared civic identity and for generating a collective will. Conversational talk can veer toward the civic and the political in many ways that would not pass muster as genuine deliberation. Bohman sees informal citizen talk as important for maintaining "a constant and vibrant interaction among cultures and subpolitics in a larger sphere of common citizenship" (Bohman, 1996:145). In his view, the character of such civic talk is reflexive: Self-creation takes place in part via such interaction. One could say that as "messy conversation" begins to take on political connotations, it becomes in some sense "civic," and activates the weak, nondecision-making public sphere.

If we accept that every day, conversational talk always harbors a civic potential, this does not mean we would thus want to study any and all contexts of verbal interaction. We would obviously have to be selective in where we aimed our analytic searchlights, trying to glean the "proto-political" – that which is beginning to percolate politically – from the simply nonpolitical, to pinpoint how, where, and under what circumstances general conversation morphs into civic talk.

If democracy is accorded a good foundation in the unpredictable talk of the life-world, it clearly needs more than this. Moving toward more explicitly political circumstances, Kohn (2000:424) suggests that democracy involves, among other things, the "possibility for various groups to work out counter projects, discuss them with authorities, and force authorities to take them into account." She suggests that deliberative democracy has most relevance for the second phase – discussions with authorities. To work out counter projects, however, often requires some kind of temporary public withdrawal, an internal working-through among like-minded citizens within specialized subaltern or counterpublic spheres, as many groups and movements have done. Introducing new values, defining new needs, and developing new social visions is difficult to attain via consensus-oriented conversation, with universalist assumptions.

Unreasonable Rationality

The Habermasian emphasis on rationality in regard to political communication makes perfectly good sense on one level. The public sphere rapidly degenerates when political debate, for example, gets locked into pie-throwing and name-calling, or when discussion and argument become reduced to monologic incantation. On another level, however, there are considerable discursive possibilities between such lows and the lofty heights of the rationalist ideals. Thus, if we turn to the settings where more formal deliberation is the suitable communicative mode (i.e., decision-making contexts), the question still remains just what such deliberation should look like. Habermasian versions are adamant that deliberation should be fully rational and strictly adhere to the literal and transparent dimensions of discourse, and should manifest impartial reasoning, that is, rest on the imperatives that all participants will see beyond their own particular interests, be open to all points of view, and ally themselves with the best arguments. Yet, there are more flexible views of deliberation.

Citing Bohman (1996), Kohn suggests that political innovation requires forming new publics, indeed, new ways of framing social reality, that foster the formulation of new issues and strategies, that problematize or "denaturalize" conventional perceptions and entrenched ideological positions. This involves the use of such communicative strategies as "irony, personal narrative, aesthetic interventions, theatricality, and visibility ..." (Kohn, 2000:425), which of course, in its emphasis on *performance*, marks a profound departure from Habermas' ideal. Further, Mayhew (1997) takes Habermas to task for positioning himself against the use of rhetoric, that is, the eloquent appeals and persuasion based on group trust, rather than on universalist discursive criteria (Garnham, 2000, Chapter 8, elaborates on this point). Mayhew claims that this is not only unrealistic, but also undesirable, since it undermines the potential richness and vibrancy of political discussion for an illusory ideal, and is likely to actually deflect civic engagement by undercutting passion, in the sense of intense enthusiasm, as I discussed previously.

In a similar vein, Gardiner (2004) contrasts Habermas with Bakhtin, who asserts that "living discourse ... is necessarily charged with polemical qualities, myriad evaluation and stylistic markers, and populated by diverse intentions. To participate in dialogue is to immerse ourselves in a plethora of alien words and discourses ..." (Gardiner, 2004:36). Dialogue is shaped by polyphonic voices, and meaning is always to some degree multiple, avoiding final closure (related themes can be found in a range of other intellectual traditions, including semiotics and deconstruction). Moreover, the demand for impartiality among the participants is quite unrealistic: People engaged in political conflict are not always so prone to behave in a neutral, truth-seeking, dispassionate, or altruistic manner.

It should be clear that this line of argument is intended as an antidote to a particular form of excessive estimation of rationality. It in no way favors an "anything goes" view of political discussion. The more commonsense understanding of deliberation as simply the application of and respect for good argument (as suggested by, e.g., Downey, 2007) is more useful in my view. The absence of such basic deliberative standards can quickly lead to dismal climates of debate: ritualistic invocation of respective ideological views, and ill-willed disparaging of political adversaries. Such atmospheres of discursive irrationality undermine not only deliberation, but also democracy as well.

Discursive Power

Another basic issue with deliberative democracy has to do with power – both discursive and social (and they are usually intertwined). Deliberative democracy asserts that meaningful political discussion can only take place if all participants are on an equal footing, that is, if respect, a pluralist outlook, and reciprocity prevail. Here's the rub: It is hard to see how this prerequisite, the leveled ground of the discussion, can be fully achieved by discussion itself. As Kohn puts it: "Reciprocity and equality . . . must be fought for rather than assumed. The dialogue itself cannot achieve its own preconditions . . ." (Kohn, 2000:417). This undercuts the universalist dimension, that is, that deliberative democracy rests on a foundation that is by definition available to all. This does not mean that we should dismiss normative concepts such as equality and reciprocity as illusions, but rather understand that in the real world they are contingent and provisional. Realistic strategies must be developed to attain them.

In fact, one could ask: Given that the distribution of communicative skills tends to follow general social hierarchies, and thereby may well serve to reinforce such hierarchies, why should we expect citizens with lower communicative skill to participate, and why should we anticipate that deliberative democracy is a good way for citizens to impact on the decisions that affect them? Public speaking often correlates with power and cultural capital, and in the context of politically subordinate and/or culturally diverse groups, the imposition of an abstract, universalist ideal of deliberation can in fact be a very power-laden move. Young (1990) argues strongly against deliberative democracy's insistence on denying difference by forcing all parties into a singular mode of discourse that may not be suitable for all. She contends that democratic politics must be able to encompass groups that are socially situated away from the mainstream or the majority, and find other ways to accord them voice in political contexts.

Moreover, if the deliberation itself appears to take place in a discursive mode that *appears* universal, neutral, and egalitarian, yet is in fact the prerogative of privileged social strata, then this mode can actually serve to conceal and legitimate its own symbolic power. Further, it has been shown many times that groups and movements, particularly if they start with little power, will effect democratic change – have more impact on the power holders who make decisions – via mobilization and collective action, rather than through discussion. The emphasis on reaching consensus through dialogue suggests an assumption that conflict basically derives from inadequate communication. Better communication is always desirable, but to suppress or deny the fact that conflicts may indeed be played out between groups with major differences in their relative power and where shared values are insufficient to generate a common understanding of what is "reasonable," will ultimately not yield better communication.

CIVIC TALK, CIVIC SILENCE: REAL-WORLD CONTEXTS

Civic talk can take many forms; as it moves out of the informal, conversational modes between people who know each other, and becomes more "public," where strangers engage with each other, particular cultural mechanisms are required to sustain it. Three decades ago Sennett (1977) noted the importance of "civility" for interaction between strangers in public spaces, something very pertinent to the conditions for talk between citizens. He meant that wearing a "mask" was important: It permits strangers to make themselves available to each other – without the burden of personal troubles, private concerns, power implications, and so on. However, such "pure sociability," he noted, runs counter to American conceptions of being open, authentic, personable.

We need to know more about the sociological realities of civic talk; research needs to follow it into its many microsettings. The research that does exist has both good news and bad news, and we can only conclude, tentatively, that the extent and character of civic talk vary enormously. Just a few snapshots from a few studies will illustrate this. The empirical work of Gamson (1992, 2001) demonstrates that at least in experimental situations, people are indeed capable of pursuing informed discussions about issues that they encounter in the media, and that such group talk often involves, where relevant, reflections on their own experiences. He finds that people can develop what he calls collective action frames, which he sees as patterns of meaning and belief that can legitimate social movement engagement.

These frames have three major components: a sense of *injustice*, that is, moral indignation at an emotional level directed toward a particular issue or theme; an *identity* component that facilitates the emergence of a we/they opposition, which thereby defines concrete political adversaries who are to be confronted, and thus brings the issue away from general abstractions; and an *agency* component that empowers people, giving them a sense of efficacy, that they can intervene collectively in a meaningful way and make a difference. His conclusion is that it is not a question of innate competence of the citizens (even if background knowledge was not always as strong as it could be), but rather the circumstances that facilitate or hinder the emergence of productive talk about politics.

Elihu Katz is one of the pioneers in media research, and some years ago he was involved in a large research project: Kim (1997), Kim, Wyatt, and Katz (1999), and Wyatt, Katz, and Kim (2000) are complementary works that derive from various constellations of cooperation around that project. It is based on extensive telephone interviews with a sample of over 1,000 citizens in the United States. The theoretic point of departure is an alignment with the position of fluid, unbounded, informal conversation as the essence of deliberative democracy; they explicitly distance themselves from the "strong" position of Schudson and like-minded colleagues.

They use a four-stage model: media exposure, talking about media output, opinion formation, and political participation; this is based on Katz's (1992) appropriation of Tarde's studies of opinion. The respondents were asked to estimate the extent to which they engaged in talk about various current affairs topics, under what circumstances, and how comfortable they felt about it. The results portray a relatively talkative citizenry. The authors find that news media use is closely associated with frequency of political conversation in daily life, both in general and issue-specific. The willingness to argue is influenced partly by majority perceptions (à la the spiral of silence theory of Noëlle-Neumann, 1993), but also correlates strongly with news media use and frequency of political talk. News media use and political conversation have positive effects on certain measures of the quality of opinions (e.g., character of argumentation, consideration of alternative opinions); in short, more talk leads to better developed opinions. News media use and political conversation are closely associated with participatory activities. In other words, media attention yields a higher payoff in terms of political discussion.

The authors report that, paradoxically, home is the site where most political conversations take place, that is, the most private space has become the most frequent site of the public sphere. The workplace is reported as the second most common site for civic interaction, and beyond the home and workplace, the spaces for civic interaction become thin. Yet we see here a robust public sphere/civil society populated by republican citizens: A key finding is that the respondents claim that they talk fairly free about politics – in the *context of informal conversation,* and thus among people they know. Katz and his colleagues conclude that informal political conversation seems to be media-fueled, and interwoven within the fabric of everyday talk.

Less encouraging is the work of Eliasoph (1998), who did an ethnographic analysis of several civic and political groups and examines how political talk is socially accomplished – and largely repressed when it enters more public contexts. While both she and Katz et al. set out to empirically study deliberative democracy in practice, they arrive at very different conclusions. If Katz et al. are encouraged by their findings, Eliasoph is both surprised and troubled by her results.

She studied three sorts of civic groups: volunteer, recreational, and activist. I cannot do justice here to the richness of her ethnographic work, but will just present some of her key points. Using among other things Goffman's scheme of front-stage/back-stage, she finds that while the citizens in these groups do talk about politics, they tend to enact an odd reversal of the public/private distinction. In front-stage settings within the groups, and not least where they are addressing a public or the media, there is a strong tendency to avoid speaking about politics. Yet, after the meetings, in private, when microphones are turned off, the talk can become very political.

Eliasoph means that within some of the groups there is the assumption that politics is divisive, painful, and generally to be avoided since it puts sociability at risk. Here Schudson and others get empirical validation for their views about the social awkwardness of political talk. Another theme is that people, when talking about politics, will often emphasize the local, close-to-home issues. They do this to the point of even repressing for themselves the obvious connections between the local and larger contexts. The issue of efficacy is at work here (though perhaps unconsciously): Defining problems at too grand a level can readily evoke feelings of powerlessness; it is best to delimit challenges so they seem do-able.

But there is more. Eliasoph goes on to show how there seems to be tacit cultural mechanisms at work that hinder the expression of any kind of ideals reflecting a public spirit and having to do with the common good, general welfare, and so on, in front-stage, that is, public, contexts. Such pronouncements are simply not treated as credible. Thus, for example, some of the ecological activists package their public arguments as the voice of "concerned mothers" worrying about the health and future of their children, rather than as spokespeople who demand a better environment for the sake of everyone living in the endangered area. It is simply assumed that all activism is based on self-interest. The back-stage becomes the site for open political expression, while in the front-stage, such talk risks being dismissed as either cynical or naïve. She sees this as a process of "political evaporation," which she summarizes as follows:

> [T]he farther back-stage the context, the more public-spirited conversation was possible . . . and the larger the audience, the less eager were speakers to ponder issues of justice and the common good, to present historical or institutional analyses, to criticize institutions, to invite debate, to speak in a publicly minded way. (Eliasoph, 1998:255)

Not surprising, she concludes that her findings do not provide a jolly prognosis for the public sphere. What is interesting is that her study puts on the agenda for deliberative democracy the issue of the cultural frameworks that shape social interaction, the unspoken "rules" that define what kind of talk is appropriate (and not) in which kind of situation. There are myriads of interactional settings for political talk, and we cannot know if they all function similarly to the ones she investigated. Walsh (2003) arrives at more encouraging conclusions: She finds that people talk about politics in many informal settings, and use these contexts to not only clarify political issues but also to develop their political identities in we-they terms. She argues that political discussion, friendship ties, and identities evolve together, generating stronger networks and social ties.

Finally, an important intervention based on extensive survey studies challenges basic conventional assumptions about the nature of political participation. Mutz (2006) picks up the theme that political discussion can be socially problematic, and in her research finds that people have difficulty being both deliberative and participative. That is, within their own networks, citizens who experience less confrontation with opposing views are more likely to be politically active, while those who are politically active are less likely to be exposed or to engage in deliberation over opposing views. This also implies, quite reasonably, that like-minded groups are good for mobilizing people, for engendering engagement and participation, but not for promoting political deliberation. As she puts it: "The kind of network that encourages an open and tolerant society is not necessarily the same that produces an enthusiastically participative citizenry" (Mutz, 2006:125).

This tension may put a dent in some contemporary theories of deliberation, in that it reiterates that deliberation is not the only form of activity for citizens. However, from the standpoint of civic agency, it simply means that different kinds of civic talk and action are more suitable in specific contexts than others. Instead of setting deliberation and participation against each other, we can simply treat deliberation as one mode of participation. However, Mutz's analysis also reminds us that different microcivic cultures may socialize citizens in different ways, promoting different forms of participation.

The range of conclusions within this little sample of studies suggests that much empirical research on civic talk still needs to be done. No doubt the vast array of possible contexts of civic talk – both face-to-face and mediated – and the different contingencies that shape them, are one of the key challenges. The specific cultures of social groups, regions, nations, and local contexts must be considered. It is easy to imagine an extensive range of various spaces and settings where ethnographic studies of civic talk could be pursued, adding to our understanding of the complexity of the dynamics that shape civic talk. We need to leave this door very open.

CIVIC AGENCY AS AGONISTIC PERFORMANCE

The perspective on citizenship as social agency, as something achieved, articulates most strongly with the republican tradition, complemented by the vision of a vigorous civil society. This understanding of citizenship necessitates, in turn, as we have seen, concerns with social and cultural patterns, identity, and other dimensions that pertain to some notion of suitable civic grooming and socialization in civil society. We have noted how the notion of the public sphere seemingly denies the socio-cultural links with the private sphere in an unfortunate and unproductive manner. The contemporary emphasis on deliberation provides important normative criteria for the enactment of democracy in particular contexts (especially formal decision-making), yet also risks downplaying the important potential of more informal forms of talk for the life of democracy, thereby bifurcating public and private in a new way. Moreover, deliberative democracy's strict adherence to rational communication and its avoidance of questions of power relationships leave it with important unresolved issues.

The few glimpses from research on civic talk that I provided show a range of possibilities as well as problems: If we look more broadly at the empirical research on deliberation, it uses various approaches, including experimental methodology. Generally it shows that deliberation has a number of positive consequences for its participants, in the form of enhanced knowledge and political efficacy, as well as improved discussion skills (see, for example, Gastil and Dillard, 1999; Lushkin, Fishkin, and Jowell, 2002; Price, Nir, and Cappella, 2002). It of course also has its problems: Delli Carpini, Cook, and Jacobs (2004), in their review of this literature, find that there is nothing automatic about its success. How well it functions is often context-specific, and sometimes it may lead to opinion polarization, frustration, or more conflict. Talk is certainly the best vehicle for resolving conflicts, for reaching compromise, and moving toward consensus. It is much preferred over violence. The upshot here is civic talk should always be encouraged, but we should avoid the impulse to dress it up in a fancy, formal deliberative suit when this is not mandatory. A chattering society is more likely to lead to participation than a tight-lipped one.

Further, deliberation should not exhaust our view of the repertoire of civic practices: There are many ways in which to embody the republican ideal. As I noted in the previous chapter, Agre (2004) argues for the importance of a range of social skills for civic engagement – the capacity to communicate in suitable ways for political purposes. He also observes that politically effective citizens or politicians will engage in a lot of behind-the-scenes work before bringing an issue to a public forum, and make use of a variety of practices well beyond deliberation, such as mobilizing, bargaining, disruption, and even civil disobedience.

Agre (2004) further posits that in most political discussions, people are in fact not actually even deliberating. In the media age, he suggests, if one listen to the arguments that people bring to bear on political matters, they are often merely repeating what they have derived from professional opinion-makers, such as politicians, columnists, scholars, pundits, or even opinion leaders they may encounter face-to-face. Most people do not have the time, energy, or the knowledge to develop their own original arguments on most issues. He suggests that even the professional opinion-makers are for the most part merely repackaging standard arguments that are already in circulation and applying them to specific situations. Agre does not denigrate the idea of civic discussion, he just wants to bring it down to earth. He suggests that what citizens largely do is pick and choose from an available marketplace of prefab ideas – and that at bottom this is not so bad. (Just how this is actually done can become an important research question about cultural and political practices.) If this view of civic talk is less noble than often found in theories of democracy, it is no doubt more in keeping with sociological realities.

If we look beyond deliberative democracy to better understand the nature and possibilities of participative practices, we can find conceptual links that harmonize better with the notions of civic agency developed here. In her critique of the notion of deliberative democracy as it appears in the Habermasian tradition, Mouffe (2000) mobilizes Wittgenstein's notion of language games. For Wittgenstein, agreement on language necessitates agreement on what he calls forms of life. This in turn projects one inevitably into issues of power and antagonism. Inevitably, rhetoric, persuasion, and compromise will characterize political discussion. There is a performative emphasis here, rather than a demand for "authenticity" in political discussion, that has echoes of Arendt (see also Benhabib, 1992, 1996; Villa, 2001). Mouffe's notion of agonistic democracy ("agonist" comes from Greek and signifies someone who is engaged in a struggle) is based not on Habermasian rational consensus, but rather on argument and performance, and the hope that one can at least reach compromise with one's opponents.

She calls this perspective agonistic pluralism, a political culture where the forms of interaction and power are compatible with democratic values, where conflict takes place between "adversaries" rather than "enemies." Mouffe's vision is predicated on shared democratic rules of the game, a minimal bedrock of unifying allegiance to democratic values and procedures. In her perspective, the goal is not to avoid conflict – on the contrary, she assumes that conflict is a built-in potential in all social relations, all social contexts, and in all kinds of talk. The resolution of old conflicts gives rise to new situations in which new antagonisms can emerge; there is no "endpoint," and we must not expect that democracy will somehow usher us in to some kind of ultimate social harmony. In this understanding of democracy's discursive dynamics, she makes a distinction between "politics"and "the political":

> By "the political" I refer to the dimension of antagonism that is inherent in all human society, antagonism that can take many forms and can emerge in diverse social relations. "Politics," on the other hand, refers to the ensemble of practices, discourses and institutions that seek to establish a certain order and to organize human coexistence in conditions that are always potentially conflictual because they are affected by the dimension of "the political." (Mouffe, 1999:754)

Politics, then, is the institutionalized arena where organized conflict takes place, be it party politics or extra-parliamentarian. If we connect this with the theme of different modes of civic discussion, it would seem that Habermas, Schudson, Warren, and others who hold a similar position about formal deliberation basically have in mind talk about *politics*, as Mouffe uses the term, and especially in its decision-making phases. Barber (1984), Walzer, and others who underscore the importance of free-wheeling conversation are referring, at least implicitly, to the potential of *the political*. They accentuate the processes by which the conversation can turn into civic talk, an ever-present potential. While it may be empirically handier to just deal with politics, given its bounded character, the political in fact allows for many avenues of interesting investigation. It is easy to imagine a schematic progression as this, from nonpolitical conversation, the introduction of a topic that takes a proto-political turn, gains momentum and becomes political, entering a public sphere. From there it might enter into the formal arena of full-fledged institutionalized politics. The women's movement is certainly a paradigmatic example of this sequence – where the final step was recently almost witnessed in Sweden, where a political network called the Feminist Initiative nearly launched a parliamentary party for the 2006 national election.

Talk, as a civic practice, can take unforeseen twists and turns, activating different subjective dimensions – including civic ones. Obviously not all talk in everyday life is politically significant, but we should always remain open to the possibilities of the political emerging – and anticipate how they might be translated into politics. The road is thus in principle clear for analyzing how talk can generate the political and thereby potentially lead toward politics – both traditional party politics and alternative politics. Still more relevant for our concerns here, this conceptual ground-clearing also allows us to investigate civic agency – political participation – as a process of becoming, conditioned by an array of factors. Civic agency has an individual dimension, but its fruition is manifested collectively, where a sense of "we" emerges to form discursive publics and, beyond that, other forms of political participation. And in all of this we should keep in mind that it is not just a question of face-to-face contexts, but also mediated ones, where performative manifestations of civic agency can be played out. (I return to this theme in Chapter 7).

What remains now is to systematize the conceptual terrain covered here, so that we can develop an integrated perspective on the major elements salient for civic engagement. This is the topic of the next chapter, where I present the concept of civic cultures, rendered as a framework for analyzing and understanding the dynamics of citizens' political participation.

CHAPTER 5

Civic Cultures: An Analytic Frame

To understand citizenship as civic agency moves the concept beyond its legal parameters and situates it within the realm of social theory. It thus involves examining the conditions and forms of such action. The previous two chapters sketched some of the socio-cultural conceptual origins of civic agency, its key attributes at the level of the individual subject, and explored aspects of such agency based in talk as well as communication in settings that exceed the standard notions of deliberation as the essential mode of civic practice. In this chapter, I pull these threads together to offer a framework that integrates civic agency into a larger perspective of civic culture. This framework is intended to help us analytically and empirically study the factors that can shape civic agency and thereby impact on citizens' engagement and participation in democracy. As I have indicated, there are an array of influences that shape engagement and participation, but here the emphasis now lands on the role of the media. I begin with an overview of the civic cultures perspective, and then discuss, in turn, each of what I see to be the six dimensions of civic cultures, concluding with a summary overview and some initial discussion relating this framework to the media.

A DYNAMIC CIRCUIT

AGENCY AND CULTURE

The concept of civic agency is premised on people being able to see themselves as participants, that they find engagement meaningful, and that they experience motivation via the interplay of reason and passion. Such agency, involving the capacity to make decisions and act in accordance with a coherent sense of self, of identity, can never emerge or function in a vacuum; it must be an integrated and dynamic part of a larger cultural environment that has relevance for politics. What I call civic cultures is a framework intended to help analyze the conditions that are necessary for – that promote or hinder – civic engagement.

Analyses around the theme of democratic engagement and disengagement have had a number of different points of departure, but it is my view that we will be able to better understand some of the dynamics involved by refracting civic agency through cultural theory. Especially if we emphasize identity as a key element in civic agency, we need to ask what are the cultural factors that can impinge on this identity, and promote (or hinder) among people such perceptions of their (multifarious) civic selves – as well as promote their civic engagement. Identities develop and evolve in an ongoing interplay with the cultural environments in which they are operative. Cultures, in turn, consist of patterns of communication, practices, and meaning; they provide taken-for-granted orientations – factual and normative – as well as other resources for collective life. They are internalized, intersubjectively among groups: They exist "in our heads," as it were, guiding and informing action, speech, and understanding, while offering affordances "out there" – concrete possibilities for action, communication, and meaning-making.

It is important to be clear about the analytic status we attribute to culture. At the conceptual level, if we were to say that a particular culture only exists at the moment of speech or action, we would be lapsing into a behaviorist view. This is because we would then be assuming that culture is only "real," can only be operationalized, at the moment of its expression. Alternatively, if we argued that such cultural patterns pre-exist all speech and action, that all action is by definition an expression of all-powerful cultural forces and steers agency in a detailed way, then we stumble into determinism. Culture thus must be analytically treated as a general orientation that can offer road markers for patterns of doing and thinking, yet it can never provide definitive predictions – not least because it is always to some degree in transition: Cultures are never entirely static. There is thus always a dimension of potentiality in cultural analysis – possibilities that we analytically assert exist, but that we can never assume always will be actualized.

Civic cultures refer to cultural patterns in which identities of citizenship, and the foundations for civic agency, are embedded. As will become evident in the discussion that follows, it is more accurate to speak of civic cultures – in the plural – since the argument rests on the assumption that in the late modern world there are many ways in which civic agency can be accomplished and enacted. In fact, given the many forms that political engagement may take, we should be open to considerable variation, and avoid defining the exact contours of any specific civic cultures in advance. They can be mapped out in a schematic way, however, and approached analytically and empirically. Civic cultures, to the extent that they are compelling, operate at the level of citizens' taken-for-granted horizons in everyday reality, or, in Habermasian terms, the life-world. (From a Bourdieu perspective one might try experimenting with a notion of "civic habitus.")

The key assumptions here is that for a functioning democracy, there are certain conditions that reside at the level of lived experiences, cultural resources, and subjective dispositions that need to be met. While the formal institutions and processes of democracy are essential, not least the state itself, these structures and processes need to be populated by real-life people with democratic inclinations. Discussions about democracy often touch upon the theme of rights and entitlements, which is as it should be. However, there is considerably less discussion about obligations, what democracy requires of citizens if it is to be viable. The notion of civic *virtue* has a somewhat quaint, old-fashioned ring to it, but we should understand that it merely expresses a simple functional logic. The notion is not addressing people's moral character in general, admonishing everyone to be some kind of a goody-goody. It simply suggests that without certain kinds of input from citizens, the quality of democracy degenerates. Achieved citizenship carries with it rights, but also necessitates responsibilities. If liberals see these responsibilities as contractual virtues that the individual accords the state (basically a "let's make a deal" relationship), republicans are prone to see them as commitments to the vision of democracy as well as to one's co-citizens.

Civic culture as a concept is not new, and my reformulation carries over some traditional elements from political science/political communication along with the more culturalist components. American researchers in the Cold War era tried to map democracy's cultural variables using large-scale survey techniques together with functionalist views on social integration (Almond and Verba, 1963, 1980). My point of departure is somewhat different; in using the concept, I wish to avoid what I take to be elements of psychological reductionism and ethnocentrism. Also, my view of culture is constructionist and materialist, rather than systemic. If the more familiar concept of the public sphere points to democracy's relevant communicative spaces, civic culture highlights those features of the socio-cultural world that serve as preconditions for people's actual participation in the public sphere and political society. In short, these preconditions involve cultural attributes prevalent among citizens that can in various ways facilitate democratic life.

The decades after World War II saw the emergence in the United States of yet another research trajectory having to do with citizens and politics, namely, political socialization. It too has lost much of its steam (but for a contemporary application, see Gimpel, Lay, and Schuknecht, 2003). In his review of this literature, Calavita (2005) finds that this tradition generally emphasizes the transfer of knowledge, values, and attitudes from one generation to another in ways that help maintain support for the political system in its current form. The mechanisms of this reproduction – or inculcation – of political culture go through such institutions as the family, school, peer groups, social networks, workplace, and religion. He observes with justifiable surprise that relatively little is said of the mass media within this tradition, though he acknowledges that during these decades, the paradigm of "limited effects" held sway over conventional thinking about mediated communication.

For our purposes, this tradition does serve to invite attention to an array of institutions that can impact on people's political horizons. However, the emphasis on an implicit top-down universe of given values, without according much importance to civic agency as such, puts decisive limits on its utility. More germane is Calavita's (2005) own innovative research, which illuminates how the dominant news media environment interplays with other significant life contexts and the developmental agency of individuals in shaping how people develop politically.

Civic cultures are thus shaped by an array of factors. Certainly family and schools lay a sort of foundation. From there, group settings, social relations of power, economics, the legal system, and organizational possibilities – all can have their impact. In terms of power, social structures, gender, and ethnicity are relevant: The resources that citizens can draw upon tend to be more abundant among the more privileged. Not least – and for our purposes here – the media, both the traditional mass media and the newer interactive media, impact directly and routinely on the character of civic cultures via their form, content, specific logics, and modes of use. In Chapter 3 it was my contention that we must not ignore the private sphere if we are to understand participation in the public sphere. Thus, we should expect that nonpublic processes also impact on civic cultures by preparing people for acting as citizens, not surprising, given that media use is very much an activity within the private sphere.

In terms of viability, civic cultures are both strong and vulnerable. They can shape citizens; they can serve to empower; citizens, in turn, via their practices, can influence the character of civic cultures. Indeed, it is not impossible that civic cultures can develop even in circumstances that may seem on the surface unlikely, as we saw when the communist system began to collapse. Alternatively, the weaknesses or absence of civic cultures is clearly disempowering, and unfavorable circumstances can readily result in suppressed or atrophied civic cultures.

I am arguing that robust civic cultures are necessary prerequisites for viable public spheres and thus for a functioning democracy: Civic cultures have thus in part a normative status. Yet they are also empirical: They can be observed and analyzed. The empirical key here is to insist on processes and contexts. Politics and the political are not simply given, but are constructed via word and deed, in specific settings, as noted in the previous chapters. For citizens, the ongoing development of civic cultures can be seen as collectively generated resources, to be used when politics and the political arise.

Civic cultures do not presuppose homogeneity among their citizens, but in the spirit of republicanism, do suggest minimal shared commitments to the vision and procedures of democracy, and that entails a capacity to see beyond the immediate interests of one's own group. Needless to say, this can be a tricky balance to maintain; the passion around a particular political goal can at times drive to the margins concerns about the common good or even loyalty to the democratic vision. However, groups and their political positions are always to some extent in flux, and individuals can embody multiple group loyalties; the boundaries of "we-ness" in heterogeneous modern democracies can shift rapidly. Yet, the fact remains that the task of making democracy work – not least in societies characterized by pervasive social differentiation and deeply conflictual group interests – is perplexing (Kymlicka, 1995; Spinner, 1994) and one of the biggest challenges it faces today.

The plural character of civic cultures should not be interpreted as suggesting that there exist rigid boundaries between the civic cultures of different groups. Rather, different groups may give differing inflections and emphasis, which can be mapped out along the lines of the six dimensions. For example, the civic culture that might characterize a group of community activists in an immigrant neighborhood will no doubt differ considerably from that of a national anti-abortion group. Yet, assuming their respective commitment to democracy, there will always be overlaps and commonalities. One could no doubt even generalize about the overarching civic culture of a nation – though it would of necessity be precisely very general – since the diversity would be lost from view.

LINKS: SOCIAL CAPITAL, SOCIAL MOVEMENTS

Treating civic cultures as resources that individuals and groups draw upon for their activities as citizens calls to mind Putnam's (2000) notion of "social capital." Edwards, Foley, and Diani (2001) indicate in their introduction to their collection analyzing Putnam's ideas about civil society and social capital that the term has a number of origins and uses. While others have also introduced the term, it is in Putnam's work where it becomes most directly relevant to the theme of democracy. Here social capital is viewed as residing in social connections within networks of reciprocal relations (Putnam 2000:21–24). These social ties involve shared values, trust, and reciprocity; they are both an individual and a social good. Putnam's notion of social capital encompasses *bonding* (exclusive, tight, intragroup ties) and *bridging* (inclusive, open links with other groups). He points out that social capital can obviously have a dark side: Bomb-planting terrorist groups, racist organizations, and so on, also manifest social capital, but in profoundly anti-democratic ways.

With his "bowling alone" metaphor, Putnam captures the decreasing communicative interaction among citizens; with social fragmentation and atomization follow declines in shared values, trust, and reciprocity, which further inhibit participation. Putnam and others look to the sociocultural landscape for explanations and find, for example, the monopolization of time that is associated in particular with television – a view that has elicited much debate (cf. the contributions in Edwards, Foley, and Diani, 2001). Also, Putnam's argument that membership in formal civil society organizations per se offers a solid preparation for political participation is questionable; it may well be that in the network society, the criterion of membership in formal groups becomes increasingly superfluous, and perhaps even delimiting. Yet, while there are such issues, Putnam's general idea of the importance of social connectivity for civic participation is beyond dispute. In the perspective I am developing here, with its "cultural turn," I would incorporate this element of social connectedness in a manner that is less wedded to the notion of formal organization – and link it more readily with the perspective of the network society more generally.

In a related vein, we can see obvious connections between the civic cultures perspective and research on the sociology of collective action and social movements. In the academic world, there are basically two loose "schools" of research in regard to social movements (Jordan, Lent, McKay, and Mische, 2005). One is called the "new social movement theory" and has its gravitational center in European social theory inspired by post-1968 thinking (see, for example, Melucci, 1989; Tourraine, 1988, 2001). It emphasizes the importance of agency, collective identities, and loose network structures; it leans toward the interactionist traditions within sociology. The other is usually termed the "political process approach" (previously known as resource mobilization theory) and has its home mostly in the United States. In the past decade, the differences between the two schools have become less pronounced, as dialogue has increased between them. My own inspiration derives more from the former, though the broad and heterogeneous research field of social movements generally has of course much to tell us about political participation and can offer insights about civic cultures.

The civic cultures framework aims to specify empirical entry points into the study of citizens' engagement and participation, and my emphasis here is on the role of the media in this regard. Conceptually, I model civic cultures as a circuit comprising six dimensions of mutual reciprocity; each of the dimensions can impact on the others in various ways, as I will suggest. The dimensions are knowledge, values, trust, spaces, practices, and identities. They are closely intertwined, and in fact, to pull them apart and identify them individually for schematic purposes may convey a misleading impression of their individual independence, but it is necessary for heuristic purposes. These dimensions can be studied in concrete circumstances to highlight their dynamic interaction and to examine how they might serve to promote or to hinder engagement.

KNOWLEDGE: ACTIVE APPROPRIATION

That citizens need knowledge in order to participate politically is obvious and basic. People must have access to reliable reports, portrayals, analyses, discussions, and debates about current affairs if they are to become civically engaged. A crucial aspect of this dimension is not just the question if citizens already have the knowledge they need, but, more important, if they are able to acquire relevant knowledge, that is, if they have viable strategies for obtaining knowledge. Thus, to speak of knowledge here includes "knowledge acquisition" – and thus this dimension is strongly related to the dimension of practices and skills. Some degree of literacy is important; people must be able to make sense of that which circulates in public spheres, and to understand the world they live in. Education, in its many forms, will thus always retain its relevance for democracy and citizenship, even if its contents and goals often need to be critically examined (see the collection by Ravitch and Viteritti, 2001). In the modern world, the media play a key role in regard to civic knowledge – a role that is problematic in many ways, as we know. Yet, precisely what kinds of knowledge are required for the vitality of heterogeneous civic cultures can never be established once and for all, but must always be open for discussion.

The theme of knowledge and civic agency has of course many potential aspects, some of which I took up at the end of Chapter 3. For one thing, it is possible to classify civic knowledge in a variety of ways. One can distinguish, for example, between background knowledge with its cognitive organization (as "schemata," structured around nodes – see, for example, Graber, 1988) and incoming new information. Thus, citizens may respond to an issue around a proposed tax raise; more background knowledge about the economy and taxes among citizens within particular civic cultures could move the discussion from a qualified "yes or no" stance toward reflections on public spending in other areas, to compare taxes on private income and corporate profits, and so on. The original issue may even evolve into something else via discussions based on such background knowledge. One could also analyze how existing knowledge bears relevance for the other dimensions of civic culture within particular groups, for example, how it impacts on that group's sense of trust and potential practices.

Certainly one important angle on civic knowledge today is the increasing ability of diverse political actors in the evolving media landscape to generate and disseminate it; activist networks, NGOs, alternative journalistic organizations, and bloggers are all a part of this rising phenomenon. As Chadwick (2006:87) discusses in the context of the Internet, political knowledge is discursive, contingent on circumstances, and, not least, changeable: It emerges via interaction with others. No doubt it would be more accurate in many cases to talk about "information" in regard to media output: It is in the process of appropriation of information – integrating it in relation to one's existing frames of reference and thereby making it personally meaningful – that information becomes "translated" into knowledge. Civic cultures can also differ in the ways and degrees to which they appropriate new information: Some no doubt tend to rest more on established background knowledge – which may even become outdated and ossified as ideological truths – while others are more continuously dealing with new information and thereby revising knowledge and even some political perceptions.

Another important feature in today's world is that information can be manifested in many ways, and the forms of appropriation – translating information into knowledge – are evolving, especially among the young, in keeping with cultural and media changes. New media technologies can promote new modalities of thought and expression, new ways of knowing. Younger generations are living in – and thinking, learning, and expressing themselves in – increasingly multimedia ways, where visual elements become more pronounced, often at the expense of linear, textual modalities. There are different communicative forms and registers among different groups, defined in terms of education, cultural background, specific circumstances, and so on.

This on the one hand speaks for democratic pluralism in regard to knowledge (and genres of journalism). On the other hand, we must be alert to the question of the efficacies of different modalities of knowledge for civic agency in situations of power relations. For example, intuitive forms of knowing and expressive modes of communication within the subaltern public spheres of some groups may be important for their group integration and political cohesion. Yet, such approaches may not always be politically effective in situations where the elite groups operate within the terms of technocratic rationality and demand formalized deliberation.

VALUES: SUBSTANTIVE AND PROCEDURAL

Democracy will not function if such virtues as tolerance and willingness to follow democratic principles and procedures do not have grounding in everyday life. Even support for the legal system (assuming it is legitimate) is an expression of such virtue: Democracy will not survive a situation of widespread lawlessness. Reports from troubled zones around the world confirm this. Just determining which are the best or real democratic values, and how they are to be applied, can of course be the grounds for serious dispute – and should be. It is precisely in such situations that the procedural mechanisms take on extra importance, offering a framework of rules where contrasting views can be wrestled with. The resolution of conflict, striving for compromise in situations where consensus is impossible, is a key task for a democratic society and requires a commitment to the rules of the game.

We can distinguish between substantive values such as equality, liberty, justice, solidarity, and tolerance, and procedural ones, like openness, reciprocity, discussion, and responsibility/accountability. Both categories should be treated as universal: In a democratic society, there cannot be exceptions to such values, whether based on ethnic traditions or religious creeds. Support for democratic values cannot cease at the moment when an individual walks in from a public space to that of a specific community enclave. Even more to the point, democratic rights cannot be contingent upon cultural milieu. Mouffe (2000, 2005), as I indicated in the previous chapter, argues for the notion of shared democratic values as a common point of departure for the playing out of political conflicts; only if such a generalized loyalty takes precedence over particular group interests will democracy be able to function.

That said, we should be fully aware that shared values per se only put people within a common communicative culture; they do not prevent antagonisms. The basic question of just how democratic values are to be applied in practice can readily become the grounds for serious dispute – and at times should be. Concrete situations, not least those concerning the relations between minority cultures to the majoritarian society, can well set certain democratic values in opposition against each other. For example, many Western European societies have been juggling the value of basic equality (for all individuals) with that of tolerance (for minority cultures) in the case of some women from non-Western minority communities who live with one foot in each world.

This is precisely why the procedural values and mechanisms take on importance: To be able to thrash out such conflicts without violence, striving for some practical compromise in situations where consensus is elusive, is a key task for a democratic society. For instance, tensions between dominant and minority cultural groups can at times be eased through laws that strive to facilitate minority group accommodation. Their realization and efficacy, however, are dependent upon a respect from all sides for the institutions and processes of the legal system.

Schudson (1998), in his historical survey of citizenship in the United States, finds that several models of democracy and citizenship have been prominent at different periods in U.S. history. He claims that today we in fact overemphasize the importance of information to the neglect of other dimensions that are important for citizenship. Of course information – and, by extension, knowledge – is important, but Schudson's point is that we can be blind to other attributes among the citizens that also are essential for the vitality of democracy. Specifically, he argues that since the 1960s, democracy in the United States has increasingly developed a rights-based dimension. This cementing of the values of individual rights offers grounds for a qualified optimism regarding democracy's future. For U.S. citizens, this means that affirming the value of rights, in a manner that has become second nature, has had an impact on the character of democracy and citizenship. Citizens have increasingly come to use the courts to secure these rights, adding the legal process to the repertoire of civic practices.

The dimension of values and the necessity that these be integrated into the taken-for-granted sensibilities of daily life remind us that, fundamentally, democracy is as much about a democratic society – how people live together and treat each other – as it is about a system of institutional frameworks. Democratic value commitment is not simply a rational-cognitive choice, but also involves an element of passion, as I discussed in the previous chapter (see also Mouffe, 2000:97). An intense enthusiasm for democratic values can evoke response, stimulate engagement, and generate action. This passion for democratic values is, in a sense, the foundation of civic virtue, the guidelines that define ideal civic behavior. This stands in sharp relief if we keep in mind that – as I discussed in Chapter 1 – economist values of profitability and managerial efficiency pose an ever-growing threat to democratic values, not least in the contexts of the institutions of everyday life where we interact with one another.

TRUST: OPTIMAL AND DIRECTED

Trust has long been seen as an important component for democracy; it has been reiterated in theory and studied empirically. It has been presented as a self-evident "good thing" – the more trust, the better, and declines in trust signal trouble. The bearers of trust are usually seen as the citizens, and the objects of trust are the institutions or representatives of government. More recently, however, the theme of trust has been explored in a number of different civic contexts (see the collection by Tonkiss, Passey, Fenton, and Hems, 2000); for our purposes here, it is especially trust among or between groups of citizens that is of interest. In this regard, Putnam (2000:136) distinguishes between "thick" trust, based on established personal relationships, and "thin" trust, the generalized honesty and expectations of reciprocity that we accord people we don't know personally but with whom we feel we can have a satisfactory exchange.

That individuals can experience some degrees of thick trust in their lives is obviously necessary for psychological and social well-being, but thin trust becomes especially relevant in civic contexts. Without a degree of thin trust, collective political action becomes impossible, undercut by suspicion even toward citizens of similar persuasions. Thin trust, then, becomes the salient mode for the loose bonds and networking relationships of civic participation; it links up with the "bridging" (rather than the "bonding") relations within Putnam's scheme of social capital. Sociology has understood society from both the perspectives of structures and interaction, yet democracy theory has tended to ignore the latter. Along with Putnam, another exception here is Tilly's (2007) expansive study on historical processes of democratization and de-democratization. He shows among other things that one of the central "master processes" of democracy is precisely the integration of networks of trust into politics, calling attention to the interactive foundations of democracy, where trust helps facilitate (civic) identities and social ties.

In getting a grasp of the complex character of trust in democracy, Warren's (1999) collection is very helpful. In his introduction (Warren, 1999:1–21), he notes that while trust is usually accorded a positive role in democracy, there are some paradoxes at work. Politics involves conflicts of interest, as well as identities in opposition, which insert an element of mistrust into these social relationships from the start. Thus, in the democratic tradition, excessive trust is unsuitable in the sense that it can suppress conflict and sustain oppressive relations. At the same time, minimum degrees of trust in society are necessary and, assuming that they are appropriate, can certainly enhance the quality of life in terms of freedom, efficiency, mobility, and less need for systematic controls. In complex societies, increasing interdependence on others and the roles they play (e.g., other drivers on the highway, the contents of pharmaceuticals we are prescribed, the quality of the products we buy) means an increasing vulnerability; we live, as we have so often been told, in "risk societies." We cannot know – and probably could not bear living with the knowledge if we did – all the possible vulnerabilities that we are exposed to. Instead, we operate to a large degree via trust.

Even in politics we cannot grasp all our possible vulnerabilities, and we choose to trust – at least to some extent. It can be argued that it is patently foolish to blindly trust political institutions, even in well-functioning democracies; there is simply too much we don't know about how they work, who is doing what and for what reason within them, and so on. So trust with a built-in antenna for scepticism seems prudent. Low trust in institutions can be ameliorated if they do a better job in telling the truth, keeping their promises, and acting with fairness and solidarity. Or, alternatively, trust can be enhanced by a growth in positive civil society experiences among citizens, thereby expanding the cultural disposition to expect positive performance. Yet high trust has a problematic aspect, aside from potential naiveté: Studies suggest a class bias, where the more affluent tend to "trust" regimes that support their position, and they act collectively in its – and their – interests, while the less well off, and not least the genuinely oppressed (or those who have collective memory of group oppression), are more likely to express distrust. We might say, in sum, that in regard to institutions and their representatives, trust operates in an ambivalent manner for civic cultures. Some degrees and forms of trust will always be necessary, but the optimal ratio of trust/mistrust has to be worked out according to specific circumstance.

What, then, of interpersonal trust? I noted in Chapter 2 that a major pillar of the civil society argument, most forcefully made by Putnam, is that participation in associations helps groom citizens for political life, in terms of both competencies and trust. While there no doubt are many qualifications in order here, certainly to act as citizens entails collective efforts, manifests the loose relations of networks, and depends on minimally functional thin trust. Interaction is perceived as holding out the possibility of mutual benefit; familiarity breeds cooperation. Without this kind of modest level of trust, activist groups, networks, social movements, and political parties would be impossible. This entails a thin, generalized trust, but I would also call it "focused," since it has to do with developing a sense of "we-ness" around specific issues or ideologies that involve like-mindedness. Such trust relates directly to the notion of democratically oriented political community, which I take up under the section "Identity."

SPACES: COMMUNICATIVE ACCESS AND CONTEXTS OF ACTION

For democracy to happen, citizens must be able to encounter and talk to each other. They need access to each other to develop their collective political efforts, and contexts in which they can act together. Citizens also must be able to contact those who represent them, and to enter into the communicative spaces where policy and decision-making are discussed. In the circumstances of everyday life there are innumerable physical spaces, sites, and settings in which people may meet and interact as citizens. The dimension of communicative spaces can thus be seen as the accessibility of viable public spheres in the life-worlds of citizens. The objective presence of public spheres is of course a prerequisite, but in the context of civic cultures, I stress their experiential proximity to citizens, that citizens feel that these spaces are available to them for civic use.

It could be argued that these civic spaces are declining, as the shopping mall becomes paradigmatic for the dominant new collective space, and large-screen televisions drown out conversation in some traditional sites for civic encounters, such as bars. We should not, however, write off physical co-presence as a mode of civic interaction: Civil society and its public spheres still offer many situations where people can talk to each other, and the political can potentially still rear its head in many such encounters, including the home, as noted in the previous chapter. Of course, in large-scale representative democracies, the representational chain may be very long, and the relevant communicative spaces may feel very remote, which is why it is crucial that decision-making structures and their various levels function and enjoy legitimacy. When such is not the case, the warning signals – not least in the form of civic disengagement – usually make themselves felt.

With the media, of course, the conditions for civic encounter expand, and potential civic communicative spaces multiply, as I will discuss in the next few chapters. The mass media contributed to the reconfiguration of private and public space, and as we continue with the interactive electronic media, we see an intensification of the sense of being co-present with others who are physically removed, contributing to the growth of "despatialized simultaneity" (Thompson, 1995), where the experience of a shared now is uncoupled from the imperatives of physical proximity. Moreover, as the new wireless telephony is joined with the Internet, mobile publicness is enhanced, with civic spaces increasingly in geographic transit.

Thus, new communicative spaces are emerging in which civic cultures can develop and flourish, and in which the political can be developed, and where politics can be pursued – even if the civic spaces that exist on the Internet are generally small in scale compared to the growing spaces occupied by the market. With the expansion of research in cultural geography and its interfaces with media and communication studies, we are now starting to see studies that explore the links between media and spatial perspectives (e.g., Couldry and McCarthy, 2004), as well as the specific spatial aspects of democracy itself (Hénaff and Strong, 2001; Barnett and Low, 2004).

The new media make it relatively easy to generate new communicative contexts. As I discuss in Chapter 7, the Internet offers its users not only vast communicative spaces in which to travel, visit, and participate, it also allows them to collectively construct new spaces, by launching Web sites, news groups, blogs, discussion forums, wikis, and so on. Further, "interspatiality," the capacity to move freely between different cyber-communicative spaces, becomes easy. Individuals are increasingly able to select from an enormous array of online output, customizing their own mix of news, opinion, and other information. Significantly, online spaces can facilitate offline activity, coordinating political interventions in "real-life" spaces. Moreover, given that these technologies are so ubiquitous in everyday life, they help foster, even at the nonpolitical level, taken-for-granted cultures of networking. People increasingly are linking up with strangers in loose networks for shared interests and activities. This development helps pave the way for networking in civic contexts.

From the standpoint of the civic cultures, these are of course attractive attributes. Knowing where to find and use these spaces, and knowing how to generate new ones, are part of the practices and skills that enhance civic cultures. The availability and accessibility of suitable communicative spaces – physical and virtual – is central; the ease of networking offers one obvious answer to the question of where and how civic agency can be enacted. Mediated networking does not replace face-to-face encounters, but to the extent that they are on the decrease, such networks certainly have the potential to complement and compensate. However, territorial parameters simply do not vanish: Governments still protect their borders, people still maintain geographically based identities, and there is still local social life to be lived. And much of social life, not least its political concerns, remains premised on place and its demarcations. At the very least, it can be argued that the growing late modern separation between the limits of territorial place and the potentials of communicative space is one of the key tensions that democracy must creatively deal with.

PRACTICES: EMBODIED AGENCY AND SKILLS

A viable and growing democracy must be embodied in concrete, recurring practices – individual, group, and collective – relevant for diverse situations. Such practices help generate personal and social meaning to the ideals of democracy, and they must have an element of the routine, of the taken-for-granted, about them if they are to be a part of a civic culture. Practices can be and are learned; they often require specific skills, especially communicative competencies. Thus, to be able to read, write, speak, work a computer, and get around on the Internet can all be seen as competencies important for democratic practices – and is closely linked with the knowledge dimension of civic cultures. Education will thus always play a key role in nurturing democracy, even if its contents and pedagogic approaches periodically need to be scrutinized and debated. To engage in practices contributes to experience, which can in turn serve to empower citizens. Not only does this solidify the specific practices as part of the civic repertoire of these citizens, but the practices also interplay forcefully with knowledge, trust, and values; practices involve defining, using, or creating suitable spaces, and also help to further foster civic identities.

Participating in elections is usually seen as the paramount concrete practice for democracy's citizens. Talk, too, has a prominent position, and has been associated with democracy and opinion formation from the start. In my discussion of deliberative democracy in the previous chapter, I emphasized that civic talk can involve a number of different practices, beyond that of formal deliberation. Agre (2004:7) argues that the key practice for civic engagement is not developing or joining networks in the abstract, but rather the capacity to use networks to connect to specific issues. This involves

[I]dentifying issues that are coming to prominence, researching and analyzing them, staking out public positions on them, and building social networks of other citizens who have associated themselves with related issues, especially those whose positions are ideologically compatible. Not only is this kind of issue entrepreneurship central to the making of public policy, but it is also central to "politics," in the broad sense, of nearly every institutional field, from industries to research fields, from professions to social movements. (Agre, 2004:7)

The same fundamental processes of issue linkages take place on all levels of politics, across all geographic entities and institutional contexts (political parities, unions, churches, professional societies, etc.). In this practical perspective of the pursuit, cultivation, and advocacy of issues, ideologies become the "connecting tissues" cementing networks and coalitions engaged in political movements. Doing politics in this way requires a minimal threshold of trust to activate and sustain the networking; a deep-rooted sense of community is not required. Yet it does presuppose considerable social and communicative skill, and a point of departure in concrete issues, framed by some sort of ideological coherence. What is useful in Agre's perspective is that it adds a sociological (and social psychological) frame to engagement and participation that enhances the generalized notion of associations and networks with concrete criteria of civic skills, ideology, and social relationships.

Thus, without denying the importance of values, Agre asserts the centrality of the capacity to define and promote issues, articulate positions on them (relating in some way to existing ideological currents), recruit support, cement relationships, and follow up with the necessary organizational skills to keep the momentum going. This is what drives engagement forward, and can embody it in participation. In this context, Agre highlights the decisive role of media technologies, especially those that can be used by citizens to actively communicate around issues.

Across time, practices become traditions, and experience becomes collective memory; today's democracy needs to be able to refer to a past, without being locked in it. New practices and traditions can and must evolve to ensure that democracy does not stagnate. We see today how the lack of civic practices, skills, and traditions is an obstacle in many societies attempting to develop their democratic character. Skills can develop through practices, and in this process foster a sense of empowerment; the dimensions of practices and identities (see the next section) are thus closely entwined.

There will always be practices used in democracy that elicit normative debate. For example, to what extent should civic practices permit less than full openness and honesty? To what extent should "doing politics" include manipulation? Just how "dirty" should we let democratic politics become? How civilly disruptive, how civilly disobedient may citizens become? At what point do problematic practices begin to threaten the basic substantive and procedural values of democracy? For such questions there can seldom be final answers. While we assert universal democratic values, their interpretation and application, as well as debate ethics, must remain part of the ongoing normative negotiations within democracy.

IDENTITIES: HETEROGENEITY, EMPOWERMENT, COMMUNITY

We return thus to identities, to the theme of people's subjective view of themselves as members and participants of democracy. As a foundation for agency, identities can be seen as the centerpiece of civic cultures (cf. Castells, 2000), with the other five dimensions contributing, reciprocally, to shaping the conditions of its existence. For example, identities build on knowledge and values, they can be reinforced by trust, and embodied in particular spaces via practices – pursuing issues by the use of civic skills – that in turn serve to reinforce identities. (Alternatively, the spiral can of course be negative, downward.) Today, identity is understood as plural: In our daily lives we operate in a multitude of different "worlds" or realities; we carry within us different sets of knowledge, assumptions, rules, and roles for different circumstances; we operate in different registers in different contexts.

To see citizenship as one component of our plural identities may also help us to avoid letting our democratic ideals generate a predefined, one-size-fits-all portrait of citizenship that is sociologically and psychologically unrealistic. There are many ways of being a citizen and of doing democracy. Identities of membership are not just subjectively produced by individuals, but evolve in relation to social milieus and institutional mechanisms; backward glances in history will remind us of ongoing changes. Civic identities are not static, but protean and multivalent. Not least, as I discussed in Chapter 1, a big challenge to civic identities in late modern democracies is that they can be overwhelmed by identities relating to consumption, which get considerably more reinforcement from the dominant media culture.

Two further general points: First, identities develop and evolve through experience, and experience is emotionally based. While the twentieth century witnessed many horrors of political passions run amok, the affective dimension of political engagement should not be automatically linked with irrationality in the destructive sense, as I discussed in the previous chapter. Affective involvement with political goals and values compatible with democracy not only poses no threat, but contributes to democracy's vibrancy – and to people's sense of their political selves. While Freud's revolutionary ideas about the unconscious dimension of emotional life may have caused moral panic in some Victorian circles a century ago, it is time that democratic theory relaxes about this fundamentally human quality.

Secondly, the salience of civic identities can vary enormously among individuals, but for most people it is low. Barnhurst (2003), in an innovative study of life narratives of young adults who spoke about their experiences of citizenship, puts his findings in stark contrast to the classic ideal of the engaged and informed citizen. That his respondents tend to follow the general pattern of low civic involvement that has been established over the past century is in itself not surprising, but his analysis of their identity processes sheds some interesting light. He finds that while the media are very much entwined with their life experiences, most political experiences take place in life zones beyond the media, and the civic self hovers largely at the margins of these people's identities. Indeed, in many cases, it even evokes a degree of contempt, precisely because it is experienced as having little personal relevance.

Yet Barnhurst suggests that if we reformulate citizenship in a more expansive way, as I suggested in Chapter 3, and as citizenship studies are trying to do, then it could conceivably take on stronger relevance. This is because many of the clashes, conflicts, and forms of resistance and problems that these young people report from their lives are seemingly viewed as personal, but could well be situated within the political. That is, the political realm could be defined in broader terms, to accord political significance to their personal experiences. Barnhurst's effort points to possible reformulations of citizenship, but even as it stands, his study reminds us that civic identity, even if it resonates with affect, comprises for most people only a small part of their overall identities. The question is if and how the civic component can be enlarged.

Received citizenship, that is, formal membership as a legitimate, equal, and recognized citizen of the state, is probably the most fundamental source of civic identity for most people, especially if they are not particularly engaged in any specific political issues. Though of a legal nature, such formalized inclusion also has important consequences at the level of subjectivity for the individuals and groups, providing an important foundation for civic identity. Feeling that one is a legally certified member of a democratic nation-state protected by rights and due procedures (and most often also shaped by its national culture), provides an important platform of psychic security, as well as situating one in a collective context. One is a bearer of concrete liberties – even if, as noted earlier, real equality and inclusion may be lacking despite their formal status.

Beyond the identity that formal citizenship can offer, I would suggest two important schematic components to civic identity that can operate in tandem with each other. The first involves the sense of being an empowered political agent. This links up explicitly with the notion of achieved citizenship, with civic agency. Resting on the security of formal membership of the state, and with its rights and safeguards, citizens are at least potentially in a position to make some kind of impact on political life. Empowerment emerges at the subjective level, and can be seen as both actualizing participation and being strengthened by it. At some point, of course, empowerment must be experienced as meaningful, that people sense that their efforts at least made a contribution in a political struggle, even if they do not win each time.

The second identity component here is membership in one or more political communities. It is difficult to feel empowered if one is alone, and civic participation is basically collective activity, people acting in concert with one another. Belonging to political communities clearly enhances the sense of empowerment. Political community involves a specific (though sometimes temporary) feeling of a "we" group, clearly defined in relation to "they" around a contested issue. Political communities are not limited to the territory of nation-states; as democracy takes on global-cosmopolitan attributes, such communities may extend, for example, to others who are part of the same global movement, or to diasporic networks seen in political terms. Dayan's (2005) point about treating issue-publics as forms of "imagined communities" bears reiteration here.

To talk about "community" in the late modern world is to dance on a conceptual minefield, but it is unavoidable. I use the concept with some reservation; it is problematic, if not downright melancholic, given that the trajectory of modernity has involved a considerable dissolution of community. What I have in mind is a kind of affinity, a minimal sense of commonality among citizens in heterogeneous late modern societies (Alexander's, 2006, notion of the "civic sphere" involves a similar trajectory of thin political community). Community-based identity here of course resonates strongly with the dimension of trust. Citizens have to deal with each other to make their common entities work; they have to cooperate with each other to make political interventions, and they have deal with their political opponents in ways that do not violate membership in a democratic citizenry, whether at the level of neighborhood, nation-state, or the global arena. Thus, in most of such contexts, the current notion of "network" can take us quite far, in that such loosely organized constellations with relatively weak social ties are quite suited for democratic engagement and for catalyzing empowerment.

Political community, just like all community, is never fully static. Communities evolve with changing circumstances, with the appearance of new issues; they will pick up new members, perhaps lose some old ones, or some members will develop multicommunity allegiances.

The boundaries may in part be contingent on circumstances. For example, in Britain, depending on the political issue and the relevant geography involved (e.g., local or national level), a person may define him/ herself as a Muslim, as an Asian, or as a Pakistani, and in some circumstances there may even be tensions between subjective positions as these.

When the political manifests itself in societal contexts, communities of "we" become delineated against "they," mobilizing identities in the form of issue-publics, for instance, around a particular piece of legislation. Once the bill is accepted or defeated, the issue is passed, and the coalescence of opinion around the issue disperses. At the same time, there are also more stable groupings that share an ideological consensus that stretches over many kinds of issues. Those who are adversaries in the particular issue must still be accorded such democratic values as recognition, respect, and reciprocity, and not seen as enemies who must be dealt with by violence; in Mouffe's (see Carpentier and Cammaerts, 2006) terms, conflict must be exercised agonistically, not antagonistically.

Many lines of we-they are drawn not just around a particular (and transitory) issue, but also around fundamental elements of identity and community that have to do with, for example, ethnicity, religion, and sexuality. These constellations usher us into the expansive field of identity politics, which can contribute both to strengthening and weakening democracy. Such politics pose a special challenge in that they raise precisely the tension between, on the one hand, commitment to one's specific community and its interests, and, on the other hand, a sense of civic solidarity toward one's opponents (the "larger democratic community" that we share), and a loyalty to the values and procedures of democracy. How adversaries relate to each other becomes a part of a civic culture. All too often the democratic ethos of reciprocity, respect, and open discussion is unfortunately lacking.

Respecting difference, according recognition to minority cultures, and harmonizing them with the broader majority, while at the same time extending genuine equality, is not a simple matter. This becomes especially difficult in cases where majoritarian communities promote undemocratic exclusion, or where some minority cultures may hold values at odds with democratic principles. Complicating factors are also found where there has been a history of oppression and exploitation by the state of such minority groups (e.g., European colonial legacies, African Americans in the United States). These situations become exacerbated, for example, when anti-democratic elements react against what they perceive to be the bewildering and threatening developments of late modernity (e.g., racist extreme right-wing parties in Europe). We can anticipate many and long struggles based on such community identities. Touraine (2000) specifies as one of the key tensions of modernity precisely this cacophony of communities that profoundly challenges democracy to deal with the couplet of equality and difference. The question he poses – "Can we live together?" – still remains to be answered. Without viable civic cultures, it will indeed be difficult.

CIVIC CULTURES, NETWORKS, AND THE MEDIA MATRIX

To pull the discussion together, let us recall that there are many factors that can impact on civic cultures, not least social class and institutionalized power relations, but in the context of late modernity, one of the most important is the complex and dynamic system of the ever-evolving media matrix. In looking at our circuit of six dimensions, all of them potentially impact on each other, and each of them in turn is shaped by developments in the other five. It is no doubt the case that their respective saliencies will vary in different contexts, and of course for individual citizens. However, we might nonetheless in a tentative manner order them in a general way in terms of their respective valence.

Sets of interviews with young political activists that were done in the context of a Swedish research project (see Dahlgren and Olsson, 2007a, 2007b, 2007c) suggest that the dimensions of trust and values function in more long-term and less visible ways, with their changes having more gradual impact; also, they would generally be less observed/analyzed by the participants themselves.

From the standpoint of civic agency, knowledge and practices/skills tend to be not only the most immediately empowering, but also the dimensions that citizens can most readily analyze in a self-reflexive way, charting one's development in such terms. Spaces of communicative access offer the necessary opportunities; they at times may become very much the focus of attention – for example, if a new space suddenly becomes accessible – or they may simply remain taken for granted. Civic identity is, perhaps paradoxically, the dimension that is least likely to be formulated, at least in verbal terms, as something pertinent by civic agents themselves, yet functions, I would argue, as the most compelling link between civic cultures and the sense of agency that engages people and can help turn them into political participants.

Looking at late modern democracies more generally, the media spread knowledge, albeit very selectively and at times in woefully inadequate ways. They also contribute to new forms of knowledge, new ways of understanding oneself and the world. The newer ICTs can be used by citizens to generate, spread, and share knowledge; to supplement; and also to challenge that which is received from the mass media. By appropriating information and making it meaningful, citizens generate their own knowledge, which they can then use in forming opinions. At the same time, there is the increasing problem of expert knowledge in late modern society, which is essential for societal development, even while this cognitive inequality creates problems for engagement.

Civic values are referred to both explicitly and implicitly; in the latter case they may be indirectly evoked and affirmed by, for example, the role they play as a baseline in political scandal. They can also be ideologically undercut, for example, where citizenship becomes collapsed into consumerism. Civic values can function as taken-for-granted background horizons that give meaning to the political world and its events, yet they can also be thematized, invoked rhetorically, and debated. At the same time, they are under threat from economist and consumerist values. Trust is seldom addressed directly in the mass media (it appears in occasional journalistic reports of trust in institutions based on opinion studies), though it is at times given much attention in the counter-public spheres using interactive media. Critics at times maintain that contemporary modes of journalistic reporting undermine trust and promote cynicism among citizens, however, via interactive media, trust can also be built up through the experiences of civic practices.

The spaces of civic culture that provide communicative access to others for civic encounters have traditionally been shaped in part by people's face-to-face encounters, and in part by the mass media. Today, the interactive media allow for many innovations where citizens are "making space" for democracy, thereby extending and transforming public spheres. The media matrix makes possible new kinds of civic practices, while at the same time demanding new skills beyond the traditional ones required for citizenship, in particular, the use of the media to identify specific issues for engagement, and for making the connections and developing networks of issue lattices.

Civic identities have an essential affective component and cannot be understood in solely rationalist terms; moreover, we understand the growing relevance of the late modern media matrix for people's identities generally. However, civic identities understandably tend to reside in the fringes of people's self-conceptions, which is congruent with the diminutive position of civic identities (compared to identities as consumers, clients, customers, or spectators) in the media milieu. Though they are diminutive, resources for civic identities are not entirely absent in the mass media, and the interactive media in particular offer many opportunities for their cultivation, especially in regard to empowerment and valorized political community.

The media can mobilize an array of identities and offer various kinds of engagement and community that can become quite strong, yet such identities often do not – at least explicitly – have much to do with politics. Mediated sports and reality television programs, for example, can generate very compelling "we-ness." However, as we probe further into popular culture (and I do this in the next chapter), we can find at least implicit links to politics even with this domain. We would be foolish to see engagement in these phenomena as somehow completely irrelevant to or entirely different from engagement in democracy. They all have to do with a mobilization of certain identity elements, a manifestation of some kind of community – as well as demonstrations of knowledge, values, trust, practices, and skills.

With the analytic horizons from this chapter now behind us, the next three chapters explore in more detail attributes of the contemporary media in regard to civic cultures.

CHAPTER 6

Television and Popular Public Spheres

In this chapter, I want to examine television in terms of its popularity and contribution to civic cultures, relating this to the traditional notion of the public sphere and updating my earlier perspectives on that theme (Dahlgren, 1995). The concept of the public sphere remains a central analytic construct in our ongoing efforts to understand the relationship between democracy and the media. And television remains the dominant medium for most people in Western democracies, despite the profound communication revolution associated with the Internet. Yet the conceptual premises of the public sphere become all the more problematic, as the media, with television in the vanguard, seemingly drift ever further in the direction of entertainment and consumption. How do we orient ourselves in this regard via the concept of the public sphere? How does the popular quality of television resonate with notions of public spheres and civic cultures?

The discussion consists of three parts. First I probe television and its media logics from the standpoint of its problematic role in the public sphere. While we can clearly specify traditional news and current affairs programming, we cannot establish a watertight barrier between politics and popular culture on television, a fact that we must incorporate into our understanding of the medium's contributions to the public sphere. Thereafter, with a focus still on television, I take up the more general debates around the relationship between popular culture and politics. There are several points of interface, which have varying relevance for passion, engagement, and civic cultures. In the final section, I draw together the arguments, stressing that the traditional bifurcation between politics, on the one hand, and popular culture and entertainment, on the other, leads us into a dead end. At the same time, we do ourselves an analytic disservice if we ignore the real tensions between them.

TELEVISION LOGIC AND THE CIVIC IDEAL

Television is constantly in transition, in terms of its industrial structures, legal frameworks, technological parameters, programming output, and audiences. In today's world it has become quite difficult to empirically generalize about television, and equally challenging to grasp it as a totality via some theoretic discourse. Television has simply become too heterogeneous in too many ways. The original terrestrial broadcast model was first refashioned with cable and satellite technologies; today, digital developments are further recasting what we mean by "television." With computers, the Internet, mobile phones, iPods, and TiVo recording becoming part of the ancillary technology, and the growing availability of on-demand services and pay-per-view, television and its audiences are in rapid transformation. Thus, I should clarify that in this chapter, when I say "television," I am mostly referring – in an imperfect manner – to its more traditional manifestations, with the largest audiences.

In terms of its socio-cultural significance, it also remains analytically a moving target for researchers (see, for example, the collections by Allen, 2004; Spigal and Olsson, 2004; Wasco, 2005). While television's programming has been an object of popular and academic criticism since its beginnings, there have been intensified discussion and research in recent years as observers try to come to terms with such global phenomena as reality television and docu-soaps (cf. Hill, 2005; van Zoonen and Aslama, 2006) and, more generally, the "trash" and "dumbing-down" character of the medium (cf. Dovey, 2000; Glynn, 2000).

While television is becoming increasingly connected to telecommunication and computer technologies, beyond this technical convergence we also witness the entwinement of television and the larger media culture. By this I mean that via its forms, contents, and self-referential character, television and the larger late modern media milieu are moving toward enhanced interconnectedness. To talk about "television" means that we get inexorably involved in talking about other elements of the media matrix as well, even if television remains one of its most prominent elements. For example, the various docu-soaps are also covered in various newspapers and weekly and fan magazines. On the Internet one can follow plot developments and take part in discussions and even in some cases vote about how conflicts are to be resolved. A number of the participants become mini-celebrities, and we can intertextually follow their (albeit usually short-lived) careers in stardom in various media. Series on television become films. Shrill tabloid headlines announce "scandals," identifying simply by their first names various television stars with the understanding that for the general public there is no mystery as to who these people are.

Visualizing News: A Real Pleasure

The dramatic developments in the formats of television over the past two decades abound with varieties of infotainment, and even the traditional news programs themselves strongly tilt toward the popular and the sensationalist. Television journalism incorporates more and more of the personal, the intimate, the sensational, the subjective, the confessional; distinguishing journalism from nonjournalism becomes all the more difficult. The technical and cultural fusion between television and other media no doubt serves to further erode the "exceptionalism" of journalism, that is, the assumption that this genre is to be produced and evaluated by sets of criteria fundamentally different from those operative in other programming.

At one level, all journalism is engaged in a kind of "translation service": It must take that which is new and convey it in terms that are recognizable and meaningful. This tension is of course a continuous challenge, in that certain events or developments cannot be truly understood with reference to the familiar. Yet, the established frames of references of audiences are usually difficult to alter, at least in the short term, and much news is in fact of a routine character. Thus a good deal of journalism consists of reiterations of the world as it is, using familiar kinds of stories with recurring elements. The highly conventionalized use of language and, in television news, visuals also enhances the impression of the everyday, the "normal" (see Cottle and Rai, 2006, for an updated discussion on the form of television news). News can thus also be analytically treated as a technology of daily civic socialization.

In the traditional television news program, the repertoire of the visuals is quite standardized, with many generic ingredients in the camerawork. The codes that define the genre are quite unmistakable. For journalists as well as audiences, this camerawork is not merely "containers" that carry information; the particular use of specific shots is part of a well-developed audiovisual discourse that can convey meaning in an efficient manner, for example, a shot of the White House is not merely an architectural representation, but signifies the presidency, government, or power of the United States. Above all, in the context of journalism, the visual dimension also embodies the aesthetics of realism: It conveys an impression of documentary "natural observation."

The camera ostensibly strives to function as the surrogate eye of the viewer, and thereby becomes in a sense "invisible," deflecting awareness from the constructed character of news. In terms of the transmission of information and the generation of knowledge, the visual dimension, with speaker texts, results in a format where cognitive comprehension is often low, and where many of the informational details are lost. At the same time, the very familiarity of news formats and their visual repertoires may help deflect the sense that we may actually be missing a good deal of the content.

Yet, this notion of visual objectivity is in a sense eroding, as audiences become more aware of how television generally gets done. Popular conceptions about objectivity, camera work, "real" versus fictive, and so on, have become more sophisticated in the wake of versions of reality television as well as the growing active involvement in amateur/home media productions of all kinds through the use of inexpensive and accessible consumer digital media equipment. This "media savviness" of the "postdeferential public," as Andrejevic (2004) terms it, becomes in fact a part of the pleasure of viewing: a sense of being hip enough to see through artifice. Such a viewer stance is, in all likelihood, far from universal among television audiences, but it is safe to assume it is most prevalent among the young, and thus growing.

At a more general level, the visual dimension is of course also strongly associated with entertainment, and even in the news visuals can readily evoke engagement via narrative, drama, personification, and spectacle. It is the visual dimension that gives television the aura of a "pleasure machine" – which from the beginning has constituted an underlying tension with the rational legacy of journalism. From the dawn of television news, producers have grappled with the fact that some stories may be of journalistic importance yet may not readily lend themselves to suitably compelling visuals (e.g., much political negotiation can be of great societal significance but visually of little interest). And, conversely, dramatic visual footage may be available but be lacking a good informative story (e.g., breathtaking images of war may be weak in terms of information).

The extensive use of compelling visuals no doubt goes far to explain the popularity of television news. Even very emotionally difficult topics can mobilize affective response and become engaging via visuals. A much-discussed instance of this is the portrayals of suffering in various parts of the world that have spurred viewers to a various kinds of actions, not least the giving of money to help support relief. The news has also paved the way for larger global media events geared to bringing in still more money for support (e.g., Live Aid). How such stories are framed are of course important: Chouliaraki (2006) shows how differing modes of representation can structure a sense of identity and social proximity for the viewer vis à vis those who are afflicted – and usually geographically remote. Such civic engagement carries with it an element of global cosmopolitanism, a sense of universal "we" toward mankind. Alternatively, it is also possible that such news coverage can result in distancing, a cementing of a sense of the "other," that at best only evokes pity for those who are not like us. The problematic issue of "compassion weariness" also emerges in this context, readily evoked by the very delimited range of agency that most viewers experience in regard to such reports (see also Boltanski, 1999; Tester 2001).

Television journalism's visuals help explain the general attraction audiences have for the genre, and, more to the point, visuals are able to mobilize civic engagement and participation in specific contexts. That such involvement tends to be sporadic and delimited is understandable given the difficulties of follow-up action. But if we reverse the perspective, and focus not on dreadful events abroad, but political life at home, why is it that television journalism, with it capacity for engaging visuals, has apparently not been successful in helping to sustain civic engagement in national politics? One answer we have encountered already in Chapter 2 in the study by Couldry, Livingstone, and Markham (2007): While exposure to news, even television news, may help citizens maintain "public connections," for most citizens it is difficult to see any practical link between the news and some form of viable political activity: They cannot easily translate journalistic information into civic knowledge and practices. This has to do chiefly with the way political life is organized, leaving little room for citizens' initiatives. However, it also has to do with how the news portrays citizens, giving very few clues to support civic identities and agency.

Civic Agency: As Seen on Television

A further study explores explicitly how citizens, their views, and their actions figure in television news reporting. Lewis, Inthorn, and Wahl-Jorgensen (2005), in their study of media portrayals of political participation, analyzed more than 5,600 television news items from the main evening programs in the United States and the UK to see how television news portrays the role of citizens in shaping political life. The data show that television journalists do take up public opinion and do discuss citizens; 30–40 percent of all news stories have some reference or at least inference to public opinion, and the vast majority of references to citizens and their views come from journalists themselves in the news items. Also, about four of ten journalistic references to the views of citizens take the form of vox populi items, that is, the short interviews with people "in the street." Moreover, the range of topics is largely of the politically serious kind, not on entertainment and celebrity themes – even if many were angled toward consumer issues. The researchers also note that editors and journalists feel that feedback from citizens is very important for their work. At this point, however, the upbeat findings unfortunately come to an end, and another picture comes into focus.

Most of the references to citizens and public opinion made by reporters are done without any substantial evidence. This is surprising, given the availability of so many current opinion polls; in fact, only 3 percent of the news items in the UK and the United States that referred to citizens had any reference to polling data. The overwhelming claims made about citizens thus present no evidence. The authors deduce that journalists are therefore relying mostly on their own impressions and assumptions of the audiences and their views. Further, these portrayals tend to be systematically more conservative or right-wing than polling results would actually support.

However, the dominant image to emerge from television news about citizens is that they have no clear place in the news. They are largely passive observers: Citizens overwhelmingly do not hold or discuss strong views. Citizens are represented as *responding* to issues and situations, but are almost never portrayed as offering political suggestions or other constructive thoughts. They are seen as expressing emotional responses – fear, anger, concern, and so on – with only 4 percent of the news items showing citizens offering any political measures that could be taken. Citizens may be represented as engaging in some commentary, but very rarely in advocacy. In terms of news dramaturgy, the main actors are government and business, not citizens. The authors suggest that the portrait of citizens that emerges here is largely in keeping with elite theories of democracy, where citizens respond and follow, but they do not initiate and participate.

Lewis, Inthorn, and Wahl-Jorgensen (2005) explain these patterns by underscoring how the ideology of consumerism has permeated the dynamics of political life, with the public seen as an object to be managed and to which politics are "sold" by the various devices of spin.

The media environment forcefully tells us daily that consumption is the domain where pleasure and freedom are to be found. The public realm, the arena of citizenship, by contrast, generally appears as uninspiring, devoid of any promise of real personal fulfilment. Also, the authors suggest that journalistic habits and constraints play an important role, especially the traditional "top-down" mode of reporting, which results in these kinds of representations. The news is based on what politicians do; it is they who set the agenda. The impression of citizens who largely lack their own policy preferences thus fits in nicely in this context. We can say that the subject position offered viewers of television news is basically that of a spectator to political life – a form of socialization for civic quiescence.

In these media images, "the public" emerges in the news as a construction, a product of journalistic, political, and scientific discourses. The public is spoken for by a variety of powerful voices, but does little speaking of its own, and is given little or no help in learning how to do so in politically effective ways via television news. Add to this the familiar laments about the nature of the contents, the swiftness of the tempo, and problems of comprehension, and we must conclude that while the contributions of television news to the public sphere remain important in many ways, they are also highly circumscribed.

Given such critical analysis, it may actually seem odd or even pointless to invoke the Habermasian tradition of the public sphere in relation to this media genre. Yet there are in fact ways of looking at television journalism's contribution to the public sphere without heading into a dead end. Scannell (1996) argues that television, at least in its national, public service context, has done a great deal to resocialize private life toward a shared public culture. The trajectory of public service broadcasting over the years has been to continually expand the topics and perspectives that can be aired and uttered in public, rendering more and more terrain as familiar and accessible to larger audiences, to be talked about and interpreted by them. In the process, television has been increasingly inclusive in incorporating audiences-as-citizens into the communicative space of the public sphere.

The golden age of public service has faded, so we can only go so far with that type of argument. Yet, as Dovey (2000) indicates, there is in this line of reasoning a potentially useful analytic kernel we should hang on to concerning television, namely, the idea of extending the public sphere, and making it accessible, despite apparent "losses" in the levels of rationality or civic socialization. This view concerns television as a whole, not just the news programs; we take the step beyond journalism to look at television's overall program output. Here the culturalist perspective becomes explicitly operative, in that we have to look beyond news and current affairs output if we are to understand political communication and mediated citizenship (see Jones, 2006, for elaborations on this theme).

PROCESSING THE PROTO-POLITICAL

I find that Ellis' (2000) view of contemporary television provides a useful frame in this regard. It realistically incorporates the basic attributes of the medium, takes seriously its public functions, is sociologically well anchored, and avoids the pitfalls of the extreme conceptual positions. While allying himself with the idea of television's potential for extending the public sphere, as illustrated by Scannell (1996), he is also fully aware of the critiques. Ellis talks of television as a "working through," of television not providing any ultimate or definitive point of view, but rather offering its viewers vast amounts of transitory glimpses, preliminary meanings, multiple frameworks, explanations, and narrative structures for processing basic private as well as public concerns, many times touching on topics that are, if not fully political, at least insipient, or proto-political. These may or may not at times coalesce as concrete political issues; often they remain at the level of perceptions and values.

Television is largely oriented to the present moment, to the experiential rather than the analytic, to the personal rather than the structural. Also, though Ellis does not make a big point of it, his approach avoids the unproductive polarization of the rational and the affective. In our everyday lives we make sense of our experiences, ourselves, and the world around us largely using a combination of our head and our heart, as I discussed in Chapter 4. There is no reason why we should – or even could – function any differently when we find ourselves connected to public spheres.

As Ellis puts it, "Television attempts definitions, tries out explanations, creates narratives, talks over, makes intelligible, harnesses speculation, tries to make fit, and, very occasionally, anthematizes" (Ellis, 2000:79). In the meanings that television offers viewers, uncertainty prevails over certainty; there is a perennial tentativeness in the voice of television. One can grasp this in the broad debates and many positions around programs such as *The Sopranos* and *Sex and the City* – which in my view echo some of Fiske's (1988) arguments about the importance of polysemy for popularity, that is, that the popularity of popular culture resides to some extent in its many meanings, which evoke different interpretations from different groups.

This working through operates via all genres and their hybrids, but is predicated on viewer familiarity with generic formulas as a key vehicle for the communication of meaning (Johansson, 2006, finds that readers of British tabloid press use these newspapers in ways very similar to what Ellis describes). Such a view does not preclude mechanisms of mainstreaming; the working through of television largely takes place within broadly hegemonic boundaries, as critics have long argued. Thus, working through does not deny the hegemonic character of television, but recognizes that such hegemony is loose, leaky, and always at risk.

Television's working through can take intensely politicized turns, as it has done in the post–9/11 era in the United States. Yet the point of the working-through perspective is that much of the meanings offered up are anchored in a transitory present; new issues and angles will emerge, there will always be a bit more cacophony than coherence – at least on the surface level that is most immediately relevant for opinions, attitudes, and practices. The more deeply rooted ideological dimensions are less transitory in character, and can be mobilized in new contexts, as new issues arise. However, even political rhetoric based on deep ideological dimensions can diminish in their impact; for example, the grip that the Bush administration's patriotic post–9/11 rhetoric had on the U.S. political climate has loosened somewhat over the years.

We can briefly contrast Ellis' view with that of Scheuer (2001), who makes the argument that there is a conservative, right-wing bias in television's modes of representation. In this analysis the tendency toward personalizing; dichotomizing; putting style over substance, the emotional and physical over the intellectual and the moral; and the general aversion toward complexity all serve to support social and political conservatism. While it is true, for instance, that the medium tends not to promote analytic response, and that personification and psychologism may work against perspectives of collective well-being and responsibility, it strikes me that this type of reading founders precisely in its adherence to a traditional textual rationality.

One can certainly appreciate Scheuer's sense of exasperation with television, and it cannot be denied that the modes of representation he criticizes often indeed carry a deeply conservative import (blatantly apparent on Fox News). However, I see no deterministic imperative that in principle precludes using such modes for progressive messages; in the border zone between journalism and comedy, *The Daily Show* does just this. Rather, I would here refer to the external social forces that impact on the contemporary output of television to explain its ideological slant – political power arrangements and economic mechanisms. Scheuer's call for better "media literacy" – to be taught in the schools and elsewhere – to enhance "critical viewing" would no doubt lead to more media-critical audiences. Yet, this appeal to education misses something essential about television's cultural power, and its capacity to engage at the affective level.

At a fundamental level, what is at stake in the public sphere perspective is the question of where the political (in Mouffe's sense) resides – where social conflict is articulated and processed – and how it is positioned against that which is deemed nonpolitical. As I have noted, the traditional view from both public sphere theory and political communication has been to maintain a strict boundary between the rational and the affective, and, by extension, between serious current affairs information and entertainment. Yet, in the notion of television serving to work through various issues via its entertainment programming, providing a daily environment where topics are raised, become contested, and take on the character of the political or at least the proto-political, this boundary begins to loosen up. Thus, the ongoing televisual treatment of value conflicts having to do with premarital sex, sexual preference, abortion, gene manipulation, interethnic relations, and so on, in such diverse genres as dramatic series, soap operas, reality television, talk shows, situation comedies, and comic monologues all are indicative of television's blurring of this basic dichotomy.

It would of course be difficult to calibrate television's exact impact here, not least because of the flowing, meandering character of themes and issues across time, yet to belittle its significance seems simply erroneous. In the case of certain identity politics, for instance, seen in the long term of the working-through perspective, many of the issues raised and positions taken by various groups found their way into television and achieved visibility and enhanced legitimacy, not least via entertainment programs. For example, the sitcom *All in the Family* from the 1970s, with its main character the working-class bigot Archie Bunker, through its humor and irony challenged discriminatory views on gay people and racial prejudice, as well as problematizing the traditional view on women's social position. (I realize that critics pointed to a certain polysemy here – that viewers who agreed with Archie could get their prejudices validated – but I would argue that in the long run the program served to undermine those positions.)

At the time, the controversies the program touched upon could reverberate with considerable electricity. More than three decades on, the visibility and legitimacy of, for example, gay men and lesbian women on television have been enormously enhanced. This is not to say that social discrimination or oppression of homosexual people is a thing of the past, but in terms of television's representations in these areas, the public sphere has been transformed, and the center of normative gravity has certainly shifted in society at large. The underlying assumptions that might frame specific issues relating to homosexuality today (for example, in regard to the right to adopt children) depart from a different set of societal dispositions that television helped engender at the popular level.

POPULAR ENGAGEMENT: LOCATING DEMOCRACY

We thus have to take seriously television's popularity, and consider how in its largely un-Habermasian modes it can promote – as well as constrict – public spheres. What has been emerging in this chapter is the importance of popular horizons, especially as mediated via television, in the life of democracy. The culturalist view underscores the importance of looking beyond news and other forms of traditional political communication, in a sense to treat the realm of popular culture as bearing relevance for democratic life. Simons expresses the view cogently: "... there is a structural and necessary relation between the popularisation of culture and the democratisation of politics ..." (Simons, 2003:186–187). How far should we extend this perspective? What is at stake in our understanding of the relationship between popular culture and political processes?

Politics and Popular Culture: Border-Crossings

The boundary between politics and popular culture has long been well defended, since it has been assumed that letting popular culture "leak into" politics will just subvert the whole enterprise of democracy and citizenship. Certainly feminists have long made the point that the private realm is not a priori devoid of political issues. In recent years, scholars working in media research and cultural studies have been recasting the relationship between politics and popular culture, trying to probe and clarify this link in new ways. Some studies in this area highlight the analytic trajectories that are now in motion. Several contributions in the collection by Corner and Pels (2003), for example, reject the firm division between these two domains, stressing the significance of the aesthetics of political image, style, and performance, with much of it being borrowed from popular culture and orchestrated by spin and PR. Thus, for example, politicians can take on an aura of "celebrity," equivalent to the stars of popular culture. In the shift away from emphasizing party ideology, the political style of individual politicians becomes central to how audiences experience them and evaluate their performance, authenticity, and political capabilities.

More broadly, Street (1997) suggests in a manner similar to Ellis that "Popular culture neither manipulates us nor mirrors us; instead we live through it and with it ... our lives are bound up with it" (Street, 1997:4). This posits what we might call an undeniable base relevance of popular culture for political life: Moral judgments are operative in culture, cultural values have relevance for politics, identities emerge within both domains. Popular culture offers images and symbols that express and evoke emotion, that we use not least in shaping our individual and collective identities; our sense of who we are; what is right, important, and so forth. These can certainly be pertinent for how politics operates and what political views emerge. Modern politics, in turn, often makes use of, and is expressed via, forms and languages of popular culture.

There is a fundamental logic linking the two spheres, having to do with "the way in which notions of representation, the people, popularity, and identity are shared between them" (Street, 1997:21). In this linkage, passion and pleasure are always present, mobilized and manifested often in very similar ways. Street structures the argument clearly: On the one hand, popular culture feeds into politics; on the other hand, politics often takes the form of popular culture. In the first case, he provides many examples of how popular culture takes on political character, and impacts on the political imagination: rock music at times expressing political resistance, or galvanizing public opinion for aid relief; movies addressing political themes; television programs doing exactly what Ellis (2000) says they do in working through important social issues; individual icons of popular culture taking a political stance; audiences making use of popular culture in developing particular identity positions in regard to, for example, gender or ethnicity. He stresses above all how popular culture can contribute to the redefinition of what constitutes politics, often extending notions of the political into the private sphere of personal relations and group contexts (today the docu-soaps can serve as a telling illustration).

In the second case, looking in the other direction, Street (1997) shows how politics takes on the forms of popular culture, as politicians and party machines resort to the same kinds of advertising strategies used to market commodities, as well as the image management associated with celebrities. Political leaders associate themselves in various ways with stars from popular culture (e.g., Bono), appear together with them, and even use popular culture formats at times in communicating with citizens, such as appearing on entertainment shows. There is of course an established school of thought that reacts vehemently to all such forms of political packaging, and while acknowledging the ever-potential problems, Street avoids simple, blanket condemnation. He invites us to instead look at these developments in the larger contexts of modern culture, mediated politics, and the options available for communicating to large audiences. In particular, he asserts that it is important to distinguish the political substance from the forms of packaging, and concludes the book by emphasizing the continual need to make judgments – in politics and popular culture. And he reminds us that such judgments are always political.

Politics as Engaging Entertainment?

Extending these lines of argument, van Zoonen (2005) further opens the gates by suggesting that politics can be made more accessible – and in a sense more democratic – by linking up with popular culture, by putting pleasure more in the forefront. Van Zoonen argues that it is particularly via personalization and dramatization (via key dramaturgical frames as the quest, bureaucracy, conspiracy, and soap) that popular culture can serve as a resource for political citizenship; these dimensions not only can help convey politics but also offer tools for reflecting on what citizenship can and should mean, as well as providing mechanisms for the enactment of politics by citizens. Thus, popular culture can process and communicate collective experience, emotion, and even knowledge; it offers opportunities for negotiating views and opinions on contested values as well as explicit political issues. It can therefore serve as a form of what we might call "metadeliberation," adding (but certainly not replacing) different forms of expression, different registers, and different emotional spectra to the more traditional forms of news and political communication. Lunt and Spenner's (2005) analysis of *The Jerry Springer Show* as an "emotional public sphere" neatly illustrates this line of thinking.

Further, van Zoonen underscores the close similarities between political engagement and pop cultural fandom (see also Gray, 2007). Fans invest avid emotional involvement and symbolic valence into the objects of their attention, deriving great pleasure from it and not seldom also taking a playful stance toward this object, be it a person/icon, a television series, or whatever. Van Zoonen relates these traits to citizenship, noting the structural similarities between fan cultures and publics, each with their shared sense of values and willingness to engage in collective actions. In highlighting the similarities, she does not suggest a complete equivalence, nor does she mean that fan cultures should or could replace political constituencies. Rather, her point is that by using the model of fan cultures, we can better understand some of the major mechanisms at work in politics, such as fantasy, imagination, and emotional intensity (the latter being very visible at, for example, political rallies).

Variants of the working-through perspective thus need not per se be restricted to just television but could be attributed to all kinds of mediated popular culture. Yet, it is in television programming where political life is perhaps most often explicitly interpreted by entertainment – that is, "politicotainment." The collection by Reigert (2007) offers a number of analyses of such programs, but also analyses of how the changing character of television's political economy, the growth of participatory technologies, and various forms of "voting" in popular programming continue to develop. An analysis of *The Daily Show with Jon Stewart* is also included (while a longer treatment of that show and other new forms of political comedy by the same author is found in Jones, 2005). The humor, not least the parodies of established forms of political communication that strip away artifice, highlight inconsistencies, and generally challenge the authority of official political discourse, offers pleasurable ports of entry to current political topics, as it contributes to the evolution of mediated political culture.

Another very suggestive angle on engagement in popular culture and its political relevance, with a focus on young people, is found in Stephen Coleman's (2006, 2007a, 2007b) research on *Big Brother* in the UK. Based on his studies of young fans of this reality television series, he concludes first that we need to understand present disengagement from traditional party politics less as a question of young citizens abandoning the political system and instead consider how the system has abandoned and/or excluded them. The way parliamentarian politics is represented – especially on television – clearly contributes to disengaging many young citizens.

Secondly, and still more provocative from the standpoint of traditional political communication, Coleman argues that forms of popular entertainment are also offering topics that engage young viewers in ways that must be understood as political, thereby redefining what "politics" is. His young viewers did have the capability to follow the news, critically reflect on politics, and participate in elections. Many in fact did so, "but they often felt themselves to be outsiders in someone else's story" (Coleman 2006:27). They felt they had little political efficacy. Instead, they found on *Big Brother* (and in many other media spaces) a large range of topics that engaged them, such as "debates about asylum seekers, inequality, cheating, bullying, anarchism, sexual identity, religious fundamentalism, and war...." (Coleman 2006:26).

For Coleman, this indicates the "hopelessly narrow conception of politics" that still prevails, one that ignores the concerns people have in their daily lives, such as ethics, identity, justice, taboos, social power relations, and an endless range of topics about the world beyond face-to-face settings. The problem in part has to do with the establishment's political agenda: Politicians seem unable to take up many issues that engage the young, while the issues they offer do not resonate deeply with such audiences. But it is also a problem of communication, of modes of representation and expression. Coleman suggests that much traditional political communication is out of step with the new generations and their media cultures. He thus argues for the need for enhanced double transparency: to make established politics more visible, compelling, and accessible to the young, while at the same time politicians need to know about, be better anchored in, the realities of young people. Such developments would involve a further decentralization of political communication – and no doubt of political power as well.

These kinds of challenging ideas receive a sort of overarching frame in the notion of cultural citizenship as recently developed by Hermes (2005). In noting that "popular culture" is much more popular than "politics" – with "popular" meaning basically of and for the people – she probes the civic qualities of popular culture and highlights a number of key attributes in this regard. Cultural citizenship as a perspective underscores the democratic potential of popular culture, while allowing that it often may not always be realized. This potential lies largely in its capacity to join us together: Popular culture makes us feel welcome and offers us a sense of belonging. It sets up few barriers, and thus can permit easy engagement. Also, it invites us to fantasize about the ideals and hopes we have for society, as well as to process things that we fear.

That is, as in Ellis' approach, cultural citizenship sees popular culture as having relevance for identity construction, ideology, and norms, aiding us to work through important contemporary ideas and issues.

Popular culture also provides guidelines for the interpretation and evaluation of actions and experiences, while also offering sites for an extensive range of emotional and mental states – while offering lots of pleasure. In short: "Cultural citizenship is the process of bonding and community building, and reflection on that bonding, that is implied in partaking of the text-related practices of reading, consuming, celebrating and criticising offered in the realm of (popular) culture" (Hermes, 2005:10).

TELEVISION, POPULAR CULTURE, AND CIVIC CULTURE

Television news in its traditional guise contributes to the public sphere in complex ways, while at the same manifesting a number of significant limitations, not least that it offers very few entry points for civic identity and agency (which in turn both derives from and reflects the dilemmas of power relations in contemporary democracy). As we move beyond news programs and look at television in broader terms, and at popular culture more generally, we find degrees of political relevance emerging in ways quite at variance with conventional conceptions of political communication. The recent interventions into the relationship between politics and popular culture that I have touched upon make a number of important points in this regard, and I would summarize them as follows:

- In the contemporary media world, popular culture and politics cannot be fully separated. They are discursively structured in many similar ways, and they inform each other, feed off each other.
- Both domains mobilize rational as well as affective response.
- The blurring and hybridization of program genres further bring them together.
- Popular culture offers a sense of easy access to symbolic communities, a world of belonging beyond oneself.
- This can at times be seen as preparatory for civic engagement, prefiguring involvement beyond one's private domain, by offering "cultural citizenship" in the media world.
- As a further step, popular culture invites us to engage – with both our hearts and minds – in many questions having to do with how we should live (and how we should live together) and what kind of

society we want. It allows us to process, to work through positions having to do with conflicting values, norms, and identities in a turbulent late modern socio-cultural milieu. It can thus lead us in to the proto-political.

- Moreover, many of the themes taken up by popular culture may seem more important and more personally relevant than the agendas on offer from mainstream politics. It can thus at times even actualize the political, i.e., highlight issues of conflict where a "we" and a "they" can be identified.

- Finally, popular culture can serve to foster alternative conceptions of what actually constitutes politics and the political, generating reflections and engagement over other kinds of concerns and issues.

DEMOCRACY: EXPANSIONS, NOT CONTRACTIONS

Taken together, these points strongly accentuate the porous character of the politics–popular culture boundary, and offer us insights into how television and other forms of popular culture can play a role in civic engagement. Can we, should we, go further than this in our understanding of the relationship between them? No doubt we can and will go further as our sense of both the political and media logics continue to evolve. However, here it can be useful to keep in mind a few distinctions.

The perspective on television and popular culture that I have been sketching suggests that the field of democracy is in the process of addition, not subtraction. That is to say, in our expanding notion of the political – the inclusion of more personally relevant political questions, identity issues, the single-issue groups with their respective agendas, the various kinds of alternative or life politics, and so on – we are basically *adding* to the realm of what is potentially political. And that is a crucial development. However, while many citizens understandably find conventional party politics uninviting, many of the key issues addressed in that context are decidedly not trivial. They have to do with such things as how taxes are set and how public funding is spent, that is, how wealth is distributed in society. Such politics concern a whole range of questions, large and small, local, national, and global, that profoundly affect the life circumstances of people.

These questions must not disappear from the public sphere – though democracy would often certainly benefit if they were framed differently. These kinds of issues can be – and certainly have been – defined and added to the formal political agenda via extra-parliamentarian contexts, which is also an important development. Yet, what is at stake here is not the particular site of politics, but the continual importance of certain categories of issues: They may not always be subjectively engaging (or "interesting"), but they remain objectively significant (i.e., "important").

Likewise, the forms of political communication are also expanding and evolving. While it would be conceptually confusing to a priori label most of popular culture as "political communication," in the light of the discussion above we should at least acknowledge its potential political relevance, recognizing its proto-political character for stimulating civic talk. Yet, as we move into the newer forms of factual television, in particular where the traditional conventions of documentary have become loosened, can we simply assume that audiences unproblematically follow along? Have their foundational assumptions about factuality and truth claims simply evolved with the newer programs? How are their coordinates of social and political reality affected by the hybridization of genres, and how do they perceive such programming?

It is important to maintain sociological contact with real, live citizens and their experiences of the changes going on – to have some grasp of how they perceive, for example, the turbulence within factual television programming. We have some important evidence of this from the comparative studies conducted by Hill (2007) in the UK and Sweden. Focusing on viewers' strategies, how they engage with and interpret the various genres, her interviews aimed to ascertain how they make their way through the chaotic mix of new and rescrambled genres, where the fictive and nonfictive have become entwined.

What she finds is a strong tendency for viewers to hold on to established conceptions of an external, objective reality and notions of documentary truth claims. Viewers are fully aware of the contemporary restyling of factual television and other genre developments; they can identify a documentary as an overarching genre and can classify many different versions of documentaries as subgenres. While there is an acceptance of the newer forms of factual television, as well as a tendency to continue to underscore a baseline conception of reality, there is a clear tendency to rank the spectacle of reality entertainment lower than more serious genres (unlike Coleman, 2005, who interviewed fans of *Big Brother*, Hill [2007] is working with representative viewer samples). For both British and Swedish viewers, the distinction between public issues and popular culture remains a compelling framework for evaluating genres of factual television.

The UK and Sweden are of course societies with a strong public service tradition in television, as Hill (2007) emphasizes, and this no doubt impacts on how viewers responded. For example, they tended to strongly rank factual public service programs higher than other kinds. Yet, the results are still of relevance for societies like the United States that lack a strong public service tradition. The genre developments in the UK and Sweden, which are similar, though not identical, have had a disruptive impact on fundamental orientations having to do with the representation of knowledge, fairness, and truth claims. This has forced audiences to come to reflect on – and come to terms with – these changes. Thus, for example, "reality television," which Hill calls in this context a "feral genre," has become reclassified in viewers' minds as "reality entertainment," reminding us of the cultural tenacity of core conceptions having to do with how we orient ourselves to the "real world," and the media we use in doing so.

Finally, we can engage in some speculation that the modes of engagement and participation facilitated by popular culture may have significance for future democratic involvement. Mediated popular culture, as found on the Internet and on the growing net-based forms of interaction prevalent on television, are contributing to the emergence of new horizons of expectation concerning communicative practices. In chatting and voting on issues around reality programs, joining online fan cultures, making use of fanzines, blogging about popular topics, utilizing such tools as Photoshop, portraying oneself online on such sites as MySpace and Facebook, people – especially younger ones – are developing strong patterns of mediated engagement and participation. The perennial question as to where the political resides follows along with these developments, but we can certainly assume that the boundary with popular culture will continue to be permeable. We must conclude that a new, very talkative mediated culture is emerging, with this "convergence culture," as Jenkins (2006) calls it, enabling many new forms of participation and collaboration. If we recall the kind of working through that broadcast television has facilitated over the past decades, one can only begin to speculate what can be done online in much shorter time frames. I will return to these themes in more detail in the next two chapters.

Popular Civic Cultures?

The public sphere perspective and political communication have both traditionally zeroed in on television journalism; the remaining programming, and popular culture more broadly, has been dismissed as at best irrelevant for concerns about democracy, and at worst outright harmful. The above discussion, and the culturalist literature on which it draws, hopefully serve to offer a more nuanced view. I conclude this chapter with some summary reflections on television as a space for civic cultures, looking at some of the dimensions of civic culture in regard to the links between politics and television. As will be apparent, it is not the case that we arrive at many easy closures in these matters.

KNOWLEDGE. While conveying detailed information in a cognitive manner has never been television's forte, it does well at evoking discussion on an endless array of themes and topics, thereby contributing to a talkative citizenry. Whether the topics should be seen as political or not can be discussed in each case, but certainly the accessible character of television, as a prominent institution of cultural citizenship, is important in foregrounding and promoting political talk. The popularity of the medium is bound up with the pleasures that it offers, even in knowledge acquisition. While there are obvious limits as to what it can reasonably provide in terms of traditional notions of knowledge, Glynn (2000) makes the point that television offers different regimes of knowing that speak, in different ways, to different groups, in particular those with less social power. It is precisely the "popularity" of television that makes it so important both as a purveyor of potentially relevant political knowledge and as a space in which viewers are free to select and define what is important to them and what indeed is political.

VALUES. Television offers a mixed bag in regard to values. Much of programming's concerns with values of course pertain to private life, private solutions, individual choice-making, consumption, and market relations. This reminds us of the hegemonic boundaries of much of television's working through. Yet, television's working through of values central to people's lives over the years would suggest that it can become a space for contestation, often with a proto-political resonance, and thus of significance for civic cultures. Also, television discourses still reiterate many of the basic values and virtues of democracy, such as individual rights and respect for the law. Such values become a baseline for generating scandal, and representations of moral deviation are often amplified through compelling dramaturgy. The portrayals of scandal may well become less convincing when scandal becomes routinized: Skepticism and cynicism take root. Yet, if scandal and indignation are one kind of response, laughter is another. Jones (2005), in analyzing the new political comedy programs from a civic cultures perspective, concludes that much of the humor builds on a values-centered way of looking at politics, and is driven by the comic appeals to return to basic democratic values.

TRUST. Television tends to show very few examples – in fiction or nonfiction – of the "thin trust" that typifies civic social bonds or cooperation that makes a political impact. The social bonds displayed lean toward romance, male bonding such as sports or action/military, social friendships, and so on. (A large-scale content analysis of this theme might yield interesting results.) Television is also known to promote fear and suspicion in some audience groups via its emphasis on crime, linking danger with public space and thereby contributing to the uncivic retreat into the private domain. On the other hand, television's continual processes of making visible a wider and wider array of social sectors, life styles, and generally unconventional personalities may be more significant than normally recognized. One might well hypothesize that the medium does an important job in both factual and fictive programming of rendering as familiar particular elements of society that many people would otherwise never encounter; television has been conveying a growing sense of society's plural character. That established politics and politicians tend to have low trust returns us to the fundamental issues of contemporary civic disengagement and mainstream media's role in this regard.

PRACTICES. One of the key practices of civic culture is discussion, a cornerstone of the public sphere perspective and civic republicanism. Different kinds of programming situate the viewing subject differently; in some cases viewers are very much invited to respond actively, take positions, even to argue, as we see in some talk shows and reality television programs. Other programming leans more toward positioning the viewer as a nondialogic receiver of information from on high (e.g., traditional news programs). What real viewers actually do is of course an empirical question. Some viewers will be left speechless by a sensationalist talk show, while others will be provoked into argumentative response by a serious documentary.

In the American context, Lembo (2000) identifies a typology of television use: "Discrete" use is selective and focused; viewing has a cohesion and coherence in relation to people's social location and to their sense of accomplishment. "Undirected" and "continuous" uses are diffuse, less the product of conscious decision. Moreover, Lembo links discrete use with a solid, modernist sense of self-formation; it is action- and productivity-oriented, and correlates with higher social power.

Undirected and continuous use has less consistency and coherence; the viewing is characterized by more context-free involvement with imagery where normative frameworks are weak. This type of engagement with television's image world generates disjuncture, where fleeting meaning does not cumulatively add up to much. The flows, eruptions, and interruptions of the viewing experience situate viewers squarely in the domain of corporate commodity culture, according to Lembo.

Even if this analysis is in part a replay of the differences in class-based cultural capital, it suggestively invites attention to the issue of watching as a practice that relates to individual autonomy, personal development, and empowerment. Set in relation to civic culture, we might say that the issue is not between watching television or not, but rather where the locus of control and definitional power lies – that is, who's in charge, so to speak. We could conclude from Lembo's study that the way we relate to television in our everyday lives correlates with the civic horizons we may develop and the sense of empowerment we may experience.

Beyond the engagement in the viewing, we should reiterate the theme of weak public connections to political practice emphasized by Couldry, Livingstone, and Markham (2007), that exposure to mainstream news mostly does not lead to political participation, because of the perceived limited access afforded by the political system itself. Together with the findings of Lewis, Inthorn, and Wahl-Jorgensen (2005) that stress the lack of enabling images of citizens on television news, we must keep in mind that the immediate civic practices and sense of empowerment to be derived from television news as such are limited.

IDENTITIES. Traditionally, it has been said that the mass media are weak in fostering identities of citizenship among its audiences. Where do we find the sense of civic "we-ness" in contemporary television? As we move from the journalism of high modernity to the late modern realms of subjective experience, it becomes quite thin. Increasingly, television and the rest of the media milieu position us as consumers: It is in the domain of consumption where we are to be empowered, where we make choices, where we create ourselves. To be sure, being a citizen and a consumer is not always antithetical: Citizens need to consume, and consumption at times can be politically framed. Yet there is a fundamental distinction between consumption, which is predicated on the fluctuations of the market, and the principles of universality embedded in the notion of the citizen.

However, this perspective is being modified by arguments from another angle – that television, as a major institution of popular culture, offers us opportunities to fantasize, and speculate, about ourselves, our lives, and our identities. Moreover, from the literature on identity in late modernity, it may be that it is more productive to see how elements of civic identities infuse other domains of our selves, how the political can enter into many areas of our lives, rather than to conceptualize a bounded "civic identity module" that we activate in limited, yet already explicitly delineated political contexts. Certainly popular culture offers us resources for exploring the political links between public and private spheres, and thus extending and multiplying our civic identities.

Television's contribution to civic cultures remains equivocal, though the picture becomes more optimistic as we shift toward the online linkages of the newer television environment. It may be that mainstream television offers largely shriveled, voting-oriented versions of civic identities. On the other hand, it provides a continuous flood of topics that touch people in various ways. Some of these topics can, especially if processed by discussion, resonate with core values, suggest practices, mobilize identities, and generate engagement in the public sphere. They can evoke contestation, and further develop the terrain of the political, thereby pumping blood into the body of democracy. Or not: We can no doubt just as easily find evidence for negative spirals. The point is not that we should try to arrive at some ultimate, once-and-for-all evaluation, but rather, to be alert for how television – despite all its familiar limitations – may at times help move us beyond the narrow definitions of politics and the public sphere, and connect us to civic cultures in subtle, surprising, and unintended ways.

CHAPTER 7

Internet and Civic Potential

The traditional mass media contribute positively in certain ways to democratic civic cultures, just as they also obstruct their development in other ways. There are also, as we have seen, elements of ambiguity, and we have to be careful with generalizations. In this chapter, I look at the Internet's potential significance for civic cultures. Again the picture will not lead to a simple black and white conclusion; if anything, the situation becomes more complex.

Political activity is usually shaped by the circumstances, resources, and practices that characterize people's lives; to engage in democracy normally does not mean to step out of one's existing frames of realities, or one's dominant habitus. The net and the overall intense development of ICTs raise a whole range of issues that have relevance for a democratic society, including privacy, security, censorship, and copyright, and there is a good deal of research on these and other areas. Given the focus of this presentation, I emphasize mainly the theme of civic engagement. The point here is that the net's significance is found not just at the level of social institutions, but also in lived experience. Cyberspace is altering how we live, providing us with very efficacious tools for social agency. These premises are important for grounding our understanding of how the net can be incorporated into civic cultures. From there I look at the Internet in terms of the spaces it affords for civic activities, underscoring the importance of its network character for democratic participation. The final section takes up the classic theme of the Internet and public spheres, engaging with and updating some of the key arguments.

TAKING STOCK OF THE NET: CIVIC HORIZONS

SITUATING THE NET IN DAILY LIFE

At this point in our collective histories of Internet experience, asserting its saturation in the societies of the West, and noting its rapid expansion in many other countries – where the statistics of its spread (see, for example, Internet World Statistics, at http://www.internetworldstats. com/stats.htm) climb with considerably more vigor than many indicators of economic growth – has lost much of its feel as bold futurology. The Internet has become pervasive; it has become an inexorable and commonplace feature of how societies, organizations, and individuals operate in the modern world. We no longer retain the (seen from today's perspective) somewhat quaint views about how "life online" and "virtual realities" are so very different – tantalizing or threatening – from our "in real life" experience. This is because the Internet has become institutionally so integrated with how society functions that the sense of its separateness, its distinction, in regard to the way we normally get things done has dissipated.

The Internet and other ICTs have not only become fixtures in our homes, we have "domesticated" them, that is, assimilated them into our household routines (Berker, Hartmann, Punie, and Ward, 2006), as well as in other domains of life. Now, about a decade and a half after the emergence of the net as a mass phenomenon, we have a young generation that has grown up with it, who cannot recall a significant period of time in their lives without it. Much like with the history of the telephone, film, radio, or any other media "revolution," the newness of the net has worn off – while it is constantly evolving at a staggering pace, offering ever new possibilities.

Research and debates about the social significance of the Internet, its use in everyday life, the character/potential of online communities, and other key topics have made considerable strides in the past decade, in the sense that what emerges is a more qualified and detailed view (see, among a vast literature, for example, Bakardjieva, 2005; Lievrouw and Livingstone, 2006; Barney, 2004; Howard and Jones, 2004; Kolko, 2003; Wellman and Haythornwaite, 2002; Slevin, 2000). It is understood that the "the Internet" is neither a unitary nor a static phenomena, but it is protean, evolving technologically and linking up with other media forms. There is a large array of use patterns, shaped by particular purposes and circumstances; its use is highly embedded. As Klang (2006) argues, some emerging uses may appear to be socially "disruptive" – for example, the dissemination of viruses, the reinter-pretation of private property online, and civil disobedience in the online environment – yet it is not always clear how such uses should best be regulated to enhance the democratic character of society.

The societal implications and transitions that configure around the net – in, for example, such domains as economic structures, patterns of social interaction, cultural practices, and political participation – are still in the process of emerging, though general patterns are now quite clear (see, for example, Cardosa, 2006, for a recent Castellsian contribution). Jenkins (2006) explores an important theme in this regard, namely, what happens in the interfaces between the new and old media. While such convergence is at bottom technological, it also brings with it cultural consequences in how we live and perceive the world. We are still charting that transformation. The "network society" heralded by Castells (1998, 2000), in the grand sweep of his trilogy from the latter part of the 1990s, is not fully in place, and there is still much we do not understand about its detailed manifestations and consequences in con-crete settings. We thus find ourselves in a sense in the middle of things, still trying to specify and interpret dramatic movements of change.

SPACE, PLACE, AND POSSIBILITIES

The humanities and social sciences have in recent years become increasingly sensitive to the spatial dimensions of social and cultural processes: The "where" is catching up in importance with the "what," the "who," the "why," and the "how." The spatial involves more than simple geography; it readily becomes a theoretic dimension in a world where space can be constituted by communication processes that may be quite indifferent to place. We sometimes say that politics "takes place" in the media, on television, in the press, and so on, but in fact we are referring to a communicative *space* shaped by these media (the collec-tion by Barnett and Low, 2004, offers insight on these themes in rela-tion to democracy). The constitution of social space via modern communication technologies, and their separation from place, can be said to have begun with the invention of the telegraph, with its proto-digital code and its capacity to travel large distances in almost no time. Such transformations of social space of course impact on social rela-tions, and these tendencies have accelerated enormously in the past century. As Giddens (2002) argues, modern communication can enact a disembedding of previous patterns of social relations from their anchoring in a specific locale, to a re-embedding in an abstractly constructed and shared space. This separation takes a very large step with the emergence of the Internet.

The Internet has become a normal feature of everyday life, shaping the way things get done in just about every sector of society. We use the net not just to access information in the broadest sense, but also for arranging all sorts of activities and encounters. Cultural production generally has gone digital and becomes increasingly centered on the Internet (Klineberg, 2005b). With the advent of what is sometimes called Web 2.0, a new generation of easily used advanced applications become available for self-publishing (e.g., blog engines, webcasting, video and music file sharing tools) and networking. Nonprofessionals, in nonmarket contexts, are increasingly blurring the distinctions between producers and consumers, rendering culture more participatory, transparent, and self-reflective (Benkler, 2006; see also Quiggin, 2006; Shirky, 2008, offers many illustrations of individual and group uses that are altering traditional organizational and professional ways of functioning).

While Web 2.0 signals some technological innovations, it also rhetorically underscores the potential for broad social participation. The demarcation between production and consumption, professionals and amateurs, work and play, and so on, become less well-defined (see Zimmer, 2008; Cormode and Krishnamurthy, 2008). For example, amateur musicians within any genre can post their audio-visual performances on sites such as YouTube and get constructive feedback from "strangers" all around the world. People can engage in more detailed self- and artistic presentation and develop tighter "communities" on MySpace or form their own social networks on Facebook. A key feature is that one can construct "closed communities" – one can define which "friends" will be included in one's network – and have access to the often rather personal information that is made available there (see Golbeck, 2007).

There is of course a vast business domain here: YouTube, for example, was launched in December 2005 by its originators, and bought by Google a year later for $1.65 billion; as of this writing, it is adding approximately 65,000 new videos each day, resulting in the largest audio-visual archive on the planet. Facebook, previously a somewhat exclusive haven for ivy-league students in the United States, has exploded to encompass millions of users around the world, now incorporating many different sectors of society, including the academic world.

One can view the emergence of wikis, or wikimedia, as a particularly civic phenomenon: Such open source, collaborative Web sites develop through the input of its users. Wikipedia, the largest and most famous, had as of August 2007 about 8 million articles in over 250 languages, with approximately 2 million being in English. While there are of course controversies about reliability and partisanship of sources, the system exercises transparent peer review and is easy to revise in the light of new knowledge. Being one of the most visited sites on the net, however, means that interested parties will inevitably try to impact on the content, even if success in this regard apparently remains very much the exception: Recently a hacker developed a tool that has revealed that both the CIA and the Vatican have doctored materials on Wikipedia (Söderberg, 2007). Of course, civic uses of the net remain modest in comparison to other forms of engagement, and much net use has to do with leisure and entertainment. Specific sites for online popular culture attract large followings that can generate immense niche communities, such as Second Life and World of Warcraft.

Thompson (2005) writes about the "new visibility," which on the one hand allows for power centers to manifest themselves and their versions of reality in the media, while on the other hand they have increasingly less control over the visibility of others who would challenge them through interventions in public space. This point – and the new technological possibilities available to citizens – are well illustrated in the case of "Loose Change," a 90-minute documentary challenging the veracity of the U.S. government's version of what actually happened during the attacks in New York and Washington on September 11, 2001. While the production itself is colored by the conspiratorial mindset of the so-called "9/11 Truth Movement," the point is that three young men in their early twenties, with little specialized training or higher education, and working with a laptop computer and minimal financial resources, were able to put together a professional-looking documentary that has been seen by millions of viewers around the world. And in so doing they offer a counterversion of reality to what has been asserted by the Bush administration, the FBI, and the CIA. That it is available on YouTube is interesting in itself: This site is no longer just a megasite for musical expression. Today it also includes political materials of many kinds, including presidential campaigning and EU public relations plugs aiming to improve citizens' participation.

The hypertext link structure of the Internet's architecture allows for very extensive "interspatiality," the capacity to move freely between different communicative spaces – sites, forums, networks. Many online services normally provide accessible data banks over previously published materials. Individuals are able to select from an enormous array of online output, customizing their own personal information packages. Indeed, the seemingly infinite degree of individual preference that the Internet provides is one of its hallmark characteristics: It is unlikely that any two individuals will have the identical mix of elements in their use of the net. The ease of interacting, reformatting, remixing, adding on to existing texts, and so forth, promotes the participatory uses of these technologies – and alters forever the traditional premises whereby mass audiences receive ostensibly authoritative, centralized information in a one-way manner. Certainly that older model is still with us, and may never fully disappear, but it has been dislodged as the dominant paradigm for political communication.

The emergence of online communication very early on raised the fear of the erosion of local contact. Yet, as Quan-Haase and Wellman (2004) remind us, the polemics around the consequences of the net in many ways recycle debates about the impact of industrialization and modernity on community. These discussions have been going on for more than a century and a half, and have encompassed all positions from the rosily optimistic to the darkly pessimistic. The view of these authors is that community has not vanished, but has instead become quite transformed. Ways of being together and doing things together have always been evolving. Based on extensive social surveys in North America, Quan-Haase and Wellman find a variety of patterns for different groups of people, but at the general level they conclude that the Internet tends to enhance social contacts in daily life, for people who are geographically both near and remote. Not least, the Internet, like the telephone, is often used to facilitate local encounters. Heavy users of the Internet continue to use the telephone and engage in face-to-face encounters as well. Quan-Haase and Wellman (2004) also underscore the net's capacity to support many-to-many communication between people who are geographically remote. They see the Internet's impact in ways similar to the telephone's: profound, but gradual.

It is important to underscore that net use does not merely follow technological development, but rather also applies the net in new and creative ways, develops new contexts of use, and, thereby, in a reciprocal fashion, transforms users' own horizons. It is via this kind of appropriation – the dialectical interplay of possibilities and their actualizations – that engenders changes in the way we live. In historical terms, fifteen years is a very short time, yet experientially it is sufficient for massive incremental changes to take place, even if we on a day-to-day basis do not necessarily notice them.

SPACES AND PRACTICES

At the same time, much of the literature about the Internet and networking tends to treat the notion of "cyberspace" in a merely metaphorical, generally underdeveloped manner. Cyberspace becomes a residual category, as a nonplace, removed from established conceptions of our "real here and now," while of course at the same time lauding all that it has to offer. The problem with this approach is that it misses an opportunity for a deeper analysis of the social transformations under way, an opportunity to anchor them not just within the framework of macrosociological patterns, but also at the level of lived experience, identity, skills, and horizons of expectation. This is inevitably even more compelling as we look at younger users of the net (see Buckingham, 2007). Such an opening would help link up the phenomena of the net with subjective experience, with dimensions that resonate with civic cultures.

Nunes (2006) opens such a line of inquiry in regard to the net's spatial attributes. He poses a key question: "Where does cyberspace take place?" In so doing, he is not indulging in clever word-play, but is rather attempting to shed light on cyberspace as a realm of practices and experience. His point of departure is to critically distance himself from the dominant, dualistic Cartesian-Kantian tradition of treating space as an inert container, a material realm radically separate from the realm of lived being (that it allegedly contains). Using the theoretical work of Henri Lefebvre, he attempts to develop a framework for analyzing cyberspace – the space of networks on the Web – as something generated by social practices – which in turn impacts on the way we live. Lefebvre asserts the incompleteness of the two dominant views on space: either as a container for objects and bodies – an a priori emptiness waiting to be filled – or as merely something in our minds, a conceptual or metaphorical construct.

Lefebvre's premise is that social space is a product of collective practices. Nunes' argumentation is dense, but the upshot is that to apply this perspective to the Internet means "to acknowledge that any spatial analysis of cyberspace must be able to account for a dynamic relation of material form, conceptual representation, and dispositional practices that produces networked social space" (Nunes, 2006:xxii). Thus, the material forms include the concrete technologies of the computer, of the software, social access to them, and the human-machine interactions around their use, notably the Internet protocols that are central to the global computer networks (Galloway, 2005). The conceptual representations encompass prevailing notions about the net – as marketplace, informational resource, leisure domain, civic tool, global society, and so on – as well as the territorial vocabularies (sites, browsers, domains, etc.) that contribute to giving it a strong degree of conceptual/semiotic stability.

The practices relevant to cyberspace are specific and extensive: from e-mailing to file-sharing, from blogging to uploading one's biographical information to get social contacts via Facebook, from moderating a forum to buying something off eBay, to participating in virtual games. And as mobile telephony becomes more integrated with the Internet and its affordances, the emerging technology and its developing usages have deep implications for not only our conceptions of space, but also for all kinds of issues about daily living, not least democracy (see, for example, Scheller and Urry, 2003; Drotner, 2005; May and Hearn, 2005; Stald, 2007; Campbell, 2007; Kleinman, 2007).

Moreover, along with offering new forms of communicative activity, these practices reconfigure the way we organize our daily lives; they offer new ways of accomplishing traditional tasks, and, significantly, I would add, they continually expand our sense of the possible as both the technologies and our command of them develop; the innovative and unexpected character of online experience can empower individuals as well as lead to new social encounters (McPherson, 2007). The dynamic and evolving relationships within this tri-partite constellation become clear: If the material forms and the conceptual representations are in a sense "given" as what we encounter from our everyday horizons, it is our enacted practices that impose the final set of attributes. Krug (2005) makes a similar argument about the interplay of technology, language, and the self from the standpoint of cultural theory and the history of media technologies. As Nunes (2006:xxiii) summarizes, ". . . cyberspace is not where we go with network technology, but how we live it." Not least in the academic world, in the past decade, digital libraries, online journals, and electronic communication have altered many of the parameters of how we do our research – and how fast – as well as our forms of collaboration.

This somewhat abstract horizon makes the claim that cyberspace is not just some vague "place" located "out there" where we go online, but rather as sets of practices using technological potential and conceptual frameworks, which actually becomes an accomplishment. We can intuitively sense the centrality of these practices, as well as the skills, knowledge, and even the identities that can galvanize around them, and their potential relevance for civic cultures. In plain terms, the practical facility to use computers and the Internet enhances people's capacities to do more things for themselves, and in cooperation with others. Moreover, the flexibility of new media means that they can be readily adopted for new forms of practices. This improved efficacy, as well as the growing habituation to loose, informal networks, structures new dispositions for social agency generally, and offers new potential for civic agency in particular.

CONNECTIONS: THE NETWORK PERSPECTIVE

As users gain experience, they generate and develop networks, in the form of vast linkages of people and organizations that are connected, albeit often loosely, in Web-based social relations. The idea of social networks is hardly a new one in the social sciences, though in recent decades the notion has explicitly become the focus of much research; in media and ICT contexts, the work of Castells has of course played an important role here. Castells (2000) argues strongly in his work that we are now being ushered into the age of the network society (see also Stalder, 2006; for recent general treatments of social networks, see Degenne and Forsé, 1999; Monge and Contractor, 2003). He claims that the "space of flows" of the emerging network society is replacing the spatial organization that has previously shaped our experience, the "space of places," and that this logic now permeates many sectors, including urban architecture. Most emblematic of this development is of course the Internet. Place as such does not become eradicated, and we still live our lives with reference to specific geographic sites, but the functionality of social relations is increasingly manifested in flows, with their network structures, including key nodal points.

Societal development over the past decade or two has to a significant degree felt the impact of new informational and communication technologies (see, for example, Cardosa, 2006, for a recent Castellsian contribution), and the argument that the media logics and architecture of the ICTs have contributed to extending and deepening the network character of society is compelling. Basically, social networks are the expression of certain kinds of social relations between people. Indeed, one could in principle simply see all forms of social relations as networks, though such a rewriting of sociology would probably not offer much of a payoff. Instead, if we think in terms of modern social net-works, at least beyond the primary and formative relations of family and clan, one definitive attribute is that they manifest forms of com-munication that are relatively stable and recurring, even if the codes and conventions may still be evolving. Participation is generally vol-untary, seen as meaningful in some way, often as serving the partic-ipants' self-interests.

The idea of networks as a dominant social morphology has been gaining ground as a useful perspective for understanding the modern world. For example, I would note that Habermas (1996, 2006), in his updates of his public sphere perspective, now stresses complexity, over-lapping spaces, and criss-crossing media and interaction; that is, while he does not make much of the Internet per se in his analysis, he is basically now working with a network model. The network lens can help illuminate – as long as we do not accord it deterministic powers. While a label such as the "Network Society" – much like the previous "Information Society" – can serve as a handy historical metaphor to highlight important developmental trends, it can also risk making the world opaque if used as a lens to see all social reality. However, making even just a few distinctions between different kinds of networks can help specify the network perspective's relevance for the Internet and civic agency. Modifying Nieminen's (2007) framework slightly, one possible typology is as follows:

- Associational networks, such as friendships, hobby or voluntary groups, based on active choice.
- Societal networks: These have a more definitive character and involve socialization and membership in a community (e.g., neigh-borhood) or professional body. Choice is involved here, too, though often membership follows directly from social circumstances.
- Issue- or interest-based networks, which aim to influence decision-making; politically engaged publics are of course an obvious example here.
- Imposed networks, which address us and define as members of nations or other large bodies – for example, as citizens – that accord rights and obligations.

Basically, it can be argued that we live much of our lives today in and through such social networks. Further, we increasingly live our network lives with the help of ICTs. Some of these networks we actively seek out and join, others we more simply "end up" in. There are mechanisms that can exclude individuals from networks – for example, class, gender, ethnicity, and sexual orientation can all impact on which networks we belong to. Moreover, larger mechanisms of power may exclude entire networks from participation in certain domains of society, for instance, marginalizing immigrant groups from certain elements of community life.

Putnam's (2000) analysis of social capital as a manifestation of one's networks – that is, the more and better connected one is, the more likely one is to participate as an effective citizen – captures the importance of networks. Generally, the more one is personally a "hub," that is, well-connected, the greater one's impact tends to be within a network. In today's world, such connections do not derive simply from personal charm, but also from how well one operates on the Internet. In accordance with the discussion in Chapter 4 about how the political can emerge in any social setting, in principle it can appear in all four types of networks, though we can assume that it is in the third type that will most often and overtly manifest civic agency, that is, issue- or interest-based networks.

PUBLIC SPHERES ONLINE: SOCIAL CONTEXTS AND MEDIA LOGIC

CIVIC CYBERSPACES: INDISPENSIBLE, BUT NO QUICK FIX

While the discussions about the poor health of democracy intensified during the 1990s, the Internet was rapidly leading a media revolution. It did not take long for some observers to connect the two phenomena. From early optimistic predictions or dismissive nonchalance, the claims being made today in the debates about the Internet's role in politics tend to be more cautious (see Chadwick, 2006, for an encompassing overview. Klotz, 2004, and Bimber, 2003, also provide useful analyses. Also, compare with the various chapters in Anderson and Cornfield, 2003, as well as in Jenkins and Thorburn, 2003). Some of this literature emphasizes traditional political parties (e.g., Bimber and Davis, 2003; Gibson, Nixon, and Ward, 2003; Gibson, Römmele, and Ward, 2004; Cornfield, 2004). Other efforts have extra-parliamentarian settings as their focus (e.g., Castells, 1998; McCaughey and Ayers, 2003; Opel and Pompper, 2003; van de Donk, Loader, Nixon, and Rucht, 2004; de Jong, Shaw, and Stammers, 2005; Kahn and Kellner, 2004; Cammaerts, 2007; Cammaerts and Carpentier, 2006; Dahlgren, 2007). Further, the theme of how young citizens in particular use the net is a growing subfield (Hébert and Wilkinson, 2001; Bennett, 2007b; Dahlgren, 2007; Loader, 2007; Dahlgren and Olsson, 2007a, 2007b, 2007c, 2008; Everett, 2007).

A more specific focus examines the net in terms of how it serves to enhance the public sphere via various forms of civic talk (cf. chapters in Shane, 2004; the theme issue of *Political Communication*, 2005). Given the variations in democratic systems and cultures around the world, and given the pace of change – social, political, and technological – we should not expect to soon arrive at some simple, definitive answers to the questions. Indeed, thus far the evidence seems equivocal; moreover, the conclusions one might derive are inexorably tied to the assumptions one has about the character of democracy.

The theme of the Internet and democracy now has a permanent place on research agendas and in intellectual inquiry for the foreseeable future. There are a number of disciplines that address this theme, though sometimes the Internet is abstracted out of its social and cultural contexts: in particular, some of the relevant literature suffers from a lack of a "media perspective," not treating the Internet as part of a larger, integrated media environment, as several authors have argued (e.g., Livingstone, 2004). In any case, the Internet is now entering the mainstream of concern for the study of political communication and taking its place alongside the established research on the traditional mass media.

We may still pose the overarching questions about the net enhancing or hampering democracy, but most research on these themes today acknowledge the overall complexity of the situation, avoid the either/or totalizing perspectives, and address more specific features within the larger landscape. Research is challenged not least in just trying to keep up with a rapidly evolving media landscape and evolutions in use patterns and strategies; we can see how even our neat and familiar categories become confounded and obsolete (e.g., should net television be classified as "Internet" or "television"?).

POLITICS ONLINE

An early argument about the Internet's role in democracy was that it would remain rather modest (e.g., Margolis and Resnick, 2000). This view acknowledged that the major political actors may engage in online campaigning, lobbying, policy advocacy, organizing, and so forth, but overall the political landscape would remain basically the same. It has also noted that even the consequences of modest experiments to incorporate the

Internet as "e-democracy" into local governments have not been over-whelming (see, e.g., Malina, 2003; Gibson, Römmele, and Ward, 2004; Chadwick, 2006; Olsson and Åström, 2006). What should be emphasized is that this "business as usual" perspective was anchored in the formal political system, and the traditional role of the mass media in that system. Indeed, much of the evidence is based on American electoral politics (cf. Hill and Hughes, 1998).

A counterpoint to this view asserts that, as I summarized in Chapter 1, big changes in democracy are in motion due to underlying socio-cultural developments, and that alterations in the media environment contribute to them. This perspective places the Internet in the frontlines of media development and sees it as a significant resource for political change. It can potentially help contribute to the long-term transformation of the institutions of democracy and the modes of participation, though there are no guarantees to this effect. Conceptually, the affordances of the Internet link readily with the empowerment of citizens, and the lines can easily be extended to republicanism and radical democracy (see Dahlberg and Siapera, 2007). Democracy today is seen to be, precari-ously, at a new historical juncture, and in this context, the impact of Internet use becomes significant. Just to be clear: Such a view situates the Internet within a larger set of reciprocal factors; it does not make a technological determinist claim that the new ICTs in themselves are altering politics. When we in verbal shorthand talk about the net's role in politics or society, we of course mean people putting the technology to social uses (see Karakaya Polat, 2005, on this theme).

The Internet is certainly playing a significant – if complicated – role in politics. Within party politics, while the importance of the mainstream mass media still prevails, Internet use is growing, especially in election campaigns. What takes place on the net can impact profoundly on mass media coverage of party politics, as the interpenetration between the two media domains proceeds. At present most observers feel that the net's role is most decisive in the realm of alternative politics. Here it has become indispensable for the growth of advocacy and issue politics, social movements, and activist networks outside parliamentarian party politics (for an overview of literature and debates, see Bentivegna, 2006).

Given the variations in democratic systems and cultures around the world, and given the pace of change – social, political, and technological – we should not hold our breath for quick, definitive answers to the questions. Thus far, the evidence seems equivocal; moreover, the con-clusions one might derive are inexorably tied to the assumptions one has about the character of democracy. In particular, we should keep in mind that while on the Internet we can find a broad array of democratic efforts to effect social and political change, we also see anti-democratic, racist, and neofascist politics as well (Roversi, 2008). There are at present innumerable *jihadi* Web sites, not only fermenting terrorism but also carrying on with the more mundane work of promoting a particular view of political Islam and the world. Further, even if the efforts of some more overtly authoritarian regimes around the world to curtail the democratic uses of the net have not been fully successful, the inventories of the control mechanisms are sobering.

The case of China is of particular interest; despite the Internet perhaps still being the most "open" medium, the government has continually managed to increase the level of sophistication in its internal filtering practices – paradoxically, both freedom and control seem to be on the rise (Lagerkvist, 2006). The collusion of Google, Yahoo, and other western suppliers of technology in this curtailment of freedom, however, remains troubling. The progressive and subversive potential of the net should not be overestimated (Kalathil and Boas, 2003) in the face of oppressive regimes determined to curtail democracy and restrict the use of ICTs; "closed systems" can short-circuit the potential gains to be had by online political conversation (Fung, 2002). However, as the net expands, control becomes increasingly difficult. In the world press during the summer of 2008 one could read how domestic Chinese bloggers have begun challenging local power abuses in the provinces. In Vietnam, the online newspaper VN-Express, offering uncensored, nonpropaganda news, established itself so quickly – it has 6 million visitors daily – that the government has thus far been reluctant to intervene (Zaremba, 2007). Yet repressive strategies toward "leaks" continue, for example, the military government of Burma during the democratic protests in the autumn of 2007, when they simply tried to close down as much of it as possible. However, for those with access and the political motivation, the Internet continues to offers possibilities for civic initiative and political intervention.

BABEL AND COCOONS

There is a concern that the sprawling diversity and fragmentation of public spheres on the net will undermine the communication patterns necessary for the functioning of democracy. Benkler (2006) tackles what he calls the "Babel" problem of assumed cacophony by using developments in network typology theory. He argues that citizens' patterns of

Internet use for public sphere purposes is actually more ordered than we might at first think. We should not expect the net to change human nature, and Benkler's premise is that in evaluating how the Internet functions as a public sphere we should not hold out some utopian vision as a baseline, but rather use as a reference that which has been, namely, the kind of public spheres offered by the system of centralized mass media.

His argument is that any single site is always very accessible – inter-cluster navigation is easy on the Web. However, patterns of selection generate clusters of more frequently visited sites. There are constant linkups between sites that share topics and interests, enhancing the mechanism of the clustering phenomenon. This takes place at both the micro level of a small network, as well as at larger cyberspace macro levels. At the micro level, individual sites become significant within the context of small networks; at the macro level, the big "superstar" sites retain visibility even for most of the individual sites in small clusters, serving as referents and filters.

Writing in a popular science mode about the physics of networks, Ball (2005) arrives at a very similar position. The growth of the World Wide Web follows the same patterns found in the organic molecular structure of bacteria and other life forms, namely, to generate networks consisting of hubs, or nodes. These hubs make the network structurally resilient and adaptable, but also provide the shortcuts that enhance interconnectivity (compared, say, to a simple randomly structured network). On the net, this means that human-scale social worlds can emerge easily: Certain Web pages/links become "famous" within any given domain of interest, and function as organizing clusters.

If we can lay aside the fear that the net will devolve into a hopelessly entropic cacophony, so too has the vision of a singular, integrated public sphere faded. In the face of the social realities of late modern society, much of the normative impetus that may have previously seen this as an ideal has passed. The goal of ushering all citizens into one unitary public sphere, with one specific set of communicative and cultural traditions, is mostly rejected on the grounds of pluralism and difference. There are thousands of Web sites having to do with the political realm at the local, national, and global levels; some are commercial, most not. We can find discussion groups, chat rooms, alternative journalism, blogs, civic organisations, NGOs, grassroots issue-advocacy sites (cf. Berman and Mulligan, 2003; Bennett, 2003b), as well as voter education sites. One can see an expansion in terms of available communicative spaces for politics, as well as an extended ideological breadth compared to what exists in the mass media.

Structurally, this pluralization constitutes a dispersion of the relatively clustered public sphere of the mass media (Bohman, 2004): There are more and more political spaces for discussion, many of them small and remote from the mainstream. Trying to arrange these various presences on the net into a neat map of distinguishable mini-public spheres would be a cyber-cartographer's nightmare of small, sometimes overlapping "public spherettes" (or, as Gitlin, 1998, calls them, "sphericules").

Spaces are required in which citizens belonging to different groups and cultures, or speaking in different registers or languages, will find participation meaningful. Differences of all kinds, including political orientation and interests, gender, ethnicity, cultural capital, and geography, can warrant specialized communicative spaces. Not least we must take into account alternative or counter-public spheres (see Fraser, 1992; Fenton and Downey, 2003; Asen and Brouwer, 2001; Dahlberg and Siapera, 2007), where political currents oppositional to the dominant mainstream can find support and expression, and flourish in a relatively secure environment.

Yet here we encounter a dilemma of a different, and more problematic, character: that of discursive isolation, rather than Babel. The politics of identity and difference that feeds a myriad of counter-public spheres can easily lose sight of the larger issues of power in society and the world, fostering an inwardly oriented fixation on the individual groups' interests. Moreover, if carried too far, such patterns threaten to undercut a shared public culture; various groups develop little contact with – or understanding of – one another, and become less capable of building alliances that could be politically effective. On a more fundamental level, Sunstein (2007) makes a strong case that such "information cocoons" are dangerous for the health of democracy, since their participants tend to screen out that which deviates from their entrenched like-minded patterns.

The fact that we can each structure on the net our own individual info-packages – resulting in what Sunstein (2007) calls the "Daily Me" – constitutes a pivotal mechanism that can render the public sphere a very personal one and thus undermine its efficacy. For both individuals and groups, the lack of confrontation with the information or arguments that may challenge existing world-views becomes in the long run debilitating for both citizens and for democracy as a whole (see also

Downey, 2007; Galston, 2003). While like-minded spheres can serve important functions such as consolidating collective identity, they also risk promoting one-dimensional mentalities. Recruitment can become increasingly difficult as the boundaries of the collective world-view become more cemented. Such mechanisms reduce the net's potential for promoting agonistic civic cultures characterized by robust civic talk (Dahlberg, 2007).

The case for the importance of deliberation is easily made here, yet as Dahlberg (2007) posits, some of the "antifragmentation" arguments derive from questionable premises. There is a fear that the phenomenon of isolated groups of like-minded activists on the net will in itself lead to "extreme" political views and polarization. Further, there is a strong assumption that consensus should be the goal of political talk, that difference per se is problematic, and there is also a tendency to conveniently ignore the often great disparities in power that separate smaller groups from the mainstream (as I discussed in Chapter 4). While we would thus do well to remind ourselves of the importance of agonistic public spheres based on contestation rather than consensus, we still end up with a dilemma that at present remains unresolved: Cyberghettos are not per se dysfunctional for democracy, yet they remain potentially problematic.

The question of dispersed, multipublic spheres also raises the issue of the links between the different spheres to the centers of decision-making. We can distinguish between "strong" public spheres where decisions are taken, and "weak" ones, which offer only the possibility of generating opinion or collective identity. With weak public spheres there is per se no guarantee that the opinions generated will feed into the decision-making processes of democracy. It is important that all kinds of political information and debate are in circulation, but there must be some kind of structural connections and procedures between these communicative spaces and the processes of decision-making, as Sparks (2001) argues.

This question is a modern rendering of the classic problem in democratic theory of what should be the optimal relationship between public opinion and political decisions. Obviously it is not an automatic, lockstep connection that is the ideal here, since that would quickly degenerate into an unstable populist situation. Yet there must be some semblance of impact, some indications that the political talk of citizens has some consequences, or else disengagement and cynicism set in – as is precisely what many observers claim has been the pattern in the mainstream, mass mediated systems of the Western liberal democracies.

Today the most notable gap between communication in the public sphere and institutional structures for binding decisions is found not surprisingly in the global arena. Transnational forums, global networking, and opinion mobilization are very much evident on the net, and global and cosmopolitan citizenship are increasingly promoted. For example, the ambitious Global Voices (www.globalvoicesonline.org) attempts to cover the global blogosphere by surveying, selecting, and translating significant blogs from around the world, in English and seven other major languages; this integrative work clearly tilts toward the idea of global public spheres. Yet, global public spheres face many familiar constraints, magnified by the transnational context, as Cammaerts and van Audenhove (2005) argue. Their research on discussion forums and mailing lists of a number of transnational civil society organizations indicates that real interaction and debate is in fact rather limited; still more problematic is the fact that the mechanisms for translating the opinions generated into decision-making politics remain very weak, given the lack of institutional democratic structures in the transnational arena.

This point was also made plain during the weekend of February 14–16, 2003, when an estimated 10 to 20 million people worldwide demonstrated against the impending United States–led war in Iraq. This massive exercise in civic participation was largely organized and mobilized by networks of groups cooperating transnationally online (see Hassan, 2004:134), with mobile phones often used to coordinate activities at the sites. Yet the channels for transforming such global opinion into policies are highly limited to say the least: There are simply few established procedures for democratically based and binding transnational decision-making. While we might see the embryonic outlines of a global civil society (cf. Keane, 2003), the full realization of a public sphere where citizens impact on global decisions is not on the horizon, even if the idea is a powerful and progressive element of the social imaginary. And even with national contexts, with a multiplicity of public spheres, the risk grows that the orbit of many spheres may pass far from the processes of political decision-making.

MULTI-SECTOR ONLINE PUBLIC SPHERES

That said, the significance of weak public spheres remains central. At some points, certain groups may require a separate space where they can work out internal issues and/or cultivate a collective identity, where they can function as a relatively closed community. Many of these groups may not even be explicitly political. Here it becomes helpful to recall what was said in Chapter 4 about the notion of the political: Conflicts of interest, issues, and antagonisms can potentially emerge in any social context. Thus, specific Web sites may at one point in time merely reflect an association's particular interests and concerns, but later it may be seen that these are in fact in conflict with another group's, or with prevailing policies or structural features of society – and discussions begin to define issues, a "them" emerges in opposition to an "us." At that point the political has manifested itself – and at that point the online activity has entered the public sphere. Thus, the public sphere – through civic talk – should ideally be seen as a phenomenon that always has the potential to arise, to manifest itself in new places, to grow and expand.

Online public spheres take many forms and can be shaped by many factors. Though there is a considerable degree of fluidity online, we might – with all suitable caution about porous boundaries and no claim for being all-inclusive – attempt to schematically specify a number of different sectors of net-based public spheres, including:

The *pre-* or *proto-political domain*, which can focus on just about any topic or theme, but gives expression to common interests, social relations, or identities. In this sprawling cyber civil society landscape, consisting of different kinds of self-publications such as personal and organizational Web sites, blogs, webcasting, as well as discussion/chat, and so on, politics is not explicit, but always remains a potential. Clearly there is no absolute way in which the boundary between the para-political and the political domains can be drawn, since it is always in part discursively constructed and changeable; with just a few words, the border can be crossed, and the political can manifest itself.

The *journalism domain:* I use "journalism" broadly here, to include editorial and opinion material. Thus we have major news organizations that have gone online such as newspapers and CNN, to net-based news organizations (usually without much of their own original reporting) such as Yahoo! News, to alternative news organizations such as Indymedia and Mediachannel, as well as online opinion magazines (e.g., Slate and Salon) and one-person current affairs–oriented weblog sites (bloggers). Some expressions of journalism lean more toward activism (and thus straddle the boundary with the alternative activist domain, while others tilt more toward personal opinion and commentary. These tensions move the journalism domain in more participatory directions, while at the same time raising fundamental questions about journalistic criteria.

The traditional *advocacy domain*, where political communication is generated by generally well-established organizations and groups that promote political values and goals geared toward shaping public opinion and influencing decision-makers. This sector includes traditional parliamentarian political parties, corporate and other organized interest groups, such as unions, as well as major NGOs. Temporary issue groups and mobilization campaigns that nonetheless emanate from, or have strong links to, the established power centers are also a part of this domain.

The alternative *activist domain*; what I am pointing to is less established, extra-parliamentarian civic networks with more grassroots foundations and less hierarchical structures. In this public sphere domain we find political expression that is more interventionist, at times more militant (from both sides of the political spectrum). The new social movements and single-issue activist groups – which can often build alliances with each other – are typical of this sector. However, this domain may be difficult at times to distinguish from traditional advocacy. Sometimes a group or network – or the position they promote – simply blurs the boundary (e.g., an established church taking a stand for global economic justice in a manner that challenges the premises of capitalism) or groups evolve, as in the case of the United States–based MoveOn.org (see Chadwick, 2006:122–124).

Manifestations of *e-government*, where governments at any level and in any context interact with citizens via their representatives or information services. This may take the form of civic discussion sites or actual e-voting, but more common are sites that simply offer information about social services and governmental administration. While interaction in this domain may be relatively constricted and may often simply involve information for citizens in their roles as individual clients or consumers of services, it can still at times serve as a sector of the public sphere.

Civic forums, where views are exchanged among citizens, where civic talk, including more formalized deliberation, can take place, are often seen as the paradigmatic model of the online public sphere. It should be understood, however, that such forums rarely exist in isolation, but rather can be found on Web sites that belong to all of the sectors (and hence, I do not specify such forums as a separate sector). This list can of course be made more elaborate, but the point here is simply to highlight the diverse character of multisector online public spheres.

Among the first research concerns to emerge in regard to the Internet's role for public spheres was the character of the discussion that takes place in its various forums: Do they serve to enhance democracy? Today there is such a vast array of communicative spaces for political discussion on the Internet that it is very difficult to generalize in any meaningful way about how it impacts on the nature of dialogue. In her extensive review of the literature on empirical studies of online discussion, Witschge (2004) first reminds us of the social factors that generally deflect people from political talk and participation, and then shows that research thus far leaves us with a rather equivocal picture. Such factors as the heterogeneity of views available on the net and the anonymity afforded by the minimal social cues involved in participation had led to high expectations of the net's democratic potential in the early years. While these hopes have not been realized, Witschge is quick to point out that there are many methodological issues involved in comparing different studies addressing different kinds of forums; in particular large concepts such as "deliberative democracy" and "participation" can be operationalized differently by different researchers.

While there are research findings such as those of Tsaliki (2002), who found a good quality of public deliberation in her comparative study of online forums in Greece, The Netherlands, and Britain, most studies aiming to ascertain whether or not online discussions follow basic Habermasian principles usually arrive at negative findings. However, such conclusions need not be per se catastrophic for democracy, given that there can be a variety of other important, if less lofty, criteria for the evaluation of civic talk and interaction (see, for example, Wilhelm, 2000; Dahlberg, 2001; Holt, 2004). Not least, the Internet seems to offer opportunities to participate for many people who otherwise find that there are too many taboos and too much discomfiture in talking about politics in their own face-to-face environments (Stromer-Galley, 2002). Here, the net seemingly can help bypass some of the factors that prompt people to avoid politics (see my discussion in Chapter 4).

CAUTION AND CAVEATS

Clearly the Internet represents a massive boost for the public sphere; it is making a positive difference in terms of political involvement. While increasingly meshing with the mainstream media, the Internet is emerging as a clear factor in promoting participation (see Shah, Cho, Everett, and Kwak, 2005, for an analysis based on advanced modeling techniques). Mossberger, Tolbert, and McNeal (2007) use extensive survey data to make the same point. Political engagement rises with the spread of the Internet. Yet, we would be wise to keep in mind a number of caveats regarding the role and the circumstances of the Internet in regard to the public sphere and civic engagement. For starters, the use of the net in daily life for political purposes is far overshadowed by other uses, such as general social contacts, entertainment, chatting, shopping, gaming, nonpolitical information, not to mention pornography (cf. various chapters in Wellman and Haythornwaite, 2002). Further, the Internet's political economy has veered unabatedly toward the commercialization that characterizes the traditional mass media. The dominant character of the cyberenvironment to a great extent fosters – like that of the mass media – a consumerist identity and offers thus largely individualist courses of action.

The Internet has become thoroughly integrated into the global media industries, which are dominated by a shrinking number of transnational conglomerates (Mosco, 2004). The net is also a decisive element in the dynamics of global capitalism (Schiller, 1999). Market logic and commodification (Mansell and Javary, 2004), together with the political economy of its infrastructure (Abramson, 2002) and its emerging legal frameworks, threaten to diminish the net as a civic communicative space (Pajnik, 2005). Further, the net is far from a free-flowing arena without borders: Geography and government control are still highly relevant aspects, with top-down pressures putting significant restrictions on it (Goldsmith and Wu, 2006) – though regulation per se certainly can have its socially beneficial aspects. Also, we should not lose sight of the fact that the use of the net and other new communication technologies by government agencies and private corporations raises many issues about surveillance, privacy, and risk (e.g., Lyon, 2003). Turow (2006) lays bare online marketing techniques and how they use personal information bases to develop "customer categorization."

Not least, the question of the "digital divide" remains very much with us. Though Internet access has seeped far down into the social hierarchy of many countries, massive inequalities remain, both within and between nations. Access itself can have several dimensions; van Dijk (2005) specifies motivational, material, skills, and usage access. The inequalities of these dimensions of access have to do with the complex interplays of individual dispositions, social location, economics, politics, and cultural and linguistic resources. Also, they manifest themselves in terms of age, class, gender, ethnicity, and geography. As societies become all the more digitally based, such exclusions have very negative consequences for democracy; in fact, the new information technology seems to be actually exacerbating traditional information cleavages in society (Warschauer, 2003).

Globally, the most marked disparities are found between the developed and less developed nations. The March 2006 report of the World Internet Usage Statistics (www.internetworldstats.com/stats.htm) reports that in terms of Internet penetration into populations, North America has about 70 percent, and Europe almost 40 percent, though within Europe there are differences, with lower levels in the south and Scandinavia hovering at about at the same level as North America. Africa has 3.6 percent, the Middle East 10 percent, and Asia almost 11 percent – but here, too, we find a very wide range of differences, with South Korea, Taiwan, Hong Kong, and Japan approximating the North American situation, and with Bangladesh, Cambodia, Laos, and Nepal registering less than 1 percent. In macro-terms, at the global level, the disparities of Internet access correlate with economic development, and for the world's poorest nations, it can be argued that their lack of Internet access functions reciprocally with other developmental factors to entrench their poverty.

Such difficult realities undercut the cheery optimism of such motifs as "the information society" (for critical treatments of this notion, see, for example, Webster, 2001). The processes of globalization are highly uneven, and economic development in particular shows many dreadful and unjust trends. The Internet on its own can offer neither a fast track to economic improvement nor a shortcut to democracy. We need to have a realistic grasp of the conditions and contexts that shape and modify the net as a resource for both economic development and for civic life; it cannot deliver any "quick fix."

To that end, I turn in the following chapter to three different contexts in which the Internet plays a key role in political communication, and look at the implications for civic engagement.

CHAPTER 8

Online Practices and Civic Cultures

The potentials and conditions of Internet use for civic purposes that I probed in the previous chapter establish some basic analytic horizons. In this chapter I take up some specific settings to explore this more concretely. The possible areas for pursuing such investigations are many; I have chosen three rather different ones in order to suggestively illustrate the range of the many kinds of dynamics at work in the Internet's possible contributions to civic cultures – as well as to indicate some of the limitations. Each of these short explorations reveals different contexts and practices of net use; each relates to civic cultures in different ways. I first take up how journalism is evolving online, and then look at the European Union, where the net is used for lobbying by NGOs, and explore what this might mean for civic identities. Finally I take up net use within the alter-globalization movements.

JOURNALISM TRANSFORMED – TO A DEGREE

ADAPTING TO THE CYBER-ENVIRONMENT

The net has, as in so many sectors, revolutionized the way journalism gets done, altering the processes of newsgathering, production, storage, editing, and distribution (see, for example, Pavlik, 2001; Boczkowski, 2005; Allan, 2006, for helpful overviews. Deuze, 2001, 2004, offers further analytic perspectives; see also Matheson, 2004; Cooke, 2005; Curran, 2003). Notably the multimedia character of news production is altering the basic patterns of production and dissemination. Newspapers and other traditional news organizations are going through a tumultuous time of difficult restructuring. Moreover, they are no longer the only news providers around: While traditional news organizations have developed their online presence, there is also a host of new actors, with competition for audience attention.

We find an array of nonpress "content providers" on the net, including the portals of Internet service providers such as Yahoo, Google, and MSN, which have little of their own original journalism (and few cultural roots in the profession), but cull from a large array of sources, structuring it in an accessible manner for people navigating the portal. Further, we find specialized providers catering to target "communities" for particular news, ads, and lifestyle information (about, for example, financial matters, hobbies, and health) as part of the new mix. Not least, there are alternative news organizations, such as www.indymedia. org, various kinds of do-it-yourself citizen-journalism such as Wikinews (www.wikinews.org), and sites that engage in critical analyses of mainstream news and information, for example, MediaChannel (www. mediachannel.org). There are many specialized sites offering versions of critical journalistic material on specific areas, such as Corporate Watch (www.corpwatch.org), which monitors the actions of major corporations and financial institutions; One World (www.oneworld.org), which emphasizes news about environmental issues and democracy; and PR Watch (www.prwatch.org), which critically scrutinizes the public relations industry.

Citizens are more and more able to circumvent the traditional packaging of journalism and retrieve – and produce – information for themselves, thus "eliminating the middleman." The historical story-telling role of journalism is being complemented by large flows of socially relevant electronic information between people and organizations outside of mainstream journalism. Organized groups with sophisticated information skills are not only providing their members with useful materials, but are in some cases functioning as sources for traditional journalists, for example, environmental groups or consumer activists who target the sweatshops of transnational corporations and serve up the information for the mainstream media. Who is and who is not a journalist in this context becomes increasingly fuzzy as a variety of information functions arise to sort, sift, and funnel data electronically in differing organizational and societal contexts. The boundaries between journalism and nonjournalism in cyberspace are become even more blurry than in the mass media.

New tools of journalism offer new practices, new possibilities; from the early "computer-assisted reporting" in the 1980s to today's multimedia production, the digital revolution has offered new modes of doing journalism, not just ways of doing old things better. However, the Internet does not simply move in and redefine the way everything works; it is largely assimilated via the already existing local and national traditions within journalism. Given that there are many factors that shape journalism, the new production technologies result in a complexity and heterogeneity of adaptability. This is illustrated in Quant, Löffelholz, Weaver, Hanitzsch, and Altmeppen (2006); in a comparison between German and American journalists who work online there is considerable diversity in regard to the profiles, professional tasks, and attitudes. Similarly, Deuze (2004) underscores the difficulties involved in multimedia practices of online journalism. The drive toward what he defines as "fully integrated multimedia newsrooms where teams of news reporters from print, broadcast and online jointly gather information, mine databases, and plan story packages intended for distribution across all media" (Deuze, 2004:141) translates into a number of problems having to do with institutional structures, organization routines, and the demand for increased "multiskilling" among journalists.

In their several years' long analysis of a European media organization and how the new technologies impact on newswork, Boczkowski and Ferris (2005) found that while technology is not deterministic, it does play a key role in shaping editorial dynamics that decide what kinds of stories get told, who gets to tell them, how they are told, and which publics are to be addressed. In the process of dramatic reorganization of a news company, where multimedia became the central axis of content production, it was found (among many insightful results) that the transition did not yield the "homogenization" of content that many observers had expected, but rather led to a more diverse, niche-market profile of their production.

In another study of a news organization, Klinenberg (2005a) found that the extensive restructuring brought on by the interplay of economic pressures and technological possibilities of multimedia convergence resulted in more work pressures on the staff, with them having less time than before the reorganizations for preparing and writing stories. The goals of productivity, efficiency, and profitability pushed traditional journalistic values even further to the margins. Clearly, in the massive transitions underway, it would be foolish to conclude that such will always be the case, but it does underscore that "better" technology does not always automatically lead to "better" journalism. Thus, while digital technologies are changing journalistic production practices, within traditional news outfits these developments do not necessarily strengthen journalistic values or quality, but rather are aimed at enhancing short-term profits (Hall, 2001).

Still, from the standpoint of civic cultures, with the proliferation of material available from so many different organizations — journalistic and otherwise — along with the easy and continual updating, accessible and extensive archives that can be searched and downloaded, this new era of journalism offers enhanced possibilities for civic knowledge and access to a broader range of ideas and debates. That is, at least for those with the motivation and not least a critical capacity for selection, the growing range of information made available by online journalism can be said to be a positive feature for civic cultures. Interactive possibilities that would have been unthinkable just a few years ago have become routine: Many journalists can be reached directly via e-mail by members of the public who may wish to correct facts, offer alternative interpretations, or provide other forms of feedback.

There is a massive civic information sharing going on in cyberspace that increasingly tends to bypass the classical modes of journalism production and dissemination. The hierarchical, top-down mass communication model of journalism is being challenged in this new media environment. Understanding that it is important to go beyond "bird's-eye perspectives" and "parachute journalism" and get detailed information about fast-breaking stories, all news organizations today invite their audiences to send in materials and get in touch. Journalism has traditionally invited its audiences to provide tips for stories, but today editors know that with the diffusion of inexpensive and sophisticated technologies, members of the audience can provide journalistic scoops with raw materials of high quality. "Are you at the scene of this event? Contact us and send us your pictures."

Alternative/Participatory Journalism Online

Alternative and activist media have a long history, and their relevance today remains undiminished (see Downing, 2000; Atton, 2002; Waltz, 2005; Ostertag, 2007, for overviews including historical perspectives). The Internet era has further amplified the possibilities, and one can find on the net a vast array of journalistic sites and activity that diverge from the mainstream mass media (Baily, Cammaerts, and Carpentier, 2007; see also Gillmor, 2006, for an enthusiastic rendering of current developments). As is often pointed out, the dichotomization of "mainstream" and "alternative" journalism is not always as obvious as one may suspect at first glance. There is evidence for varieties of "crossover" in terms of actual practices, suggesting that treating the distinctions as characterized by a continuum rather than a rupture makes good sense, not least given the emergence of a small but growing cadre of "hybrid" journalists, with one foot in each sector (Harcup, 2005). Thus, for example, it has been found that while alternative journalism not surprisingly makes more use of ordinary citizens as sources, there is also evidence suggesting the use of relatively well-established groups of "alternative elite" sources (Atton and Wickenden, 2005).

Yet, certainly it would be foolish to minimize the contrasts between mainstream news media and those who explicitly challenge its worldviews, such as www.alternet.org, www.zmag.org, and www.fair.org. The network established by the Independent Media Centers – Indymedia (www.indymedia.org) – is the most extensive and well-known of the online alternative news services. Palton and Deuze (2003) argue in their analysis that the basic model on which Indymedia is based is fundamentally different from and incompatible with profit-based corporate news organizations. Similarly, Pickard (2006) finds that the network structure and strategies, the lack of formal hierarchy, as well as the participatory practices that characterize Indymedia generate a quite different kind of news organization. We should also add that, journalistically, Indymedia sees itself as an oppositional force, offering a decidedly alternative world-view to that found in the mainstream commercial media.

Indymedia emerged in conjunction with the demonstrations in Seattle in November 1999 against the WTO (see Downing, 2003; Kidd, 2003). Prior to and in preparing for the demonstrations, a group of activists, with volunteers and some donations, set up the Independent Media Center, equipping it with Internet technology relevant for journalistic activity. Its success at this event is famous, as it circumvented the corporate media and provided the outside world with net-based journalistic coverage of the events (see also the Center for Communication and Civic Engagement's Web site www.engagedcitizen.org for more background). As Hyde (2003) frames it, Indymedia can be understood in part as a response to the profit-driven journalism of the corporate media, and at the same as a manifestation of the tradition of the alternative press in the United States that has now gone online.

The readiness of many journalist volunteers to join in, and the rapid spread of Indymedia across the globe – there are now over 150 Independent Media Centers around the world – attest to the attractiveness of a Web-based "people's newsroom." Today, the volunteer infrastructure remains intact, and Indymedia focuses on grassroots reporting using online multimedia technology. It offers outlets to a vast array of groups and individuals whose understanding of the world has been ignored by the dominant media. Success seems not to have undercut the original vision, even if it today must struggle with all the pragmatic issues any large-scale organization must cope with – a challenge perhaps made all the more compelling given its commitments to minimal hierarchy and democratic openness (see Beckerman, 2003).

In an effort to conceptualize the differing journalistic orientations present in today's media environment, Nip (2006) offers a typology of journalism that takes as its conceptual point of departure the famous "public journalism" movement that appeared in the United States in the 1990s. This movement struggled for a reflexive critique of the state of journalism coupled with new efforts to dialogue with its publics. In Nip's scheme, "citizen journalism" is typified by Indymedia: In this model, "people are responsible for gathering content, visioning, producing and publishing news product ... professionals are not involved at all (unless in the capacity of citizens but not as paid employees)" (Nip, 2006:218). In "participatory journalism," on the other hand, citizens are invited to generate content, while the professionals also generate content, as well as remain in charge of the overall production, distribution, and marketing. Participatory journalism can take many forms, from the public's feedback on published stories to the initiation of new stories, and supplying materials such as visuals.

The distinction is not merely an exercise in semantics, because these two models suggest two different kinds, or degrees, of civic engagement. Citizen journalism requires extensive commitment and fine-honed skills; it can be seen as an "elite" realm in terms of civic engagement. Participatory journalism, however, is in principle readily accessible to most citizens, and does not per se have to be sustained, with daily effort. Moreover, this kind of broad interaction with the public builds in a dynamic loop between journalism professionals and their publics. Both forms can, under the best circumstances, be seen as maintaining a critical dialogue with mainstream journalism, be it at the level of particular facts around a given story – where people as technologically equipped eyewitnesses can add to stories or correct inaccuracies – or whether they offer a competing frame in which to understand the political world. It is easy to see how it potentially can deepen civic culture; it touches base with all six dimensions, not least being based on knowledge and offering practices that depend on computer and net skills that many citizens now have.

AMBIGUITIES OF THE BLOGOSPHERE

In Nip's (2006) terms, political blogging can be seen as a form of citizen journalism (usually of the opinion/commentary kind) – it fills all the criteria, albeit normally on the small scale of a single-person activity. Sullivan (2002) underscores the significance of blogging in a more dramatic way. Invoking Marx, he argues that bloggers have taken the means of journalistic production into their own hands:

> It's hard to underestimate what a huge deal this is. For as long as journalism has existed, writers of whatever kind have had one route to readers: They needed an editor and a publisher. Even in the most benign scenario, this process subtly distorts journalism. You find yourself almost unconsciously writing to please a handful of people – the editors looking for a certain kind of story, the publishers seeking to push a particular venture, or the advertisers who influence the editors and owners. Blogging simply bypasses this ancient ritual. (Sullivan, 2002)

Such infectious enthusiasm is driven by the possibilities inherent in the technology itself, and while describing what is in principle possible and what does take place to a degree, it ignores some of the other, more complex features of the development that derive from social and cultural factors (see, for instance, Haas, 2005). In the late 1990s, freely available software for weblogs helped expand the number of regular bloggers in the world from approximately 30,000 to today's several million. In the realm of alternative politics and journalism, the blogging activity inspired by the establishment of Indymedia at the demonstrations against the Seattle WTO meeting was a historic moment in the evolution of activist versions of this genre (Kahn and Kellner, 2004). Yet, looking at the blogosphere today, we find a sprawling terrain for which U.S. data suggest that news and current affairs topics account for less than one-fifth of all blogs (Haas, 2005) – hardly surprising, given what we know about the position of politics on the net. There are many possible ways in which to classify the blogosphere – a genre analysis, for example, is found in Miller and Shepherd (2004) – but the point is that journalism is but one of many orientations for blogging.

Among blogs with a current affairs or political profile, alternative political perspectives are obviously present, and certainly blogs from military personnel and civilians in the Iraq war challenging the official view from Washington are a particularly noteworthy recent subgenre (see, for example, Wall, 2005). However, analyses of journalistic blogs show that they to a great extent follow and feed off mainstream media (Reese, Rutigliano, Hyun, and Jeong, 2007; Lowrey, 2007; Haas, 2005), reproducing much of the dominant horizons. Indeed, journalistic blogging is no longer a journalistic activity done from the margins: Big-name journalists, pundits, and commentators at major media organizations have all joined in the game over the past several years – even if many still adapt a kind of "outsider" image. The journalistic blogosphere seems to have a relatively stable structure that parallels the general nodal pattern of the Internet discussed earlier. Some key players, perceived as elites, get much attention and dominate the discussions in various domains; below them is a larger, second-level tier reflecting more modest stature and/or media and discursive clout, and, finally, is the massively large popular sector of the blogosphere.

The tiers become linked, as news, ideas, and debates filter downward, but even on occasion upward, as topics from the "ground level" snowball toward the more prestigious sectors of the blogosphere – and can thus begin to impact on political agenda setting, not least via the links that blogs provide (Delwiche, 2005). Even the elite press is making increasing use of the blogosphere (Meesner and Watson DiSato, 2008); political blogging is on its way to becoming an important sector of the mediated public sphere. At the same time, evidence suggests that a complex evolution is now under way within journalism, as mainstream journalists increasingly make use of the blog format. Journalists try to assert their authority via traditional norms and professional horizons in their encounter with citizen (nonprofessional) bloggers, and thus strive to incorporate or "normalize" blogging. Yet, the frequent blending of fact, opinion, debate, and analysis found in blogs, together with the cooperative production that emerges as journalists interact with other bloggers, seem to be impacting on prevailing notions of how journalism should be done. Journalists are drawn into new forms of practices that are gaining legitimacy and thereby altering some traditional notions of how journalism should be done (cf. Singer, 2005; Robinson, 2006).

The evolution of journalism in the wake of the Internet has several dimensions, and certainly opens up new spaces for civic participation in the journalistic activity. The increasing "joint production," where citizens cooperate in various ways with mainstream journalists, is one area; the growing field of citizen journalism is another, represented by both activist organizations and individual bloggers. Individual blogging, however, in many ways reproduces the ambiguities about what constitutes journalism – and even politics, for that matter – found in mass-mediated popular culture. As with much online activity, blogging often simply leans toward the personal, yet, alternatively, can also serve to problematize traditional conceptions of private and public.

In the at least moderately affluent areas of the world, people, especially younger ones, are spending a lot of time online. Keren (2006), in his analysis of U.S. bloggers, finds civic engagement, but also large doses of "political passivity," "withdrawal," and "melancholy." He notes that blogs often have a monologic character; they often become a format for self-expression. Being thus visible in the media is taking on increased importance in the lives of many young people, and it could be argued that the more ambitious of these net participants are engaging in a sort of mini-performance, where they are the "stars" of their own "shows," thereby solidifying a net-based sense of self. Here we can see emerging aspirations toward celebrity culture, which Cashmore (2006) understands as the interweaving of contemporary consumerism, the potential of new ICTs, and the late modern currents of individualism. Keren (2006) introduces the theme of narcissism in his analysis of online activities. Indeed, this view of the contemporary, media-shaped self has been with us for a few decades (see, for example, Lasch, 1991). This concept is used not as a dismissive, rhetorical device, but rather seeks analytically to further specify the attributes of the more extreme forms of individualization that characterize the late modern psyche (see Chapter 1; see also Tyler, 2007), even if there is a lingering sense of stigma attached to it.

Narcisstic or not, young people are doing many things with the Internet, but among the key activities is socializing – spending time with others online who in some way are a part of one's social circles. Some of these contacts may be people they meet face-to-face, others may be persons they have only encountered in cyberspace. But in using such sites as Facebook and MySpace, or even in diary blogging about their lives, they are not only socializing but also affirming and confirming their identities. Politics sometimes emerges in these contexts, civic agency may be mobilized, but in many contexts it is not likely, and would involve a clear violation of the shared understanding of the purposes of the site and the interaction on it. As in the mass media, journalism in the blogosphere and on the net generally remains a small patch on a much larger field.

Generally, we may well anticipate that journalism will continue to become more plural in its forms, its functions, and its practitioners. It will become more difficult to distinguish it from advocacy political communication, public relations, alternative and participatory civic information, personal commentary, popular culture, and so on. The traditional referent of "objectivity" will recede as a compelling professional referent and ideological strategy for professional legitimation. We may need to come to terms with a more prismatic notion of truth, founded on what we might call a "multiepistemic order," where it becomes more generally understood that all story-telling is situated, all perspectives on society are contingent – not in least in a world where political communication is dispersed within a complex media matrix of global character. And at the same time we will continue to need workable criteria for distinguishing better stories from less good ones, accurate accounts from distortions, truths from falsehoods. Perhaps new such criteria will emerge; in any case, the journalistic function within late modern democracy will remain a terrain of difficulty and contention, but hopefully also of creativity.

NGOS AS CIVIC EU NETWORKS

CIVIC DISENGAGEMENT IN THE EU: FAMILIAR DILEMMAS AMPLIFIED

The European Union is a daunting project, regardless of whether one prefers to see it as a complexly integrated confederation of states or as a more ambitious attempt that is moving in the direction of supranational federalism. Either way, given the public and official commitment of the EU to democracy, both versions evoke a concern with the political orientation, loyalties, and participation of the citizens within this transnational construction. It seems almost impossible to frame any discussion on the European Union in terms of democracy without the vocabulary of "deficit," "dilemmas," and "legitimation problems" arising. This is not just discursive habit, but signals a very serious situation that threatens to undercut, at the very foundation, the very real progress toward democratic integration being made on an array of fronts (Kaitatzi-Whitlock, 2005).

The statistics speak for themselves: If we simply look in terms of participation in the elections of the Parliament, in the most recent election in 2004, while 90 percent of Belgian voters went to the polls, almost all the other countries had less than 50 percent turnout, with many even below 40 percent. (European Parliament statistics [www.europarl.eu/elections], 2004). The defeat of the draft of the proposed Constitution in 2005 was another severe blow. Certainly the democratic malaise around the EU is but a more pointed variant of what researchers, journalists, civic activists, and other observers say about democracy within the context of the nation-state, where such themes as low voter turnouts, poor media performance, civic indifference, and political cynicism are frequently noted. And, as within nation-states, the low civic engagement among citizens in the EU is not necessarily always underserved.

Given the scale and ambitions of the EU, the problems too become amplified. In the long term, without the general acceptance of the citizens of the member states and without a minimal degree of their engagement in EU affairs, democracy as such will be an empty shell, and the EU itself will be dangerously hampered by a lack of popular legitimacy (see, for example, Bohman, 2007; Magnette, 2003; Trenz and Eder, 2004; Koopmans, Friedhelm, and Pfetsch, 2002; Eriksen, 2006; Nieminen, 2007). Historically it may simply not work; normatively some wish for success, others for failure. My own sense is that, given the enormous implications of this venture, we would surely be ill advised not to do our utmost to try to enhance its democratic character.

These difficulties are no secret, yet their persistence is striking. The European Commission's *Governance in the EU: A White Paper* (http://ec.europa.eu/governance/index_en.htm) from 2001 addressed democratic participation of the citizens of the EU with a normative argument for this development. Not surprisingly, it served its internal bureaucratic functions without making much of a dent on the outside world. On page 1 we can read, "The White Paper is about the way in which the Union uses the powers given to it by its citizens," a formulation that may well elicit cynical smirks from those with any grasp of where power in the EU resides.

The fate of the democratic initiative of the Commission's vice-president Margot Wallström of Sweden is instructive. She launched the so-called Plan D, aiming to stimulate more grassroots participation in the decision-making of the EU (Communication: "The Commission's contribution to the period of reflection and beyond: Plan D for Democracy, Dialogue and Debate, COM [2005] 494 final [13 Oct. 2005]"). This program sought to stimulate national debates in the parliaments, civil society, and media of the member states, with the aim of feeding this information back to the Commission. It comprised thirteen specific proposals, including support for European citizens' projects, and a drive for more openness of Council proceedings, a stronger presence of Commissioners in national Parliaments, and renewed support for projects to increase voter participation. It seems that not only was the Commission itself somewhat less than enthusiastic about it, but national governments and media did not give it much play, not even in Sweden, where the media usually acclaim a national son or daughter who makes a big splash in the outside world. This lack of support for democratic reform no doubt has many explanations, but the upshot is that too many significant actors seem indifferent to it.

With more than twenty official languages, assertive national identities, and differing political cultures, all thoughts of unified "European identities" or "pan-European communicative space" lack realism (see Schlesinger, 2003). In the present situation, "the EU public sphere" is filtered through the journalism of the national media, and generally the prospects for a democratic EU, accountable to its citizens, remain problematic (see Fossum and Schlesinger, 2007, for a recent collection of perspectives on these themes; see also Sarkikakis, 2007. For an overview of research of media coverage of the EU, see Slaatta, 2006; see also Golding, 2006; Risse and Van de Steeg, 2003; Kevin, 2003; Machill, 2006; Downey, 2006). Though there are some exceptions, the findings are generally dismal, underscoring that the EU is much underrepresented in the coverage, that the journalistic angles often accentuate national interests, and that the media thus contribute to a woefully underinformed and largely indifferent EU citizenry. This in turn solidifies the EUs democratic deficit. One could argue that the problem is not just a case of a lack of information: The EU as such simply does not figure in the socio-political imaginary of most of its citizens.

Research on national coverage of the EU, instructive as it may be, often misses an important point, namely, that journalism does not simply follow a completely independent path, but is rather well-integrated into the political culture of each member state (Slaatta, 2006, develops this argument). And these political cultures have at best only lukewarm interest in giving the EU the time and space it warrants (evidenced not least by the reception of Plan D). Thus, the political agendas and power of the national political elites are also central factors that shape the current situation. But there is more. The problem extends to the horse's mouth, so to speak: The EU itself, particularly the Commission, has shown itself to be highly reluctant to actively stimulate debate.

There is a bit of irony in the EU, or at least the Commission, bemoaning its democratic deficit. In practice, as Magnette (2003) underscores, its notion of "participation" consists largely of consultation with selected groups; it does not extend to any real decision-making (see Brügger-man, 2005, for an analysis of the EU's communication strategies). Moreover, the groups deemed worthy for consultation are well-established interest organizations. "Citizens," "the public," "the people," and so on, figure largely as rhetorical dressing. Further, the EU is hampered by it prevailing internal culture of consensus, which leads to "finished" policy proposals and offers little in the way of ongoing issues for civic debate. This kind of paralysis seems only to have increased with the recent enlargement with more member states. The challenge of attaining internal consensus increases with the number of members. Thus, under the present circumstances, the EU is constrained both at its source as well as at the national outlets, seriously constricting the development of EU civic cultures.

EMERGING NETWORKS. The EU has of course discovered – and been discovered by – the Internet, chiefly in regard to the net's attributes as a mass medium for reaching large audiences. For example, EurActiv (www.euractiv.com) is an independent media portal dedicated to EU affairs. Based on a business model, its coverage of EU affairs concentrates on policy positions of elite EU actors trying to influence policies already in the prelegislative phase, before a Commission proposal. In a less traditional mode, on the youth-oriented YouTube we find EUX.TV (www.youtube.com/watch?v=iqEPqSbvzio), which is a private, news-oriented channel devoted to the EU. Perhaps still more striking is that the Commission has now opened up its own channel on YouTube (www.youtube.com/EUtube).

However, if we return to the network model of society, we should keep in mind that EU integration proceeds not just via nation-states and formal institutions, but also via informal networks (Schlesinger, 2003). There has been a strong tendency to devote analytic energy to the major arenas and actors of European politics, often ignoring the less institutionalized sectors. As I noted earlier, we should not see networks as merely a product of ICTs, even if they certainly can amplify the possibilities for such modes of social interaction. Not least in the case of Europe, we have a long history of a "network society." Even before the establishment of nation-states, the church, universities, guilds, commerce (e.g., the Hansaetic League in the Middle Ages), traveling performers, and so on, were networking Europe – in the absence of a common language, identity, and communication system (Nieminen, 2007). To be sure, the advent of the Internet has enhanced the opportunities for contemporary networking.

Moreover, I would affirm that it is the net's character for facilitating networking that will ultimately be significant for civic agency within the EU. While net-based politics within the context of the EU at present is not as manifest as in other political contexts, it is clearly emerging. We may even speculate whether the EU can continue to exist in its present form as the network character of European society (and politics) continues apace in the decades ahead. But for the present, there are indications of an embryonic stage of network reconfiguration.

In contemporary alternative politics, along with social movements, particularly in the areas of alter-globalization, ecology, feminism, peace, and social self-help, we also find a large number of more established advocacy NGOs that can mobilize citizens' engagement, even across national borders. Generally, there are few social movements or ad hoc activist groups that target the EU in any sustained way (see Wimmer, 2005, however, for a discussion of some exceptions to this). Instead, it is NGOs that become relevant here. There are literally tens of thousands of NGOs registered in the world; it is fair to say that NGOs are generally more stable organizations, with more traditional structures than the activist social movements engaged in alternative politics. Like all advocacy groups, NGOs can build coalitions between themselves and other groups, reach out to new potential citizen participants, debate with opponents, and provide access to spectator publics. What makes them particularly relevant in terms of the EU is that they are often engaged in lobbying and opinion-building in order to influence policy decisions.

There are some formal structures regarding NGOs and the EU. A recent reorganization has led to the launch in June 2008 of a new Web site, The European Commission and Civil Society (www.ec.europa.eu/civil_society/apgen_en.htm). Here one can read about the legal frameworks for consultation, its processes and scope, definitions and standards, principles of openness, and so on. We read that the Commission values civil society organizations for maintaining a broad policy dialogue with citizens and underscores the importance of including them in consultation. The EU Commission regularly takes counsel from civil society organizations, which include trade unions and employee federations, social and economic players (from industry), community-based organizations (CBOs), and NGOs. While we should not forget the Commission's general disinclination for genuine participation, NGOs are seen as specifically promoting the common good, are nonprofit, and are independent of governments and political parties. We find various listings of NGOs operating at the EU level, representing European civil society interests; we should note, however, that the European Commission makes no distinction between "civil society" groups and other "interest groups." Both are treated as "interested parties," thereby ignoring the distinction between those with economic interests and those of a more civic kind.

In brief, at least in formal terms, it is thus apparent that NGOs have a rather well-institutionalized role to play in the EU. Indeed, the EU annually awards something on the scale of €1.5 billion in funding to various NGOs (Kitsing, 2003). Aside from those NGOs with whom the EU has formal consulting agreements, there are many others that actively engage in lobbying within the EU to promote their causes and attempt to impact on policy in a wide variety of areas; many NGOs are in fact organized into large sector consortiums to enhance their lobbying clout.

One need not idealize NGOs – they, for example, are not a priori beyond corruption (Kitsing, 2003), and they do not always maintain the close contacts with their grassroots support as might be expected (Greenwood, 2004). Also, they tend to be less "communicative" than the more loosely structured social movement organizations. In an international study of a large number of NGOs, mostly with well-established, mainstream profiles, Brundin (2008) found that their use of the Internet was overwhelmingly monological. They used the net in a one-way manner to spread their messages to the outside world, but only on a very few of these Web sites were there any mechanisms for internal discussion. Moreover, a "responsiveness test" showed that the number of these NGOs willing to respond to inquiries by outsiders was disappointingly small.

Globally, English is the dominant language in NGO contexts, even if others are also used. And even if something like 70 percent of all EU lobbyists work for corporate interests and only 20 percent for NGOs – with the remaining 10 percent promoting the interests of regions, cities, and international institutions (Bianchi, 2004) – it is obvious that NGOs offer important communicative links both horizontally (connecting citizens between various member states) and vertically (transmitting views upward at the EU level and intervening in policy questions).

To illustrate some of the range of NGO concerns, I offer a quick sketch of five different ones, each of which is a sector network that in turn coordinates many member NGOs:

- European Environmental Bureau (EEB) (www.eeb.org): The EEB aims to promote knowledge and understanding of the current and potential EU environmental and sustainable development policies among the general public in the EU, so that this will lead them generally to mobilize for continued improvement. The EEB is a federation of more than 140 environmental citizens' organizations based in all EU member states as well as in a few neighboring countries.

- European Federation for Transport and Environment (T&E) (www.t-e.nu): T&E is Europe's principal environmental organization campaigning specifically on transport. Members are drawn from forty NGOs in nearly every European country. T&E argues that many political decisions at the EU level impact on the environmental damage caused by transport, and thus strives to influence decisions in such areas as price levels, vehicle emission limits, fuel quality standards, taxes, funding of infrastructure, and air quality standards.
- The European Women's Lobby (EWL) (www.womenlobby.org): The EWL is the largest coordinating body of national and European nongovernmental women's organizations in the EU, with over 4,000 member organizations in the 25 member states. The EWL's goal is to achieve equality between women and men in Europe and to serve as a link between political decision-makers and women's organizations at the EU level.
- European Network Against Racism (ENAR) (www.enar-eu.org): The ENAR, a network of European NGOs working to combat racism in all the EU member states, is a major outcome of the 1997 European Year Against Racism. The ENAR, with over 600 anti-racist NGOs, functions as a network to share information and influence policies across the EU through campaigns.
- CONCORD (www.concordeurope.org): CONCORD is the European NGOs Confederation for Relief and Development. Its 18 international networks and 19 national associations from EU member states represent more than 1,500 European NGOs. The main objective of the Confederation is to enhance the impact of European development NGOs by combining expertise and accountability; not least it coordinates NGOs from the North and the South in shaping the agenda of cooperation. The Confederation's key features are its ability to adopt common positions, the sharing of knowledge, and capacities to deal with major issues relating to European development policy.

What we should note with all of these NGOs, aside from the large number of organizations that they each in turn encompass in their networks, is that unlike many activist social movements, they are firmly oriented to the EU and operate mostly within its boundaries. Moreover, these and most NGOs tend to manifest a more traditional vertical organizational structure than contemporary social movements organizations. Larger NGOs, those more global in scope of their operations, will organizationally structure themselves so that there is a designated EU section, for example, Friends of the Earth Europe (www.foeerope.org) and Climate Action Network Europe (CAN Europe) (www.climatenetwork. org). In the case of CAN, its European office is one of thirteen around the world.

If one goes to the Web sites of these NGOs, what one finds is not any plea for European identity, no appeals to European civilization, not even any extended defense of the EU. Rather, one encounters an engagement with particular kinds of issues that affect Europe, or affect Europe's relationship to, and impact on, the rest of the world, especially developing nations. While there no interpellation of the citizen to join or support the EU, there is on the contrary clear calls to act within the confines of the EU to get things done.

THE EU AND "PROJECT IDENTITY"

How might we understand such engagement within the EU in terms of the perspective of civic agency and identity, and what might be required to further strengthen such participation? Castells (1998, Chapter 5) offers some hints for thinking about this with his notion of "project identity." He suggests that, on the one hand, the EU must minimally be able to "deliver the goods" in terms of material well-being for at least a large majority of its citizens. This means helping to ensure social security, work-life stability, and enhancement of living standards. On the other hand, the EU must absolutely demonstrate its allegiance to key democratic values, such as equality, justice, social solidarity, and universal human rights. This involves establishing not only the formal structures and apparatus of a democratic arrangement – with a variety of democratic forms – but also contributing to the generation of an everyday life where such democratic values can find expression, for example, in social solidarity, ethnic pluralism, and responsibility for the poor. If these two "criteria" of a material baseline and democratic values can be met, suggests Castells, then people's normative horizons will gravitate toward a "project identity" that supports the EU, and mobilize their identity as EU citizens within this project, generating and cementing various relevant practices in the process. This project identity – at both the individual and collective levels – would presumably not compete with people's affective allegiances to nation, since it would be more practical and normative rather than emotive, more rational than affective.

In simple terms: Citizens need not feel passionate about the EU per se, but about their own interests and about democratic values. The more citizens realize that the EU has far-reaching impact on their lives, and the more knowledge they gain about it, the more they will become involved. And, I would hypothetically add, the more they develop practices in relation to such engagement, the stronger will be this identity. We can note that project identity has an affinity with Habermas' (1996) call for "constitutional patriotism" – an allegiance to the values and procedures of EU democracy that does not directly compete with the emotionality of national identities. Castells sees the main immediate actors here as national governments, particularly via their participation in the Council of Ministers; civic agency would thus be at first mostly directed toward national governments' EU politics.

To suggest that this is not an easy undertaking is an understatement, and Castells makes no effort to gloss over the many obvious difficulties involved; it is a qualified agnostic view. Yet, the classic model of republicanism suggests precisely that this loyalty to democracy and its values must take precedence over ethnic and cultural loyalties (as well as group interests). The kind of EU project identity Castells has in mind can be seen as a variant of civic identity, projected to the supranational level, where the motivational impetus takes the form of self-interest guided by democratic loyalties. The dimension of values is pivotal for EU citizens' self- and collective understanding: Loyalty to the substantive and procedural values of democracy becomes the bedrock of the EU civic identities. To thus conceptualize identities as potential "cosmopolitan citizens" – since this is indeed what we have on our horizons – leads us into the challenging terrain of launching citizenship beyond the borders of the nation-state. Optimistic perspectives are found in Delanty (2000) and Beck (2007); a more pessimistic/sober account is offered by Miller (2000).

Still, we can see glimmerings of Castells' project identity on these NGO Web sites. They manifest an instrumental relationship to the EU, based on the understanding that this is an arena and a power center that must be addressed in order to enact desirable change in the world.

From the perspective of civic cultures, the values propagated are firmly democratic. There is a commitment to the ideals of democracy, as well as a strategic engagement with its procedures. Looking at the Web sites, they are strong on knowledge: They can equip the citizen with resources to better understand and to better engage in the world. One can find, variously, publications, newsletters, databases, other online resources and documents, bookstores, and libraries. In some cases, concrete competencies, in the form of digital skills, are offered. The networking involved promotes trust and affinity – there are always efforts to reach out to recruit new members; this in turn manifests an open communicative climate.

The civic practices that are fostered include discussion and internal debate; mobilization in various EU contexts; meetings, seminars, conferences, and various mechanisms for expressing opinion and – for a select few – lobbying, where pressure is directly applied to decision-makers. In short, what we have here are what we might call NGO-EU civic cultures, facilitated by the Internet. If the political climate and culture within the Commission should change – perhaps out of desperation as the present modus operandi becomes untenable – then at least some important structures fostering EU-oriented civic cultures will already be in place. In the meantime, the EU will have to make do with more modest levels of commitment to democratic values in the foreseeable future.

ONLINE ACTIVISM: GLOBAL HORIZONS

It is difficult to imagine that the current manifestation of alternative politics and oppositional world-views could have spread so extensively in the absence of the Internet. Both technologically and economically, access to the net (and other ICTs, such as mobile phones) has helped facilitate the growth of massive, coordinated digital networks of engaged activists. The ease and adaptability of use permit those with less relative social power to participate as citizens in political activities. They can more readily express their views, and counter those of the more powerful, not least as expressed in the dominant mass media.

The open and accessible character of the net means that traditional centers of power have less informational and ideational control over their environment than previously. It is thus an ideal tool for politically activist social movement organizations (SMOs) and needs to be defended and expanded as a civic resource (Atton, 2005). Not least, global activism – directed at political issues of a transnational kind – is growing, and is increasingly making use of the Internet (see, for example, Amoore, 2005; Aronowitz and Gautney, 2003; McDonald, 2006; Eschele, 2001; Eschele and Maiguashca, 2005; Danaher and Mark, 2003; Tarrow, 2005; Della Porta and Tarrow, 2004). Though there still exist variations in terminology, the notion of "social movement organizations" is often used to refer to the loose and fluid activist networks that arise in and characterize these contexts.

SOCIAL MOVEMENTS AND NET USE

In their opening statement with the launch of the new journal *Social Movement Studies* (Jordan, Lent, McKay, and Mische, 2005), the editors observe that forms of collective action are "common means of expressing political and cultural needs in societies around the world. The power of movement and collective identity is integral to a globalizing world, as it is often the only way in which communities or activist groups can express their choices and needs. . . ." There is an extensive literature on social movements, and various traditions of research, with a focus on the popular politics of protest from an array of perspectives, for example, feminist, ethnic, anarchist, queer, and postcolonial, being added in recent years to the more established approaches. One surprising feature about all the research work done on SMOs is that so very little of it deals with the communication practices and strategies, not even in recent years, when the Internet has taken on such a central role. This topic has instead largely been pursued by media and communication scholars.

In an attempt to generate an initial typology of SMOs in terms of their online presence, Cammaerts (2008) distinguishes between a number of basic kinds of organizations (and uses one organization to illustrate each category). I simplify his scheme somewhat to yield three basic categories:

1) There are a few large umbrella, or "hub," organizations, such as the Association for Progressive Communication (www.apc.org), which serves a coordinating function for many other member groups. They are generally advocative and try to ecumenically represent the broad interests of alternative groups. They also do much to actively promote the use of new media by pooling expertise and resources. We can also take note of Global Exchange (http://globalexchange.org/), an umbrella site dedicated to "building

people-to-people ties"; it not only has links to such broad themes as the global economy and to many ongoing campaigns, but also to sites offering "Education for Action" and "Reality Tours." Further, Action Without Borders (www.idealist.org), another civic clearinghouse, has links to 27,000 organizations, 186 ongoing campaigns, and approximately 6,800 volunteer opportunities. Other hub organizations function as portals or clearinghouses for more issue-specific domains; LabourStart (www.LabourStart.org) is one such organization.

2) Advocacy organizations are groups that provide a virtual platform for interaction, organization, communication, and mobilization. There are countless such organizations and Web sites; Attac (www.attac.org) is a typical and well-known one. While the use of the net is crucial, such groups often have local chapters and encourage face-to-face interaction as well. They actively try to develop alternative discourses, influence public opinion (not least by interfacing with the dominant mass media), and, to varying degrees, impact on policies.

3) Web organizations serve as key information centers. They can offer forums, mailing lists, networking, mobilization, and alternative information and points of view. Cammaerts uses Indymedia as his example, but there are innumerable others, such as CorporateWatch and MediaWatch.

Taking a few steps back and looking at the main attributes of such activist networks, Bennett (2003b) summarizes their characteristic features. They are largely decentralized: The organizations are in themselves fluid in terms of membership. These networks can be rapidly "reconfigured" as groups and memberships come and go. Organizationally, they tend to be "flat" and nonhierarchical: They are markedly different from traditional, top-steered organizations. Ideologically, they are thin, in the sense that the sentiment of "anti-ism" is strong. But interviews (e.g., Dahlgren and Olsson, 2007a) have revealed among activists personal discourses rich in terms of individual identity and lifestyle narratives. The connection between engagement and personal values is strong. "Ideology" here functions more at the level of shared normative perspectives on particular issues.

Finally, these networks are typified by maintaining porous boundaries with the traditional mass media. Activist networks can impact on the information provided by the mass media. Movements use micromedia (e.g., e-mail) and mesomedia net channels such as organization sites, alternative news, blogs, and e-zines. Materials from these outlets have at times been picked up by the dominant macro- (mass) media. Increasingly, also, activist media serve as journalistic sources – and continue the erosion of neat definitions of who is/is not a journalist.

For such activist organizations, their internal net-based communication activities are closely related to their loose network form; they are also relevant for the building of coalitions between them, outreach to potential participants, strategic communication with opponents, access to spectator publics, and mobilization for various actions. There are of course also drawbacks to the fluid character of these net-based SMOs: The ease of joining is matched by the ease of pulling out. It can thus be difficult at times to maintain organizational control or coherent frames of collective identity. Also, the norms of openness and participation can result in blunting the direction, agendas, and goals of the group. The very fluid nature of the groups and their memberships means that organizations can unintentionally morph into something its original members had not intended, as transitory membership results in a new profile.

There are many focus points for net-based online activism, but clearly one that mobilizes many groups, and is conducive to broad alliance-building, is what is called the anti-globalization or, more accurately, the alter-globalization movement. The neoliberal hegemony in the contemporary processes of globalization is being challenged by extensive groupings of SMOs and more institutionalized NGO global reformers. The alter-globalization movement has grown rapidly and made its presence felt in the centers of political and economic power. Given the loose, overlapping, interwoven, and at times transitory character of the networks involved, it is difficult to specify in any detail the boundaries of the alter-globalization movement. For example, some environmental and feminist groups clearly place themselves in this camp, while others do not.

From the standpoint of the dimensions of civic cultures, we can at least say that, despite considerable heterogeneity, these fluid groups share very similar sets of values in regard to their views on democracy and social justice; such commonality is expressed, for example, in the sprawling constellations of the World Social Forum (www.worldsocialforum.org) (see Smith, 2004; Waterman, 2005; De Sousa Santos, 2006), as well as in its many regional, national (Kavada, 2005), and even local spinoffs.

Within the World Social Forum we can observe the emergence of the kinds of alliances between different groups with compatible aims that Mouffe discusses (see Chapter 4). While the strengths associated with Internet technology – and the organizational ideals of democratic decenteredness – generally far outweigh the disadvantages, their long-term political efficacy cannot be ensured.

Fenton (2006, 2008) argues eloquently that, in the long run, what is at stake is if the collective political identities of resistance found within these polycentric movements can coalesce into more coherent and sustainable political projects. However, the idea of a shared political vision for an alternative future society at the global level has in today's world very much the ring of traditional, albeit leftist, politics. Yet, she concludes, while making injustices visible is vitally strategic, more effort must be spent on political interventions to make real changes, and this in turn requires ". . . a social imaginary . . . that will be flexible, inclusive, and visionary . . ." (Fenton, 2006:238).

Practices, On- and Offline

The Internet affords these and other activist groups a potent tool for political participation, providing an inexpensive, fast, and simple means for multimedia communication. The externally oriented opinion activities of advocacy groups can take a variety of forms. Along with the mass demonstrations and ongoing criticisms of national governments and transnational institutions such as the World Bank and the International Monetary Fund, one of the most common is the "permanent campaign." This is usually directed at specific global corporations. Through criticism, and argumentation, these groups attempt to generate publicity that will result in pressure leading to changes in corporate policies. A key strategy here is humor, particularly in what is called "culture jamming," which derives from traditions dating back to the 1960s. Culture jamming makes use of dominant media imagery to subvert political or commercial messages, in a kind of parody-infused semiotic warfare (see Harold, 2004; Cammaerts, 2007).

Also, political interventions into consumption, especially boycotts, have become a common strategy, that is, targeting corporations and products for reasons having to do with working conditions, child labor, or environmental issues (see, for example, Micheletti, Follestad, and Stolle, 2003; Scammel, 2003). Given the broad range of groups and strategies, one will in fact find a mix of new, alternative political practices with more traditional ones like lobbying (Norris, 2002).

One can distinguish between those online practices that are aimed at general internal cohesion, information, and collective identity, and those that are directed toward mobilizing members for various kinds of offline actions. Further, there are online activities that strive to impact on opinion and decision-making, that is, communication directed outside the network: to the general public, decision-makers, and/or economic power holders. Much of the alternative political movements can be witnessed online, via Web sites aimed at various aspects of neoliberal policies and specific corporate actors. The communicative approaches can vary, though most have a diversity of current materials, archives, and downloadable materials to be used in different ways. Civic forums for discussion are not always present, suggesting that there is still a good deal of one-way communication going on even among the alternative movements.

While an understanding of what is technically possible to do with the net is an important first step, we cannot simply assume that this is how most SMOs actually function online. Detailed empirical research on their communicative practices is just recently becoming available. In an ambitious study of seventy-four United States–based SMOs, Stein (2007) analyzed their communication practices. She notes that the sample is drawn from a listing that includes more established, traditional SMOs, rather than the looser, more fleeting (and possibly more politically radical) SMOs that exist largely online. Yet the results are telling. She identifies six basic communication functions: providing information, assisting action and mobilization, promoting dialogue, making lateral linkages with other groups, furthering internal organizational activities, and serving as an outlet for cultural production.

Keeping in mind that these SMOs vary greatly in their size, resources, organizational orientation, and networking patterns with other SMOs, she still found it interesting that, generally, the use of the net for communication remains much underutilized and underdeveloped: There is still a great untapped potential. While the performance of the SMOs was generally high on providing information and lateral links, it was significantly lower on the other functions: Only a small number actually engaged in, for example, dialogue and mobilization, and cultural production was very rare.

The net-based communication functions or strategies of SMOs can be classified in a variety of ways; Cammaerts (2006), for example, notes that along with recruiting members and sustaining the organization, movement activists face the outward communication challenges of getting attention in the mainstream media, mobilizing beyond those who already are sympathetic, overcoming obstructive social control and repression from the power centers of society, and impacting on state and public policy. Yet he and others also underscore the importance of offline interaction. While many SMOs have geographically widespread memberships, they can often be found clustered in particular places, making face-to-face contacts feasible. Various kinds of meeting, social, and cultural activities, and just informal get-togethers, play an important role in maintaining collective identities – a point sometimes lost in the emphasis on Internet use (Juris, 2005).

Conway (2004) makes the point that the World Social Forum (WSF), as a new form of public space, has a territorial existence via the scheduled large gatherings they organize, but that the movement as a whole exists in accessible cyberspace. Kavada (2005), in her analysis of the regional European Social Forum, observes that face-to-face contact in fact prevails over net-based communication, even while the latter is crucial. If attention to the net has led to a certain degree of exaggeration of its actual use, here again, the complementary nature of on- and offline communication is underscored. The net can be used precisely to bring together; certainly big demonstrations and other forms of collective action are coordinated using ICTs. Moreover, it is not surprising that a massive undertaking such as the WSF manifests tensions between its democratic visions of horizontal, participatory democracy and its practical need for more effective vertical organizational structures.

Even among SMOs with similar orientations one can find significant differences in communication strategies. For example, in a recent study (Jokiniemi, 2006) of six Web sites with explicit anti-WTO positions, it was found that there is wealth of different forms of information, and wide-ranging arguments against WTO policies, though only one of the six actually had a discussion site, namely RTMARK (www.rtmark.com), a rather radical outfit. The other sites were Public Citizen (www.citizen.org), World Development Movement (www.wdm.org.uk), Global Exchange (www.globalexchange.org), Institute of Agriculture and Trade Policy (www.tradeobservatory.org), and Peoples' Global Action (www.nadir.org). While these are not necessarily representative of the alter-globalization movement, together they do provide a sense of the diversity of communication styles involved. Another, larger study of nine anti-corporate Web sites (Rosenkrands, 2004) found that they had different priorities, and that they could be classified as either information-oriented, mobilization-oriented, or community-oriented.

So-called hacktivism represents yet another area of net activity, one that raises ethical and legal questions. As implied by the name itself, it is a merger of computer hacking with political activism (see Samuel, 2004; Jordan and Taylor, 2004). Hacktivism uses computer technology for a variety of different practices to impact on opinion, influence decisions, and even to disrupt or undermine political opponents. It can include information theft and information redirection, Web site sabotage, setting up and circulating false and subversive Web sites, or merely creating parodies, and even the spread of net viruses. A good deal of hacktivism is what Samuels (2004:129) calls performative: It is often enacted by people with backgrounds in art or theater, and aims to make a symbolic statement rather than to have a technological impact. The development of useful software and specialized codes, on the other hand, has the goal of providing tools that enhance activists' technological capacities, sometimes in ways that are legally questionable. Some political hackers underscore the difference between their activities and what is sometimes called "cracking," criminal computer activity that often does not have any political import, only economic gain or baleful cybervandalism.

Pulling together this overview of different kinds of practices among activists, we can surmise that the net constitutes an important factor in the emergence of civic cultures that potentially support radical forms of alternative politics. This has to do, of course, in part with the character of the technology, but also with how this technology interfaces with contemporary socio-cultural trends of political import. Late modern patterns of dispersion of cultural heterogeneity and the processes of individuation are seemingly more congruent with versions of alternative politics. Moreover, the decentered and contingent late modern self emerges as a key feature of the agonistic, democratic pluralism that Mouffe (2000, 2005) envisions.

NETWORKS AND CIVIC CULTURES

In considering the dimensions of civic cultures in relation to the alter-globalization movement, I would highlight a few basic points. Even a cursory examination of the kinds of civic communications present on the Internet – and the engagements and activities beyond the net to which such communications often point – will reveal a vast array of serious and highly competent political manifestations. These reflect and promote robust reconfigurations of the prevailing civic culture. There are clear implications for our six civic culture dimensions; most obviously, of course, is that the net, along with the various platforms and applications for communication, constitutes vast and easily accessible civic spaces that facilitate political participation.

Knowledge is a strongly highlighted dimension in this expansive political terrain. Most of these Web sites have some form of updates, news, analyses, links to resources, and so on; information-sharing tools are common (including Internet skills), and there is often a climate of self-help that suggests learning by both doing and studying. On many of these Web sites there is not only a sharing of information and experience, but also coverage of current events – often, of course, specific to the focus of the Web site. Ambitious forms of vigorous and serious alternative journalism are also a part of this terrain, as are sites dedicated to critically monitoring the mainstream media (e.g., www.mediachannel.org and www.fair.org) and sites that promote not only critical views but also media skills (www.alternet.org). It seems that there is both a strong emphasis on practically useful as well as analytic knowledge that implicitly and not infrequently explicitly challenges the dominant frames of reference and lines of interpretation that are found in the mass media. In many cases, though not all, the knowledge and competence derive "horizontally," that is, they are shared among engaged citizens, and have less of a hierarchical, professional register.

The actors behind the Web sites have widely different profiles; they range from NGOs and foundation-sponsored nonprofit organizations to social movements, political activist groups, labor unions, church groups, professional collectivities from various fields, and even, in some cases, commercial entrepreneurs who believe that business can be combined with progressive social values (e.g., www.workingforchange.com). That most of these Web sites and those they link to support general democratic values is obvious, but they clearly also encourage values that are congruent with specifically participatory versions of democracy. The insistence on activism, engagement, networking, community, and so on, point to values that differ markedly from those found in the mainstream media, where collective civic and political action outside the formal political arena is usually treated with considerable restraint, if not scepticism.

The emphasis on networking, information sharing, and alliance-building also underscores the sense of trust and affinity that is central to these civic cultures. There is a strong neorepublican tone that strives to promote a climate of solidarity and trust among activists, a feeling of commonality between those who in various ways are struggling for progressive social change. One is continuously invited to join these communities of activists. At the Institute for Global Communication (IGC) (www.igc.org), which functions as a hub organization, there are in turn links to PeaceNet, EcoNet, WomensNet, and Anti-racismNet, suggesting sets of alliances predicated on shared values and political horizons.

In terms of practices, there are of course many that are advocated. It could be argued that knowledge and competency development are indeed among the foremost practices here. A list of the kinds of practices fostered would be both long and unsurprising; we could simply summarize by saying that the kind of citizenship envisioned on these Web sites is one that is constituted *in and through* practices: Democracy is something that is *done,* enacted by citizens in various contexts. This sense of doing democracy is obviously integral to the kinds of identities found. It is through the many forms of civic activity in cooperation with others that one constructs and maintains citizen identities. One can sense a classic dialectic hovering between the lines on many of these Web sites: They intend to provide the knowledge and competencies needed to participate; the thus-empowered citizen engages in practice, leading to new knowledge and competencies – as well as a strengthened civic identity.

The use of the net helps create new conditions for democratic engagement, and citizenship as social agency has found new forms of expression in this milieu. The sense of empowerment that *can* follow from net activism supports newer forms of citizen identity. These are emerging in tandem with newer ways of enacting democratic politics. Not least, these civic cultures are increasingly global in character. At the same time, the loose character of membership suggests that civic identity itself is not necessarily anchored in organizations per se. We may speculate that some forms of civic identity are more shaped by issue clusters or ideology – while reciprocally supported via the interplay with the other dimensions of civic cultures. Knowledge and competencies are being shared and spread through activist networks. The activist networking continually reiterates core democratic values, which in turn support the civic affinity needed to participate in network-based politics; organizational, communicative, political, and political practices in turn can further solidify identity and foster agency. Yet, the upward surge of civic identities here clearly has delimiting sociological parameters: The numbers remain relatively small, though the political efficacy may indeed be proportionally much larger. And of course there are also many strong political actors on the net who espouse very different kinds of politics.

MEDIA GENERATIONS

At one level it is self-evident that the future of democracy lays in its youth – such has always been the case. Yet today, the factor of generation takes on special importance, because many of the trends we see in regard to media use, political horizons, and democratic participation are shaped by changes that have to do with specific patterns among younger age cohorts. In the United States, Zukin, Keefer, Andoliona, Jenkins, and Della Carpini (2006), in their research, summarize some key features in regard to what they call the Dot.Net generation, those between fifteen and twenty-eight years of age. In keeping with other research findings, the authors conclude that this generation clearly manifests less involvement in traditional politics. They also find that Dot.Nets generally view the corporations and the private sector as having more influence over their lives than government or the public sector; for these young people, market mechanisms thus tend to deflect political participation, because such centers of social power are seemingly beyond democratic accountability. Further, these younger citizens are less likely than older generations to assert that democracy involves obligations, and they manifest less interpersonal trust than their elders. These findings, I would underscore, make sense in the light of what was discussed in Chapter 1 about the altered relations of power between the state, capital, and labor. At the same time, this age cohort is the first one to grow up with the Internet and the other ICTs as part of their normal environment, and their competencies here not surprisingly surpass older generations.

From the standpoint of civic cultures, these patterns are troubling. While the skills and potential practices are fine-honed in regard to the net and other ICT spaces, the motivation to seek political knowledge, and the values, trust, and identities necessary to promote and sustain political participation, are weak. As mentioned previously, we do not have a firm grasp of the number of young people involved in online political engagement, but all indications are that it remains a small, if at times vocal and effective minority. In short, they have the skills and tools, yet a big majority lack the motivation. However, Zukin et al. (2006) also observe that this cohort continues to engage in civic voluntary work almost as much as their elders; we can assume that these kinds of activities may at times be at least proto-political in character, though these young people tend to not define such engagement as "political" in any sense. Such social involvement may at least serve to leave the door a little ajar, allowing perhaps for the continual evolution of perceptions about the political and civic practices. At the same time, it also reminds us of the need to rethink and reframe the way we analytically approach democracy. The established horizons seemingly lead us into a wilderness where we lose our bearings.

Findings such as these illustrate in a concrete manner the fundamental changes confronting democracy. These patterns suggest that deep structural, social, and cultural transformations are making themselves felt in how young people navigate the world and their lives, and this has profound implications for participation. We can only speculate on the profile of the next age cohort: If we fast-forward fifteen years, what will democracy look like for these citizens? What kinds of civic cultures will be operative? The complexities of successful democracy extend in many directions, and I can only reiterate the importance of grasping democracy as a historically contingent undertaking, and trying to keep abreast of the basic conditions that shape the way it functions, not least the development of the media.

Robert Dahl, one of the senior statesmen of democracy theory, has called for a sort of reformation of democracy, enabling it to function better in a world shaped by globalization and new electronic media:

> [O]ne of the imperative needs of democratic countries is to improve citizens' capacities to engage intelligently in political life . . . I don't mean to suggest that the institutions of civic education should be abandoned. But I do believe that in the years to come these older institutions will need to be enhanced by new means for civic education, political participation, information, and deliberation that draw creatively on the array of techniques and technologies available in the twenty-first century. We have barely begun to think seriously about these possibilities. . . . (Dahl, 1998:187–188)

He wrote that a decade ago, yet it has lost none of its relevance. Today the importance of the media for civic cultures and political participation continues to grow; media policy and efforts to enhance media as civic resources become all the more crucial. Despite still deep digital divides around the world, vast numbers of citizens – via the Web and net-linked mobile phones equipped with audiovisual as well as textual capacities – are in a position to politically engage themselves through the media matrix in issues that range all across the social terrain. They can support, modify, and challenge the information and frames of reference of main-stream media and established power centers; they can develop counter-public spheres and mobilize opinion and action in local contexts as well as across continents.

Tomorrow's media technologies will no doubt be still more breath-taking. Yet, at bottom, democracy simply cannot exist without input from its citizens – their participation. The character and forms of par-ticipation are evolving but can never be taken for granted. We cannot know what kinds of media-based civic cultures will develop in the future, but the struggle for democracy, for present and future generations, will remain inexorably political.

References

Abramsom, Bram Dov (2002) "Internet globalization and the political economy of infrastructure." In Greg Elmer, ed. *Critical Perspectives on the Internet*. Lanham, MD: Rowman & Littlefield, pp. 183–202.

Adler, Richard P. (2005) "What do we mean by 'civic engagement'?" *Journal of Transformative Education* 3(3) 236–253.

Agre, Philip E. (2004) "The practical republic: Social skills and the progress of citizenship." In A. Feenberg and D. Barney, eds. *Community in the Digital Age*. Lanham, MD: Rowman & Littlefield, pp. 201–223.

Alasuutari, Pertti, ed. (1999) *Rethinking the Media Audience*. London: Sage.

Alexander, Jeffey C. (2006) *The Civil Sphere*. New York: Oxford University Press.

Allan, Stuart (2004) *News Culture*, 2nd ed. Maidenhead, UK: Open University Press.

Allan, Stuart (2006) *Online Journalism*. Maidenhead, UK: Open University Press, pp. 67–82.

Allen, David S. (2005) *Democracy, Inc.: The Press and the Law in the Corporate Rationalization of the Public Sphere*. Urbana-Champagne: University of Illinois Press.

Allen, Robert, ed. (2004) *The Television Studies Reader*. New York: Routledge.

Almond, Gabriel and Sidney Verba (1963) *The Civic Culture*. Princeton: Princeton University Press.

Almond, Gabriel and Sidney Verba, eds. (1980) *The Civic Culture Revisited*. Princeton, NJ: Princeton University Press.

Altheide, David and Snow, Robert. (1991) *Media Worlds in the Post-Journalism Era*. New York: Aldine de Gruyter.

Amoore, Louise, ed. (2005) *The Global Resistance Reader*. London: Routledge.

Anderson, David A. and Michael Cornfield, eds. (2003) *The Civic Web: Online Politics and Democratic Values*. Lanham, MD: Rowman & Littlefield.

Andrejevic, Mark (2004) *Reality TV: The Work of Being Watched*. Lanham, MD: Rowman & Littlefield.

Arendt, Hannah (1958) *The Human Condition*. Chicago: University of Chicago Press.

Armitage, John, ed. (2000) *Paul Virilio: From Modernism to Hypermodernism*. London: Sage.

Armitage, John and Roberts, Joanne, eds. (2003) *Living with Cyberspace*. New York and London: Continuum.

Aronowitz, Stanley and H. Gautney, eds. (2003) *Implicating Empirer: Globalization and Resistance in the 21st Century*. New York: Basic Books.

Artz, Lee and Yahya R. Kamalipour, eds. (2003) *The Globalization of Corporate Media Hegemony*. Albany: State University of New York Press.

Asen, Robert and Daniel C. Brouwer, eds. (2001) *Counterpublics and the State*. Albany: State University of New York Press.

Atton, Chris (2002) *Alternative Media*. London: Sage.

Atton, Chris (2005) *An Alternative Internet: Radical Media, Politics and Creativity*. New York: Columbia University Press.

Atton, Chris and Emma Wickenden (2005) "Sourcing routines and representation in alternative journalism: A case study approach." *Journalism Research* **6**(3): 347–359.

Axford, Barry and Richard Huggins, eds. (2001) *New Media and Politics*. London: Sage.

Bagdikian, Ben (2005) *The New Media Monopoly*. Boston: Beacon Press.

Baily, Olga, Bart Cammaerts, and Nico Carpentier (2007) *Undertsanding Alternative Media*. Maidenhead, UK: Open University Press.

Bakardjieva, Maria (2005) *Internet Society: The Internet in Everyday Life*, London: Sage.

Baker, C. Edwin (2002) *Media, Markets and Democracy*. New York: Cambridge University Press.

Baker, C. Edwin (2006) *Media Concentration and Democracy: Why Ownership Matters*. New York: Cambridge University Press.

Ball, Philip (2005) *Critical Mass: How One Thing Leads to Another*. London: Arrow Books.

Barber, Benjamin (1984) *Strong Democracy: Participatory Politics for a New Age*. Berkeley: University of California Press.

Barber, Benjamin (2004) *Fear's Empire: War, Terrorism, and Democracy*. New York: Norton.

Barber, Benjamin (2008) *Consumed: How Markets Corrupt Children, Infantilize Adults, and Swallow Citizens Whole*. New York: Norton.

Barnett, Clive (2003) *Culture and Democracy: Media, Space and Representation*. Edinburgh: Edinburgh University Press.

Barnett, Clive and Murray Low, eds. (2004) *The Spaces of Democracy: Geographical Perspectives on Citizenship, Participation and Representation*. London: Sage.

Barney, David. (2004) *The Network Society*. Cambridge: Polity Press.

Barnhurst, Kevin (1998) "Politics in the fine meshes: Young citizens, power and media." *Media, Culture and Society* **20**(2): 201–218.

Barnhurst, Kevin (2002) "News geography and monopoly: The form of reports on US newspaper Internet sites." *Journalism Studies* **3**(4): 477–489.

Barnhurst, Kevin (2003) "Subjective states: Narratives of citizenship among young Europeans." *Multilingua* **22**: 133–68.

Bauman, Zygmunt (1999) *In Search of Politics*. Cambridge: Polity Press.

Bauman, Zygmunt (2000a) *Globalization. The Human Consequences*. New York: Columbia University Press.

Bauman, Zygmunt (2000b) *Liquid Modernity*. Cambridge: Polity Press.

Bauman, Zygmunt (2005) *Liquid Life*. Cambridge: Polity Press.

Bauman, Zygmunt (2006) *Liquid Fear*. Cambridge: Polity Press.

Beck, Ulrich (1998) *Democracy Without Enemies*. Cambridge: Polity Press.

Beck, Ulrich (2005) *Power in the Global Age.* Cambridge: Polity Press.

Beck, Ulrich (2007) *Cosmopolitan Europe.* Cambridge: Polity Press.

Beck, Ulrich and Elisabeth Beck-Gernsheim (2002) *Individualization: Institutionalized Individualism and its Social and Political Consequences.* London; Thousand Oaks, CA; and New Delhi: Sage.

Beckerman, Gal (2003) "Emerging alternatives – edging away from anarchy: Inside the IndyMedia collective, passion vs pragmatism." *Columbia Journalism Review* no. 5, Sept./Oct., www.cjr.org.

Beiner, Ronald, ed. (1995) *Theorizing Citizenship.* Albany: State University of New York Press.

Benhabib, Seyla (1992) "Models of public space: Hannah Arendt, the liberal tradition, and Jürgen Habermas." In C. Calhoun, ed. *Habermas and the Public Sphere.* Cambridge, MA: MIT Press.

Benhabib, Seyla, ed. (1996) *Democracy and Difference.* Princeton, NJ: Princeton University Press.

Benhabib, Seyla (2004) *The Rights of Others: Aliens, Residents and Citizens.* Cambridge: Cambridge University Press.

Benkler, Yochai (2006) *The Wealth of Networks: How Social Production Transforms Markets and Freedom.* New Haven, CT: Yale University Press.

Bennett, W. Lance (1998) "The uncivic culture: Communication, identity, and the rise of lifestyle politics." *Political Science and Politics* 31(4): 741–761.

Bennett, W. Lance (2003a) "Lifestyle politics and citizen-consumers: Identity, communication and political action in late modern society." In John Corner and Dick Pels, eds. *Media and Political Style: Essays on Representation and Civic Culture.* London: Sage, pp. 137–150.

Bennett, W. Lance (2003b) "New media power: The Internet and global activism." In N. Couldry and J. Currans, eds. *Contesting Media Power.* Lanham, MD: Rowman & Littlefield, pp. 17–37.

Bennett, W. Lance (2004a) "Global media and politics: transnational communicatrion regimes and civic cultures." *Annual Review of Political Science* 7:125–148.

Bennett, W. Lance (2004b) "Communicating global activisim." In van de Donk, et al., eds. *Cyberprotest: New Media, Citizens and Social Movements.* London: Routledge, pp. 123–146.

Bennett, W. Lance (2006) *News: The Politics of Illusion,* 7th ed. New York: Longman.

Bennett, W. Lance (2007a) "Civic learning in changing democracies: Challenges for citizenship and civic education." In Peter Dahlgren, ed. *Young Citizens and New Media: Learning for Democracy.* New York: Routledge.

Bennett, W. Lance, ed. (2007b) *Civic Life Online: Learning How Digital Media Can Engage Youth.* Cambridge, MA: MIT Press. Available online: http://mitpress.mit.edu/catalog/browse/browse.asp?btype=6&;serid=170

Bennett, W. Lance and Robert Entman, eds. (2001) *Mediated Politics in the Future of Democracy.* Cambridge: Cambridge University Press.

Bennet, W. Lance, Regina G. Lawrence, and Steven Livingston (2007) *When News Fails: Political Power and the News Media From Iraq to Katrina.* Chicago: University of Chicago Press.

Bennulf, M. and Hedberg, P. (1999) *Utanför demokratin. Om det minskade valdeltagandets sociala och politiska rötter. I Valdeltagande I förändring.* Stockholm: SOU, p. 132.

Bentivegna, Sara (2006) "Rethinking politics in the world of ICTs." *European Journal of Communication* **21**(3): 331–343.

Berker, Thomas, Maren Hartmann, Yves Punie, and Katie J. Ward, eds. (2006) *Domestication of Media and Technology*. Maidenhead, UK: Open University Press.

Berman, Jerry and Deidre K. Mulligan (2003) "Issue advocacy in the age of the Internet." In David A. Anderson and Michael Cornfield, eds. *The Civic Web: Online Politics and Democratic Values*. Lanham, MD: Rowman and Littlefield, pp. 77–93.

Bianchi, Stefania (2004) "EU: Corporate lobbying grows." Available online: www.globalpolicy.org/socecon/tncs/2004/1222murky/lobby.htm.

Bimber, Bruce (2003) *Information and American Democracy: Technology in the Evolution of Political Power*. New York: Cambridge University Press.

Bimber, Bruce and R. Davis (2003) *Campaigning Online: The Internet in U.S. Elections*. New York: Oxford University Press.

Bird, S. Elizabeth (2003) *The Audience in Everyday Life*. New York: Routledge.

Blaug, R. (1999) *Democracy, Real and Ideal: Discourse Ethics and Radical Politics*. Albany: State University of New York Press.

Blumler, Jay and Gurevitch, Michael (1995) *The Crisis of Public Communication*. London: Routledge.

Boczkowski, Pablo (2005) *Digitizing the News: Innovation in Online Newspapers*. Cambridge, MA: MIT Press.

Boczkowski, Pablo J. and José A. Ferris (2005) "Multi media, convergent processes, and divergent products: Organizational innovation in digital media production at a European firm." *The Annals of the American Academy of Political and Social Science* **597**: 32–47.

Boggs, Carl (2000) *The End of Politics: Corporate Power and the Decline of the Public Sphere*. New York: Guilford Press.

Bohman, James. (1996) *Public Deliberation: Pluralism, Complexity and Democracy*. Cambridge, MA: MIT Press.

Bohman, James (2000) "The division of labor in democratic discourse: Media, experts, and deliberative democracy." In Simone Chambers and Anne Costain, eds. *Deliberation, Democracy, and the Media*. Lanham, MD: Rowman & Littlefield.

Bohman, James (2004) "Expanding dialogue: The Internet, public sphere, and transnational democracy." In Peter M. Shane, ed. *Democracy Online*. London: Routledge, pp. 47–61.

Bohman, James (2007) "Democratizing the transnational polity – The European Union and the presuppositions of democracy." Available at: www.reconproject.eu/main.php/RECON_wp_0702.pdf?fileitem=5456958.

Boler, Megan, ed. (2008) *Digital Media and Democracy*. Cambridge, MA: MIT Press.

Bolin, Göran (2007) "The politics of cultural production: The journalistic field, television, and politics." In K. Reigert, ed. *Politcotainment: Television's Take on the Real*. New York: Peter Lang Publishers, pp. 59–81.

Bollier, David (1995) *Public Assets, Private Profits: Reclaiming the American Commons in an Age of Market Enclosure*. Washington, D.C.: New American Foundation.

Boltanski, Luc (1999) *Distant Suffering: Morality, Media and Politics*. Cambridge: Cambridge University Press.

Borjesson, Kristina, ed. (2002) *Into the Buzzsaw: Leading Journalists Expose the Myth of a Free Press*. Amhurst, NY: Prometheus Books.

Brennan, Theresa (2003) *Globalization and Its Terrors: Daily Life in the West*. London: Routledge.

Brüggerman, Michael (2005) "How the EU constructs the European public sphere: Seven strategies of information policy." *Javnost/The Public* 12(2): 57–74.

Brundin, Pia (2008) *Politics on the Net: NGO Practices and Experiences*. Dissertation, Dept. of Social Sciences, Örebro University, Örebro, Sweden.

Buckingham, David, ed. (2007) *Youth, Identity and the Digital Media*. Cambridge, MA: MIT Press. Available online: http://mitpress.mit.edu/catalog/browse/browse.asp?btype=6&;serid=170

Calavita, Marco (2005) *Apprehending Politics: News Media and Individual Political Development*. Albany: State University of New York Press.

Cammaerts, Bart (2006) "Media and communication strategies of globalised activists: Beyond media-centric thinking." In B. Cammaerts and N. Carpentier, eds. *Reclaiming the Media: Communication Rights and Expanding Democratic Media Roles*. Bristol, UK: Intellect, pp. 265–288.

Cammaerts, Bart (2007) "Jamming the political: Beyond counter-hegemonic practices." Continuum: *Journal of Media and Cultural Studies* 21(1): 71–90.

Cammaerts, Bart (2008) *Transnational Civil Society Activism and Their Media Strategies*. Lanham, MD: Lexington Books/Rowman & Littlefield.

Cammaerts, Bart and Leo van Audenhove (2003) *Transnational Social Movements, the Network Society and Unbounded Notions of Citizenship*. Amsterdam: ASCoR, University of Amsterdam.

Cammaerts, Bart and Leo van Audenhove (2005) "Online political debate, unbounded citizenship, and the problematic nature of a transnational public sphere." *Political Communication* 22: 179–196.

Cammaerts, Bart and Nico Carpentier, eds. (2006) *Reclaiming the Media: Communication Rights and Democratic Media Roles*. Bristol, UK: Intellect Books.

Campbell, Scott W. (2007) "A cross-cultural comparison of perceptions and uses of mobile telephony." *New Media and Society* 9(2): 343–363.

Cardosa, Gustavo (2006) *The Media in the Network Society: Browsing, News, Filters and Citizenship*. Lisbon: Centre for Research and Studies in Sociology.

Carpentier, Nico (2007) "Coping with the agrophobic media professional." In Bart Caemmerts and Nico Carpentier, eds. *Reclaiming the Media: Communication Rights and Democratic Media Roles*. Bristol, UK: Intellect Books, pp. 157–175.

Carpentier, Nico and Bart Cammaerts (2006) "Hegemony, democracy, agonism and journalism: An interview with Chantal Mouffe." *Journalism Studies* 7(6): 964–975.

Cashmore, Ellies (2006) *Celebrity Culture*. London: Routledge.

Castells, Manuel (1998) *The Power of Identity*. London: Blackwell.

Castells, Manuel (2000) *The Rise of the Network Society*, 2nd ed. Oxford: Blackwell.

Chadwick, Andrew (2006) *Internet Politics: States, Citizens and New Communication Technologies*. New York: Oxford University Press.

Chambers, Simone (2000) "A culture of publicity." In Simone Chambers and Anne Costain, eds. *Deliberation, Democracy and the Media*. Lanham, MD: Rowman & Littlefield.

Chambers, Simone (2002) "A critical theory of civil society." In S. Chambers and W. Kymlicka, eds. *Alternative Conceptions of Civil Society*. Princeton, NJ: Princeton University Press, pp. 90–110.

Chambers, Simone and Will Kymlicka, eds. (2002) *Alternative Conceptions of Civil Society*. Princeton, NJ: Princeton University Press.

Chester, Jeff (2007) *Digital Destiny: New Media and the Future of Democracy*. New York: New Press.

Chouliaraki, Lilie (2006) *The Spectatorship of Suffering*. London: Sage.

Clarke, Paul Barry (1996) *Deep Citizenship*. London: Pluto.

Clift, James (2003) "E-democracy: Lessons from Minnesota." In D. A. Anderson and M. Corfield, eds. *The Civic Web: Online Politics and Democratic Values*, pp. 157–165 Lanham, MD: Rowman & Littlefield.

Cohen, Jean and Andrew Arato (1992) *Civil Society and Political Theory*. Cambridge, MA: MIT Press.

Coleman, Stephen (2005) "The lonely citizen: Indirect representation in an age of networks." *Political Communication* 22(2): 197–214.

Coleman, Stephen (2006) "How the other half votes: Big Brother viewers and the 2005 British General Election Campaign." *International Journal of Cultural Studies* 9(4): 457–479.

Coleman, Stephen (2007a) "From big brother to Big Brother: Two faces of interactive engagement." In Peter Dahlgren, ed. *Young Citizens and New Media: Learning for Democratic Participation*. New York: Routledge, pp. 21–39.

Coleman, Stephen (2007b) "How democracies have disengaged from young people." In Brian Loader, ed. *Young Citizens in the Digital Age: Political Engagement, Young People and New Media*. London: Routledge, pp. 166–185.

Conway, Janet (2004) "Citizenship in a time of empire: The World Social Forum as a new public space." *Citizenship Studies* 8(4): 367–381.

Cooke, Lynne (2005) "A visual convergence of print, television and the Internet: Charting 40 years of design change in news presentation." *New Media and Society* 7(1): 22–46.

Cormode, Graham and Balachander Krishnamurthy (2008) "Key differences between Web 1.0 and Web 2.0." *First Monday* 13(6). Available online: www.uic.edu/htbin/cgiwrap/bin/ojs/index.php/fm/article/view/2125/1972.

Corner, John and Dick Pels, eds. (2003) *Media and the Restyling of Politics*. London: Sage.

Cornog, Evann (2005) "Let's blame the readers." *Columbia Journalism Review* Jan/Feb. www.cjr.org/issues/2005/1/cornog-readers.asp?printerfriendly (printed 2005-11-10).

Corrigan, Peter (1997) *The Sociology of Consumption*. London: Sage.

Cornfield, Michael (2004) *Politics Moves Online: Campaigning and the Internet*. New York: The Century Foundation.

Cottle, Simon, ed. (2003) *News, Public Relations and Power*. London: Sage.

Cottle, Simon and Mudha Rai (2006) "Between display and deliberation: Analyzing TV news as communicative architecture." *Media, Culture and Society* 28(2): 163–189.

Couldry, Nick (2000) *The Place of Media Power*. London: Routledge.

Couldry, Nick (2004) "The productive 'consumer' and the dispersed 'citizen.'" *International Journal of Cultural Studies* 7(1): 21–32.

Couldry, Nick and Anna McCarthy, eds. (2004) *Mediaspace: Place, Scale and Culture in a Media Sage*. London: Routledge.

Couldry, Nick, Sonia Livingstone, and Tim Markham (2007) *Media Consumption and Public Engagement: Beyond the Presumption of Attention*. Basingstoke, UK: Intellect.

Croiteau, David and William Hoynes (2001) *The Business of Media: Corporate Media and the Public Interest*. Thousand Oaks, CA: Pine Forge Press.

Curran, James (2002) *Media Power*. London: Routledge.

Curran, James (2003). "Global journalism: A case study of the Internet." In N. Couldry and J. Curran, eds. *Contesting Media Power: Alternative Media in a Networked World*. Oxford: Rowman & Littlefield, pp. 227–242.

Dahl, Robert (1998) *On Democracy*. New Haven, CT, and London: Yale University Press.

Dahlberg, Lincoln (2001) "The Internet and democratic discourse: Exploring the prospects of online deliberation forums." *Information, Communication and Society* 4(4): 615–633.

Dahlberg, Lincoln (2007) "Re-thinking the fragmentation of the cyber-public: From consensus to contestation." *New Media and Society*.

Dahlberg, Lincoln and Euginia Siapera, eds. (2007) *Radical Democracy and the Internet*. Basingstoke, UK: Palgrave Macmillan.

Dahlgren, Peter (1995) *Television and the Public Sphere*. London: Sage.

Dahlgren, Peter (1997) "Cultural studies and media research." In J. Corner, P. Schlesinger, and R. Silverstone, eds. *An International Handbook of Media Research*. London: Routledge.

Dahlgren, Peter, ed. (2007) *Young Citizens and New Media: Learning for Democracy*. London: Routledge.

Dahlgren, Peter and Colin Sparks, eds. (1992) *Journalism and Popular Culture*. London: Sage.

Dahlgren, Peter and Tobias Olsson (2007a) "From public spheres to civic cultures: Young citizens' Internet use." In Richard Butsch, ed. *Media and Public Spheres*. Basingstoke, UK: Palgrave Macmillan, pp. 198–211.

Dahlgren, Peter and Tobias Olsson (2007b) "Young activists, political horizons, and the Internet: Adapting the net to one's purposes." In Brian Loader, ed. *Young Citizens in the Digital Age: Political Engagement, Young People and New Media*. London: Routledge.

Dahlgren, Peter and Tobias Olsson (2007c) "Facilitating political participation: Young citizens, internet and civic cultures." In S. Livingstone and K. Drotner, eds. *The International Handbook of Children, Media and Culture*. London: Sage.

Dahlgren, Peter and Tobias Olsson, eds. (2008) *Young Citizens, ICTs and Democracy*. Gothenborg, Sweden: Nordicom.

Danaher, Kevin and Jason Mark (2003) *Insurrection: Citizen Challenges to Corporate Power*. London: Routledge.

Davis, Aeron (2002) *Public Relations Democracy: Politics, Public Relations and the Mass Media in Britain*. Manchester, UK: Manchester University Press.

Dayan, Daniel (2005) "Mothers, midwives and abortionists: Genealogy, obstetrics, audiences and publics." In S. Livingstone, ed. *Audiences and Publics: When Cultural Engagement Matters for the Public Sphere*. Bristol, UK: Intellect, pp. 43–76.

Dean, Jodi, Jon W. Anderson, and Geert Lovink, eds. (2006) *Reformatting Politics: Information Technology and Global Civil Society.* London: Routledge.

Delanty, Gerard (2000) *Citizenship in a Global Age.* Buckingham, UK: Open University Press.

Della Porta, Donatella and Sidney Tarrow, eds. (2004) *Transnational Protest and Global Activism.* Lanham, MD: Rowman & Littlefield.

Delli Carpini, Michael and Scott Keeter (1996) *What Americans Know About Politics and Why It Matters.* New Haven, CT: Yale University Press.

Delli Carpini, Michael X., F. L. Cook, and L. R. Jacobs (2004) "Public deliberation, discursive participation, and citizen engagement: A review of empirical literature." *Annual Review of Political Science* 2004, 315–344.

Delwiche, Aaron (2005) "Agenda-setting, opion leadership, and the world of web logs." *First Monday* 10(12). Available online: http://firstmonday.org/issues/issue10_12/delwiche/index.html.

Demers, David (2002) *Global Media: Menace or Messiah?* Cresskill, NJ: Hampton Press.

De Sousa Santos, Boaventura (2006) *The Rise of the Global Left: The World Social Forum and Beyond.* London: Zed Books.

Deuze, Mark (2001) "Online journalism: Modeling the first generation of news media on the World Wide Web." *First Monday:* www.firstmonday.org/issues/issue6_10/deuze/index.htm.

Deuze, Mark (2004) "What is multimedia journalism?" *Journalism Studies* 5(2): 139–152.

Deuze, Mark (2007) "Convergence culture in the creative industries." *International Journal of Cultural Studies* 10(2): 243–263.

Dewey, John (1923) *The Public and its Problems.* Chicago: The Swallow Press.

van Dijk, Jan A. G. M. (2005) *The Deepening Divide: Inequality in the Information Age.* London: Sage.

Domhoff, G. William (2005) *Who Rules America? Power, Politics and Social Change* 5th ed. Columbus, OH: McGraw-Hill Higher Education.

Domke, David (2004) *God Willing? Political Fundamentalism in the White House, the "War on Terror," and the Echoing Press.* London: Pluto Press.

van de Donk, Wim, Brian D. Loader, Paul Nixon, and Dieter Rucht, eds. (2004) *Cyberprotest: New Media, Citizens and Social Movements.* London: Routledge.

Dovey, J. (2000) *Freakshow: First Person Media and Factual Television.* London: Pluto Press.

Downey, John (2006) "Is there a European public sphere?" *European Journal of Communication* 21(2): 165–187.

Downey, John (2007) "Participation and/or deliberation? The Internet as a tool for achieving radical democratic aims." In Lindoln Dahlberg and Euginia Siapera, eds. *Radical Democracy and the Internet.* Basingstoke, UK: Palgrave Macmillan, pp. 108–127.

Downie, Leonard, Jr. and Robert G. Kaiser (2003) *The News About the News.* New York: Vintage.

Downing, John (2000) *Radical Media: Rebellious Communication and Social Movements.* London: Sage.

Downing, John (2003) "The Independent Media Center Movement and the anarchist socialist tradition." In Nick Couldry and James Curren, eds. *Contesting Media*

Power: Alternative Media in a Networked World. Lanham, MD: Rowman & Littlefield, pp. 243–258.

Doyle, Gillian (2006) "Financial news journalism: A post-Enron analysis of approaches towards economic and financial news production in the UK." *Journalism* 7(2): 238–254.

Drotner, Kirsten (2005) "Media on the move: Personalised media and the transformation of publicness." In S. Livingstone, ed. *Audiences and Publics: When Cultural Engagement Matters for the Public Sphere*. Bristol, UK: Intellect.

Dryzek, John S. (1990) *Discursive Democracy: Politics, Policy and Political Science*. Cambridge: Cambridge University Press.

Dryzek, John S. (2000) *Deliberative Democracy and Beyond*. Oxford: Oxford University Press.

Edwards, B., M. W. Foley, and M. Diani, eds. (2001) *Beyond Tocqueville: Civil Society and the Social Capital Debate in Comparative Perspective*. Hanover, NH, and London: University Press of New England.

Edwards, Michael (2004) *Civil Society*. Cambridge: Polity Press.

Ehrenberg, John (1999) *Civil Society: The Critical History of an Idea*. New York: NYU Press.

Eliasoph, Nina (1998) *Avoiding Politics: How Americans Produce Apathy in Everyday Life*. Cambridge: Cambridge University Press.

Elliott, Anthony and Charles Lemert (2006) *The New Individualism: The Emotional Costs of Globalization*. London: Routledge.

Ellis, John (2000) *Seeing Things: Television in the Age of Uncertainty*. London and New York: I. B. Taunis Publishers.

Eriksen, Erik Oddvas (2006) "Conceptualizing the EU public sphere." Available online: http://ideas.repec.org/p/erp/arenax/p0020.html.

Eriksen, Erik Oddvar and John Erik Fossum (2005) "Europe in transformation – How to reconstitute democracy in Europe?" Available online: http://www.reconproject.eu/main.php/RECON_wp_0701.pdf?fileitem=5456091.

Eschele, Catherine (2001) *Global Democracy, Social Movements, and Feminism*. Boulder, CO: Westview Press.

Eschele, Catherine and Bice Maiguashca, eds. (2005) *Critical Theory, Intenational Relations, and the "Anti-Globalisation Movement."* London: Routledge.

Etzioni, Amitai (1993) *The Spirit of Community: The Reinvention of American Society*. New York: Simon and Schuster.

Everett, Anna (2007) *Learning Race and Ethnicity: Youth and Digital Media*. Cambridge, MA: MIT Press. Available online: http://mitpress.mit.edu/catalog/browse/browse.asp?btype=6&;serid=170

Ewen, Stuart (1996) *PR! A Social History of Spin*. New York: Basic Books.

Fallows, James (1997) *Breaking the News*. New York: Vintage Books.

Feenberg, Andrew and David Barney, eds. (2004) *Community in the Digital Age*. Lanham, MD: Rowman & Littlefield.

Fenton, Natalie (2006) "Contesting global capital, new media, solidarity, and the role of the social imaginary." In Bart Cammaerts and Nico Carpentier, eds. *Reclaiming the Media: Communication Rights and Democratic Media Roles*. Bristol, UK: Intellect Books, pp. 225–242.

Fenton, Natalie (2008) "Mediating solidarity." *Global Media and Communication* **4**(1): 37–57.

Fenton, Natalie and John Downey (2003) "Counter public spheres and global modernity." *Javnost/The Public* **10**(1): 15–32.

Fenton, Tom (2005) *Bad News: The Decline of Reporting, the Business of News, and the Danger to Us All.* New York: HarperCollins.

Fishkin, J. (1991) *Democracy and Deliberation.* New Haven, CT: Yale University Press.

Fiske, John (1988) *Television Culture.* London: Routledge.

Fossum, John Erik and Philp Schlesinger, eds. (2007) *The European Union and the Public Sphere: A Communicative Space in the Making?* London: Routledge.

Fornäs, Johan (1995) *Cultural Theory and Late Modernity.* London: Sage.

Frank, Thomas (2000) *One Market Under God.* New York: Vintage.

Franklin, Bob (2004) *Packaging Politics: Political Communication in Britain's Media Democracy,* 2nd ed. London: Edward Arnold.

Fraser, Nancy (1992) "Rethinking the public sphere: A contribution to the crtitique of actually existing democracy." In Craig Calhoun, ed. *Habermas and the Public Sphere.* Boston: MIT Press, pp. 109–142.

Fraser, Nancy (2007) "Transnationalizing the public sphere: On the legitimacy and efficacy of public opinion in a post-Westphalian world." In Seyla Benhabib, Ian Shapiro, and Danilo Petranovic, eds. *Identities, Affiliations and Allegiances.* New York: Cambridge University Press, pp. 45–66.

Fraser, Nancy and Axel Honneth (2003) *Redistribution of Recognition? A Political-Philosophical Exchange.* London: Verso.

Friedland, Lewis A., Thomas Hove, and Hernando Rojas (2006) "The networked public sphere." *Javnost/The Public* **13**(4): 5–26.

Fung, Anthony (2002) "One city, two systems: Democracy in an electronic chat room in Hong Kong." *Javnost/The Public* **9**(2): 77–94.

Galloway, Alexander R. (2005) "Global networks and the effects on culture." *The Annals of the American Academy of Political and Social Science* **597**: 19–31.

Galston, William A. (2003) "If political fragmentation is the problem, is the Internet the solution?" In D. A. Anderson and M. Cornfield, eds. *The Civic Web.* Lanham, MD: Rowman and Littlefield, pp. 35–44.

Gamson, William A. (1992) *Talking Politics.* New York: Cambridge University Press.

Gamson, William A. (2001) "Promoting political engagement." In L. Bennett and R. Entman, eds. *Mediated Politics: Communication and the Future of Democracy.* New York and Cambridge: Cambridge University Press, pp. 56–74.

Gandy, Oscar (2001) "Dividing practices: Segmentation and targeting in the emerging public sphere." In L. Bennett and R. Entman, eds. *Mediated Politics: Communication and the Future of Democracy.* Cambridge: Cambridge University Press, pp. 141–159.

Gans, Herbert (2003) *Democracy and the News.* New York: Oxford University Press.

Gardiner, Michael E. (2004) "Wild publics and grotesque symposiums: Habermas and Bakhtin on dialogue, everyday life and the public sphere." In N. Crossly and J. M. Roberts, eds. *After Habermas: New Perspectives on the Public Sphere.* Oxford: Blackwell Publishers, pp. 28–48.

Garnham, Nicholas (2000) *Emacipation, the Media and Modernity: Arguments About the Media and Social Theory.* Oxford: Oxford University Press.

Gastil, J. and J. P. Dillard (1999) "Increasing political sophistication through public deliberation." *Political Communication* **16**: 3–23.

Gavin, Neil, ed. (2001) *The Economy, Media and Public Knowledge*. London: Continuum International Publishers.

Gellner, Ernest (1994) *Conditions of Liberty: Civil Society and Its Rivals*. London: Allan Lane/Penguin Press.

Gibbens, John R. and Bo Reimer (1999) *The Politics of Postmodernity*. London: Sage.

Gibson, Rachel, P. Nixon, and Stephen J. Ward, eds. (2003) *Political Parties and the Internet: Net Gain?* London: Routledge.

Gibson, Rachel K., Andrea Römmele, and Stephen J. Ward, eds. (2004) *Electronic Democracy: Mobilisation, Organisation and Participation via New ICTs*. London: Routledge.

Giddens, Anthony (2002) *Runaway World. How Globalization Is Reshaping Our Lives*. London: Routledge.

Gillmor, Dan (2006) *We the Media: Grassroots Journalism by the People, for the People*. Sebastopol, CA: O'Reilly Media.

Gimpel, James G., J. Celeste Lay, and Jason E. Schuknecht (2003) *Cultivating Democracy: Civic Environments and Political Socialization in America*. Washington, DC: Brookings Institution Press.

Ginsbourg, Paul (2004) *Silvio Berlusconi: Television, Power and Parsiminy*. London: Verso.

Gitlin, Todd (1998) "Public spheres or public sphericules." In Tamar Liebes and James Curran, eds. *Media, Ritual and Identity*. London: Routledge, pp. 168–74.

Gitlin, Todd (2001) *Media Unlimited: How the Torrent of Images and Sounds Overwhelms Our Lives*. New York: Metroplitan Books/Henry Holt and Company.

Glasser, Theodore L., ed. (1999) *The Idea of Public Journalism*. New York: Guilford Press.

Glasser, Ted L. and Charles T. Salmon, eds. (1995) *Public Opinion and the Communication of Consent*. New York: Guilford Press.

Glynn, Kevin (2000) *Trash, Taste, Popular Power, and the Transformation of American Television*. Durham, NC: Duke University Press.

Golbeck, Jennifer (2008) "The dynamics of Web-based social networks: Membership, relations, and change." *First Monday* **12**(11). Available online: www.uic.edu/htbin/cgiwrap/bin/ojs/index.php/fm/article/view/2023/1889.

Golding, Peter (2006) "Eurocrats, technocrats and democrats." *European Societies* **9**(5): 719–734.

Goldsmith, Jack and Tim Wu (2006) *Who Controls the Internet? Illusions of a Borderless World*. New York: Oxford University Press.

Graber, Doris (1988) *Processing the News: How People Tame the Information Tide*. New York: Longman.

Gray, Jonathan (2007) "The news: You gotta love it." In J. Gray, C. Sandvoss, and C. L. Harrington, eds. *Fandom: Identities and Communities in a Mediated World*. New York: New York University Press, pp. 100–118.

Greenwood, J., (2004) "The world of EU NGOs and interest representation." Available online: www.euactiv.com/Article?tcmuri=tcm:29-118102-16&;type=Analysis.

van Gunsteren, Herman R. (1998) *A Theory of Citizenship*. Boulder, CO: Westview Press.

Guttman, Amy and Dennis Thompson (1996) *Democracy and Dissagreement.* Cambridge, MA: Belknap.

Guttman, Amy and Dennis Thompson (2004) *Why Deliberative Democracy?* Princeton, NJ: Princeton University Press.

Haas, Tanni (2005) "From 'public journalism' to the " 'public's journalism' "? Rhetoric and reality in the discourse on weblogs." *Journalism Studies* 6(2): 387–396.

Haas, Tanni and Linda Steiner (2006) "Public journalism: A reply to critics." *Journalism* 7(2): 238–254.

Habermas, Jurgen (1984, 1987) *Theory of Communicative Action.* 2 vol. Cambridge: Polity Press.

Habermas, Jurgen (1989) *Structural Transformation of the Public Sphere.* Cambridge: Polity Press.

Habermas, Jürgen (1996) *Between Facts and Norms.* Cambridge, MA: MIT Press.

Habermas, Jürgen (2006) "Political communication in mediated society." *Communication Research* 16(4): 411–426.

Hagemann, Carlo (2002) "Participants in and contents of two Dutch political party discussion lists on the Internet." *Javnost/The Public* 9(2): 61–76.

Hall, Cheryl (2005) *The Trouble with Passion: Political Theory Beyond the Reign of Reason.* New York: Routledge.

Hall, Jim (2001) *Online Journalism: A Critical Primer.* London: Pluto Press.

Hallin, Dan (1992) "The passing of the 'high modernism' of American journalism." *Journal of Communication* 42(3): 14–25.

Hallin, Daniel C. and Paolo Mancini (2004) *Comparing Media Systems: Three Models of Media and Politics.* New York: Cambridge University Press.

Harcup, Tony (2005) " 'I'm doing this to change the world': Journalism in alternative and mainstream media." *Journalism Studies* 6(3): 361–374.

Harold, Christina (2004) "Pranking rhetoric: 'culture jamming' as media activism." *Critical Studies in Media Communication* 21(3): 189–211.

Hassan, Robert (2004) *Media, Politics and the Network Society.* Maidenhead, UK: Open University Press.

Hatchen, William A. (2005) *The Troubles of Journalism*, 3rd ed. Mahwah, NJ: Lawrence Erlbaum.

Hatchen, William A. and James F. Scotton (2007) *The World News Prism: Global Information in a Satellite Age*, 7th ed. Malden, MA, and Oxford: Blackwell.

Hébert, Yvonne M. and Lori A. Wilkinson (2001) "Values for pluralistic democratic societies." In M. Montane and Y. Bernaerdt, eds. *Towards Active Citizenship: Connecting Young Citizens across Europe and the World.* Barcelona: Universal Forum of Cultures and UNESCO, pp. 59–74.

Held, David (2006) *Models of Democracy*, 3rd ed. Cambridge: Polity Press.

Held, David and Anthony McGrew (2002) *Globalization/Antiglobalization.* Cambridge: Polity Press.

Hénaff, Marcel and Tracy B. Strong, eds. (2001). *Public Space and Democracy.* Minneapolis: University of Minnesota Press.

Henry, Neil (2007) *American Carnival: Journalism Under Seige in an Age of New Media.* Berkeley: University of California Press.

Herman, Edward and Robert McChesney (1997) *The Global Media.* London: Cassell.

Hermes, Joke (2005) *Re-reading Popular Culture.* Oxford: Blackwell.

Hertz, Noreena (2001) *The Silent Takeover: Global Capitalism and the Death of Democracy.* New York: Arrow Books.

Hetherington, Kevin (1998) *Expressions of Identity: Space, Performance, Politics.* London: Sage.

Hiley, David R. (2006) *Doubt and the Demands of Democratic Citizenship.* New York: Cambridge University Press.

Hill, Annette (2005) *Reality TV: Audiences and Popular Factual Television.* London: Routledge.

Hill, Annette (2007) *Restyling Factual Television: News, Documentary and Reality Television.* London: Routledge.

Hill, Kevin A. and John E. Hughes (1998) *Cyberpolitics: Citizen Activism in the Age of the Internet.* Lanham, MD: Rowman & Littlefield.

Hindess, Barry (2002) "Neo-liberal citizenship." *Citizenship Studies* 6(2): 127–143.

Holt, Richard (2004) *Dialogue on the Internet: Language, Civic Identity, and Computer-Mediated Communucation.* Westport, CT: Praeger.

Honneth, Axel (1995) *The Struggle for Recognition: The Moral Grammar of Social Conflicts.* Cambridge, MA: MIT Press.

Howard, Philip and Steve Jones, eds. (2004) *Society Online.* London: Sage.

Hyde, Gene (2003) "Independent media centers: Cyber/subversion and the alternative press." *First Monday: Peer-Reviewed Journal on the Internet.* www.firstmonday.org/issues//issue7_4/hyde/index.htm

Inglehart, Ronald (1997) *Modernization and Postmodernization: Cultural, Economic and Political Change in 43 Societies.* Princeton, NJ: Princeton University Press.

Isin, Engin F. and Bryan S. Turner, eds. (2002) *Handbook of Citizenship Studies.* London: Sage.

Isen, Engin F. and Patricia K. Wood (1999) *Citizenship and Identity.* London: Sage.

Janoski, T. (1998) *Citizenship and Civil Society.* Cambridge: Cambridge University Press.

Jenkins, Henry (2006) *Convergence Culture: Where Old and New Media Collide.* New York: New York University Press.

Jenkins, Henry and David Thornburn, eds. (2003) *Democracy and New Media.* Cambridge, MA: MIT Press.

Johansson, Sofia (2006) "Reading Tabloids: A Study of Readers of the Sun and the Daily Mirror." Unpub. PhD dissertation, University of Westminster, UK.

Jokiniemi, Päivi (2006) "Anti-WTO Websites: Political Information, but Little Dialogue" (in Swedish). Unpub. senior thesis, Dept. of Media and Communication Studies, Lund University, Sweden.

Jones, Jeffrey (2005) *Entertaining Politics: New Political Television and Civic Culture.* London: Sage.

de Jong, Wilma, Martin Shaw, and Neil Stammers, eds. (2005) *Global Activism, Global Media.* London: Pluto.

Jordan, Tim and Paul A. Taylor (2004) *Hacktivism and Cyberwars: Rebels with a Cause?* London: Routledge.

Jordan, Tim, Adam Lent, George McKay, and Ann Mische (2005) "Social movement studies: Opening statement." www.tandf.co.uk/journals/titles/CSMS_opening.asp

Juris, Jeffrey S. (2005): "The new digital media and activist networking within anti-corporate globalization movements." *The Annals of the American Academy of Political and Social Science* **597**: 189–208.

Kahn, R. and Doug Kellner (2004) "New media and Internet activism: From the 'Battle of Seattle' to blogging." *New Media and Society* **6**(1): 87–95.

Kaitatzi-Whitlock, Sophia (2005) *Europe's Political Communication Deficit*. Bury St Edmunds, UK: Arima Publishing.

Kalathil, Shanthi and Taylor C. Boas, eds. (2003) *Open Networks, Closed Regimes*. Washington, D.C.: Carnegie Endowment for International Peace.

Kantola, Anu (2003) "Loyalties in flux: The changing politics of citizenship." *European Journal of Cultural Studies* **6**(2): 203–217.

Kantola, Anu (2007) "On the dark side of democracy: The global imaginary of financial journalism." In Bart Cammaerts and Nico Carpentier, eds. *Reclaiming the Media: Communication Rights and Democratic Roles*. Bristol, UK: Intellect, pp. 192–215.

Karakaya Polat, Rabia (2005) "The Internet and political participation." *European Journal of Communication* **20**(4): 435–459.

Katz, E. (1992) "On parenting a paradigm: Gabriel Tarde's agenda for opinion and communication." *International Journal of Public Opinion Research* **4**: 80–85.

Kavada, Anastasia (2005) "Exploring the role of the Internet in the 'movement for alternative globalization': The case of the Paris 2003 European Social Forum." *Westminster Papers in Communication and Culture* **2**(1): 72–95.

Keane, John (1998) *Civil Society: Old Images, New Visions*. Cambridge: Polity Press.

Keane, John (2003) *Global Civil Society?* Cambridge: Cambrige University Press.

Kellner, Douglas (2003) *From 9/11 to Terror War*. Lanham, MD: Rowman & Littlefield.

Kellner, Douglas (2005). *Media Spectacle and the Crisis of Democracy: Terrorism, War, and Election Battles*. New York: Paradigm.

Keren, Michael (2006) *Blogosphere: The New Political Arena*. Lanham, MD: Lexington Books.

Kevin, D. (2003) *Europe in the Media: A Comparison of Reporting, Representation and Rhetoric in National Media Systems*. Mahwah, NJ: Lawrence Erlbaum.

Kidd, Dorothy (2003) "Indymedia.org: A new communications commons." In Martha McGaughey and Michael Ayers, eds. *Cyberactivism: Critical Theories and Practices of Online Activism*. New York: Routledge, pp. 47–69.

Kim, J. (1997) "On the Interactions of News Media, Interpersonal Communication, Opinion Formation, and Participation: Deliberative Democracy and the Public Sphere." *Dissertation.Com*.

Kim, J., R. O. Wyatt, and E. Katz (1999) "News, talk, opinion, participation: The part played by conversation in deliberative democracy." *Political Communication* **16**: 361–385.

Kitsing, M. (2003) "Behind corruption: From NGO's to the civil society." Available online: http://www.eumap.org/journal/features/2003/july/behindcorruption.

Kivisto, Peter and Thomas Faist (2007) *Citizenship: Discourse, Theory and Transnational Prospects*. Malden, UK: Blackwell.

Klang, Mathias (2006) *Disruptive Technology: Effects of Technology Regulation on Democracy*. Gothenborg, Sweden: Dept. of Applied Information Technology, University of Gothenborg.

Klein, Naomi (2007) *The Shock Doctrine: The Rise of Disaster Capitalism*. New York: Henry Holt.

Kleinman, Sharon, ed. (2007) *Displacing Place: Mobile Communication in the 21st Century*. New York: Peter Lang.

Klinenberg, Eric (2005a) "Convergence: News production in a digital age." *The Annals of the American Academy of Political and Social Science* **597**: 48–64.

Klinenberg, Eric, ed. (2005b) "Cultural Production in the Digital Age." Theme issue of *The Annals of the American Academy of Political and Social Science* **597**.

Klinenberg, Eric (2007) *Fighting for Air: The Battle to Control America's Media*. New York: Metropolitan Books.

Klotz, Robert J. (2004) *The Politics of Internet Communication*. Lanham, MD: Rowman & Littlefield.

Kohn, Margaret (2000) "Language, power, and persuasion: Towards a critique of deliberative democracy." *Constellations* **7**(3): 408–429.

Kolko, Beth, ed. (2003) *Virtual Publics: Policy and Community in an Electronic Age*. New York: Columbia University Press.

Koopmans, Ruud, N. Friedhelm, and B. Pfetsh (2002) "*Conditions for the Constitution of a European Public Sphere.*"Available online: ftp://ftp4.cordis.lu/pub/improving/docs/ser_citizen_koopmans.pdf.

Kovach, Bill and Tom Rosentiel (2001) *The Elements of Journalism: What Newspeople Should Know and the Public Should Expect*. New York: Three Rivers Press/Random House.

Krug, Gary (2005) *Communication, Technology and Cultural Change*. Thousand Oaks, CA: Sage.

Kymlicka, Will (1995) *Multicultural Citizenship: A Liberal Theory of Minority Rights*. Oxford: Clarendon Press.

Laclau, Ernesto (1993) *Emancipations*. London: Verso.

Laclau, Ernesto and Chantal Mouffe (1985) *Hegemony and Socialist Strategy*. London: Verso.

Lagerkvist, Johan (2006) *The Internet in China: Unlocking and Containing the Public Sphere*. Lund, Sweden: Lund University, Dept. of East Asian Studies.

Lasch, Christopher (1991) *The Culture of Narcissism*. New York: Norton.

Lazarsfeld, Paul and Elihu Katz (1955) *The People's Choice*. New York: Columbia University Press.

Lembo, Ron (2000) *Thinking Through Television*. Cambridge: Cambridge University Press.

Lessig, Lawrence (2006) *Code: Version 2.0*. New York: Basic Books.

Leys, Colin (2003) *Market-Driven Politics: Neoliberal Democracy and the Public Interest*. London: Verso.

Lewis, Justin (2001) *Constructing Public Opinion*. New York: Columbia University Press.

Lewis, Justin, Sanna Inthorn, and Karin Wahl-Jorgensen (2005) *Consumers or Citizens? What the Media Tell Us About Political Participation*. Maidenhead, UK: Open University Press.

Lievrouw, Leah A. and Sonia Livingstone, eds. (2006) *The Handbook of New Media*, 2nd ed. London: Sage.

Lippmann, Walter (1922) *Public Opinion*. New York: Macmillan.

Lister, Ruth (2003) *Citizenship: Feminist Perspectives*, 2nd ed. London: Macmillan.

Livingstone, Sonia (2004) "The challenge of changing audiences: Or, what is the audience researcher to do in the age of the Internet." *European Journal of Communication* **19**(1): 75–86.

Livingstone, Sonia, ed. (2005a) *Audiences and Publics: When Cultural Engagement Matters for the Public Sphere*. Bristol, UK: Intellect.

Livingstone, Sonia (2005b) "On the relation between audiences and publics." In S. Livingstone, ed. *Audiences and Publics: When Cultural Engagement Matters for the Public Sphere*. Bristol, UK: Intellect, pp. 17–41.

Livingstone, Sonia (2005c) "In defence of privacy: Mediating the public/private boundary at home." In S. Livingstone, ed. *Audiences and Publics: When Cultural Engagement Matters for the Public Sphere*. Bristol, UK: Intellect, pp. 163–185.

Livingstone, Sonia and Peter Lunt (1994) *Talk on Television*. London: Routledge.

Llewellyn, Kristina R., Sharon Cook, Joel Westheimer, Luz Alison Molina Girón, and Karen Suurtamm (2007) *The State and Potential of Civic Learning in Canada: Charting the Course for Youth Civic and Political Participation*. Ottawa: Canadian Policy Research Networks. Available online: CPRN_State of Civic Learning in Canada_Oct2007_EN.pdf.

Lloyd, Mora (2005) *Beyond Identity Politics: Feminism, Power and Politics*. London: Sage.

Loader, Brian, ed. (2007) *Young Citizens in the Digital Age: Political Engagement, Young People and New Media*. London: Routledge.

Louw, Eric (2005) *The Media and Political Process*. London: Sage.

Lowrey, Wilson (2007) "Mapping the journalism-blogging relationship." *Journalism* **7**(4): 477–500.

Lull, James and Stephen Hinerman, eds. (1997) *Media Scandals: Morality and Desire in the Popular Culture Marketplace*. New York: Columbia University Press.

Lunt, Peter and Paul Stenner (2005) "The Jerry Springer Show as an emotional public sphere." *Media, Culture and Society* **27**(1): 59–81.

Lushkin, R. C., J. S. Fishkin, and R. Jowell (2002) "Considered opinions: Deliberative polling in Britain." *British Journal of Political Science* **32**: 455–488.

Lyon, David, ed. (2003) *Surveillance as Social Sorting: Privacy, Risk and Digital Discrimination*. London: Routledge.

Machill, Marcel (2006) "Europe-topics in Europe's media." *European Journal of Communication* **21**(1): 57–88.

Magnette, Paul (2003) "European governance and civic participation: Beyond elitist citizenship?" Available online: www.blackwell-synergy.com/doi/pdf/10.1111/1467-9248.00417?cookieSet=1

Malina, Anna (2003) "e-Transforming democracy in the UK. Considerations of developments and suggestions for empirical research." *Communications: The European Journal of Communication Research* **28**(2): 135–155.

Mansell, Robin and Michèle Javary (2004) "New media and the forces of capitalism." In Andrew Calabrese and Colin Sparks, eds. *Toward a Political Economy of Culture*. Lanham, MD: Rowman & Littlefield, pp. 228–243.

Margolis, Michael and David Resnick (2000) *Politics as Usual: The Cyberspace "Revolution."* London: Sage.

Marquand, David (2004) *Decline of the Public: The Hollowing Out of Citizenship.* Cambridge: Polity Press.

Marshall, T. H. (1950) *Citizenship and Social Class.* Cambridge: Cambridge University Press.

Matheson, Donald (2004) "Weblogs and the epistemology of the news: Some trends in online journalism." *New Media and Society* 6(4): 443–468.

May, Harvey and Greg Hearn (2005) "The mobile phone as media." *International Journal of Cultural Studies* 8(2): 195–211.

Mayhew, Leon H. (1997) *The New Public.* Cambridge: Cambridge University Press.

McCaughey, Martha and Michael D. Ayers, eds. (2003) *Cyberactivism: Online Activism in Theory and Practice.* London: Routledge.

McChesney, Robert (1999) *Rich Media, Poor Democracy: Communication Politics in Dubious Times.* Champaign: University of Illinois Press.

McChesney, Robert (2004) *The Problem of the Media: US Communication Politics in the Twenty-First Century.* New York: Monthly Review Press.

McChesney, Robert (2007) *Communication Revolution: Critical Junctures and the Future of the Media.* New York: The New Press.

McCombs, Maxwell (2004) *Setting the Agenda: The Mass Media and Public Opinion.* Cambridge: Polity Press.

McDonald, Kevin (2006) *Global Movements: Action and Culture.* Oxford: Blackwell.

McManus, John H. (1994) *Market-Driven Journalism.* London: Sage.

McNair, Brian (2000) *Journalism and Democracy: An Evaluation of the Political Public Sphere.* London: Routledge.

McNair, Brian (2005) "The emerging chaos of global news culture." In S. Allan, ed. *Journalism: Critical Issues.* Maidenhead, UK: Open University Press, pp. 151–163.

McPherson, Tara, ed. (2007) *Digital Youth, Innovation and the Unexpected.* Cambridge, MA: MIT Press. Available online: http://mitpress.mit.edu/catalog/browse/browse.asp?btype=6&;serid=170.

McQuail, Denis (1997) *Audience Analysis.* London: Sage.

McQuail, Denis (2000) *Mass Communication Theory: An Introduction*, 4th ed. London: Sage.

McQuail, Denis (2003) *Media Accountability and Freedom of Publication.* Oxford: Oxford University Press.

McQuail, Denis and Karen Siune, eds. (1998) *Media Policy: Convergence, Concentration and Commerce.* London: Sage.

Meehan, Johanna, ed. (1995) *Feminists Read Habermas.* London: Routledge.

Meesner, Marcus and Marcia Watson DiSato (2008) "The source cycle: How traditional media and weblogs use each other as sources." *Journalism Studies* 9(3): 447–463.

Meijer, Irene Costera (2001) "The public quality of popular journalism: Developing a normative framework." *Journalism Studies* 2(2): 189–205.

Meijer, Irene Costera (2007) "The paradox of popularity: How young people experience the news." *Journalism Studies* 8(2): 96–116.

Melucci, Alberto (1989) *Nomads of the Present: Social Movements and Individual Needs in Contemporary Society.* Philadelphia: Temple University Press.

Mestrovic, Stjepan (1997) *Postemotional Society.* London: Sage.

Meyer, Phillip (2004) *The Vanishing Newspaper: Saving Journalism in the Information Age*. Columbia: University of Missouri Press.

Meyer, Thomas (2002) *Media Democracy: How the Media Colonize Politics*. Cambridge: Polity Press.

Micheletti, Michele, Andreas Føllestad, and David Stolle, eds. (2003) *The Politics Behind Products: Exploring Political Consumption Past and Present*. New Brunswick, NJ: Transaction Books.

Miles, Steven (1998) *Consumerism as a Way of Life*. London: Sage.

Mill, John S. (1998/1861) *On Liberty and Other Essays*. Oxford: Oxford University Press.

Miller, Carlyn R. and Dawn Shepherd (2004) "Blogging as social action: A genre analysis of weblogs." *New England Journal of Medicine*, Nov. Available online: www.nejm.org.

Miller, David (2000) *Citizenship and National Identity*. Cambridge: Polity Press.

Miller, David, ed. (2004) *Tell Me Lies: Propaganda and Media Distortion in the Attack on Iraq*. London: Pluto.

Milner, Henry (2001) *Civic Literacy: How Informed Citizens Make Democracy Work*. Hanover, NH: University Press of New England.

Mindich, David T. Z. (2005) *Tuned Out: Why Americans Under 40 Don't Follow the News*. New York: Oxford University Press.

Morley, David (2000) *Home Territories: Media, Mobility and Identity*. London: Routledge.

Morley, David and Kevin Robins (1995) *Spaces of Identity: Global Media, Electronic Landscapes, and Cultural Boundaries*. London: Routledge

Monge, Peter R. and Noshir S. Contractor (2003) *Theories of Communication Networks*. Oxford: Oxford University Press.

Mosco, Vincent (2004) "Capitalism's Chernobyl? From Ground Zero to cyberspace and back again." In Andrew Calabrese and Colin Sparks, eds. *Toward a Political Economy of Culture*. Lanham, MD: Rowman & Littlefield, pp. 211–227.

Mossberger, Karen, Caroline J. Tolbert, and Ramona S. McNeal (2007) *Digital Citizenship: The Internet, Society and Participation*. Cambridge, MA: MIT Press.

Mouffe, Chantel, ed. (1992) *Dimensions of Radical Democracy*. London: Verso.

Mouffe, Chantal (1993) *The Return of the Political*. London: Verso.

Mouffe, Chantal (1999) "Deliberative democracy or agonistic pluralism?" *Social Research* **66**: 745–758.

Mouffe, Chantal (2000) *The Democratic Paradox*. London: Verso.

Mouffe, Chantal (2005) *On the Political*. London: Routledge.

Muetzelfeldt, Michael and Gary Smith (2002) "Civil society and global governance: The possibilities of global citizenship." *Citizenship Studies* **6**(1): 55–75.

Mutz, Diana (2006) *Hearing the Other Side: Deliberative vs. Participatory Democracy*. New York: Cambridge University Press.

Negrine, Ralph, Paolo Mancini, Christina Holtz-Bacha, and Stylianos Papathananas-sopoulos, eds. (2007) *The Professionalization of Political Communication*. Bristol, UK: Intellect.

Negt, Oskar and Alexander Kluge (1993) *The Public Sphere and Experience*. Minneapolis: University of Minnesota Press.

Nichols, John and Robert W. McChesney (2005) *Tragedy and Farce: How the American Media Sell Wars, Spin Elections, and Destroy Democracy*. New York: The New Press.

Nieminen, Hannu (2007) "Europe of networks or the European public sphere? Four plus one approaches." Paper presented at the 50th Congress of the International Association for Media and Communication Research, Paris, July 22–25.

Nip, Joyce Y. M. (2006) "Exploring the second phase of public journalism." *Journalism Studies* 7(2): 212–236.

Noelle-Neumann, Elizabeth (1993) *The Spiral of Silence*, 2nd ed. Chicago: University of Chicago Press.

Norris, Pippa (1999) *Critical Citizens: Global Support for Democratic Government*. New York: Oxford University Press.

Norris, Pippa (2002) *Democratic Phoenix: Reinventing Political Activism*. Cambridge: Cambridge University Press.

Nunes, Mark (2006) *Cyberspaces of Evetryday Life*. Minneapolis: University of Minnesota Press.

Olsson, Jan and Joachim Åström, eds. (2006) *Democratic eGovernance: Approaches and Research Directions*. Stockholm: Almqvist and Wiksell International.

Olsson, Tobias, Håkan Sandström, and Peter Dahlgren (2003) "An information society for everyone?" *Gazette* 65(4–5): 347–63.

Opel, Andy and Donnalyn Pompper, eds. (2003) *Representing Resistance: Media, Civil Disobedience, and the Global Justice Movement*. Westport, CT: Praeger.

Ostertag, Bob (2007) *People's Movements, Peoples Press: The Journalism of Social Justice Movements*. Boston: Beacon Press.

Pajnik, Mojca (2005) "Citizenship and mediated society." *Citizenship Studies* 9(4): 349–367.

Pateman, Carole (1989) *The Disorder of Women: Democracy, Feminism and Political Theory*. Cambridge: Polity Press.

Pavlik, John V. (2001) *Journalism and New Media*. New York: Columbia University Press.

Petit, Phillip (1997) *Republicanism: A Theory of Freedom and Government*. Oxford: Clarendon Press.

Phillips, Ann (1993) *Democracy and Difference*. Cambridge: Polity Press.

Pickard, Viktor W. (2006) "United yet autonomous Indymedia and the struggle to sustain a radical democratic network." *Media, Culture and Society* 28(3): 315–326.

Platon, Sara and Mark Deuze (2003) "Indymedia journalism a radical way of making, selecting and sharing news?" *Journalism* 4(3): 336–355.

Plummer, Ken (2003) *Intimate Citizenship*. Seattle and London: University of Washington Press.

Poster, Mark (2006) *Information, Please: Culture and Politics in the Age of Digital Machines*. Durham, NC: Duke University Press.

Preston, P. W. (1997) *Political/Cultural Identity*. London: Sage.

Price, Vincent, L. Nir, and J. Cappella (2002) "Does disagreement contribute to more deliberative opinion?" *Political Communication* 19: 95–112.

Project of Excellence in Journalism (2004, 2005, 2006, 2007) State of the News Media, annual reports. (www.stateofthemedia.org).

Putnam, Robert (2000) *Bowling Alone: The Collapse and Revival of American Community*. New York: Simon & Schuster.

Quan-Haase, Anabel and Barry Wellman (2004) "How does the Internet affect social capital?" In M. Huysman and V. Wulf, eds. *Social Capital and Information Technology.* Cambridge, MA: MIT Press, pp. 113–131.

Quant, Thorsten, Martin Löffelholz, David H. Weaver, Thomas Hanitzsch, and Klaus-Dieter Altmeppen (2006) "American and German online journalists at the beginning of the 21st century." *Journalism Studies* 7(2): 171–186.

Quiggin, John (2006) "Blogs, wikis and creative innovation." *International Journal of Cultural Studies* 9(4): 481–496.

Rancier, Jacques (2007) *Hatred of Democracy.* London: Verso.

Rantenen, Terhi (2005) *The Media and Globalization.* London: Sage.

Rasmussen, Claire and Michael Brown (2002) "Radical democratic citizenship: Amidst political theory and geography." In E. F. Isin and B. S. Turner, eds. *Handbook of Citizenship Studies.* London: Sage, pp. 175–188.

Ravitch, Diane and Joseph P. Viteritti, eds. (2001) *Makiung Good Citizens: Education and Civil Society.* New Haven, CT: Yale University Press.

Rawls, John (1972) *A Theory of Justice.* Oxford: Oxford University Press.

Reese, Stephen D., Lou Rutigliano, Kidseuk Hyun, and Jaekwan Jeong (2007) "Mapping the blogosphere: Professional and citizen-based media in the global news arena." *Journalism* 8(3): 235–261.

Reigert, Kristina, ed. (2007) *Politicotainment: Televison's Take on the Real.* New York: Peter Lang Publishers.

Risse, T. and M. Van de Steeg (2003) "An emerging European public sphere? Empirical evidence and theoretical clarifications." Paper presented at the conference "Europeanizatoin of Spheres, Political Moblization, Public Communication and the European Union." Available online: http://www.fuberlin.de/atasp/texte/030624.

Robinson, Susan (2006) "The mission of the j-log." *Journalism* 7(1): 65–83.

Rosanvallon, Pierre (2006) *Democracy Past and Future.* New York: Columbia University Press.

Rosen, Jay (2001) *What Are Journalists for?* New Haven, CT: Yale University Press.

Rosenkrands, Jakob (2004) "Politicizing *Homo economicus*: Analysis of anti-corporate websites." In Wim van de Donk, Brian D. Loader, Paul G. Nixon, and Dieter Rucht, eds. *Cyberprotest: New Media, Citizens and Social Movements.* London: Routledge, pp. 57–76.

Ross, Karen and Virginia Nightingale (2003) *Media and Audiences: New Perspectives.* Maidenhead, UK: Open University Press.

Roversi, Antonio (2008) *Hate on the Net: Extremist Sites, Neo-fascism On-line, Electronic Jihad.* Aldershot, UK: Ashgate.

Samuel, Alexandra (2004) "Hacktivism and the future of democratic discourse." In Peter Shane, ed. *Democracy Online: The Prospects for Political Renewal Through the Internet.* London: Routledge, pp. 123–140.

Sandel, Michael J. (1996) *Democracy's Discontent.* Cambridge, MA: Harvard University Press.

Sanders, Lynn (1997) "Against deliberation." *Political Theory* 25(3): 347–376.

Sarkikakis, Katarina (2007) *Media and Cultural Policy in the European Union.* Amsterdam: Rodopi.

Sassen, Saskia (2002) "Towards post-national and denationalized citizenship." In E. F. Isen and B. S. Turner, eds. *Handbook of Citizenship Studies*. London: Sage, pp. 277–291.

Scammel, Margaret (2003) "Citizen consumers: Towards a marketing of politic?" In John Corner and Dick Pels, eds. *Media and the Restyling of Politics: Consumerism, Celebrity and Cynicism*. London: Sage, pp. 117–136.

Scannel, Paddy (1996) *Radio, Television and Modern Life*. Oxford: Blackwell.

Scheller, Maria and John Urry (2003) "Mobile transformations: 'Public' and 'private' life." *Theory, Culture and Society* **20**(3): 107–125.

Scheuer, Jeffrey (2001) *The Sound Bite Society*. London: Routledge.

Schiller, Dan (1999) *Digital Capitalism*. Cambridge, MA: MIT Press.

Schiller, Dan (2007) *How to Think About Information*. Urbana: University of Illinois Press.

Schlesinger, Philip (2003) "The Babel of Europe? An essay on networks and communicative spaces." Available online: http://ideas.repec.org/p/erp/arenax/p0062.html.

Schudson, Michael (1997) "Why conversation is not the soul of democracy." *Critical Studies in Mass Communication* **14**: 297–309.

Schudson, Michael (1998) *The Good Citizen: A History of American Civic Life*. New York: Martin Kessler Books.

Schudson, Michael (2003) *The Sociology of News*. New York/London: Norton.

Self, Peter (2000) *Rolling Back the Market: Economic Dogma and Political Choice*. New York: St. Martins Press.

Sennett, Richard (1977) *The Fall of Public Man*. New York: Knopf.

Shah, Dhavan V., Jaeho Cho, William P. Everett, and Nojin Kwak (2005) "Information and expression in a digital age: Modelling Internet effects on civic participation." *Communication Research* **32**(5): 531–565.

Shane, Peter (2004) *Democracy Online: The Prospects for Political Renewal Through the Internet*. London: Routledge.

Shirky, Clay (2008) *Here Comes Everybody: The Power of Organizing Without Organizations*. New York: Allen Lane.

Simons, Jon (2003) "Popular culture and mediated politics: Intellectuals, elites and democracy." In J. Corner and D. Pels, eds. *Media and the Restyling of Politics: Consumerism, Celebrity and Cynicism*. London: Sage.

Singer, Jane B. (2005) "The political j-blogger: Normalizing a new media form to fit old norms and procedures." *Journalism* **6**(2): 173–198.

Skocpol, Theda (2004) *Diminished Democracy: From Membership to Management in American Civic Life*. Norman: University of Oklahoma Press.

Slaatta, Tore (2006) "Europeanization and the news media." *Javnost/The Public* **13**(1): 5–24.

Slater, Don (1997) *Consumer Culture and Modernity*. Cambridge: Polity Press.

Slevin, Jan (2000) *The Internet and Society*. Cambridge: Polity Press.

Sloan, Tod (1996) *Damaged Life: The Crisis of the Modern Psyche*. London: Routledge.

Smith, Anne Marie (1998) *Laclau and Mouffe's Radical Democratic Imaginary*. London: Routledge.

Smith, Jackie (2004) "The World Social Forum and the challenges of global democracy." *Global Networks* **4**(4): 413–421.

Söderberg, Karen (2007) "CIA ändrade uppgifter i Wikipedia." *Sydsvenka Dagbladet*, August 15, p. A15.

Sörbom, Adrienne (2002) *Vart tog politiken vägen?* Stockholm: Almqvist & Wiksell International.

Sparks, Colin (2001) "The Internet and the global public sphere." In W. L. Bennett and R. M. Entman, eds. *Mediated Politics: Communication in the Future of Democracy.* New York: Cambridge University Press, pp. 75–95.

Sparks, Colin and John Tulloch, eds. (2000) *Tabloid Tales: Global Debates Over Media Standards.* Lanham, MD: Rowman & Littlefield.

Spigal, Lynn and Jan Olsson, eds. (2004) *Television After TV: Essays on a Medium in Transition.* Durham, NC: Duke University Press.

Spinner, Jeff (1994) *The Boundaries of Citizenship: Race, Ethnicity, and Nationality in the Liberal State.* Baltimore and London: Johns Hopkins University Press.

Splichal, Slavko (1999) *Public Opinion: Developments and Controversies in the Twentieth Century.* Lanham: MD: Rowman & Littlefield.

Splichal, Slavko, ed. (2001) *Public Opinion and Democracy: Vox Populi – Vox Dei?* Cresskill, NJ: Hampton Press.

Stald, Gitte (2007) "Mobile monitoring: Questions of trust, risk and democracy in young Danes' uses of mobile phones." In Pteer Dahlgren, ed. *Young Citizens and New Media: Learning for Democratic Participation.* New York: Routledge, pp. 205–225.

Stalder, Felix (2006) *Manuel Castells and the Theory of the Network Society.* Cambridge: Polity Press.

van Steenberger, Bart, ed. (1994) *The Condition of Citizenship.* London: Sage.

Stein, Laura (2007) "National social movement organizations and the World Wide Web: A survey of web/based activities and attributes." Paper presented at the 50th Congress of the International Association for Media and Communication Research, Paris, July 22–25.

Stevenson, Nick (2003) *Cultural Citizenship: Cosmopolitan Questions.* Maidenhead, UK: Open University Press.

Stewart, Angus (2001) *Theories of Power and Domination.* London: Sage.

Strangelove, Michael (2005) *The Empire of Mind: Digital Piracy and the Anti-Capitalist Movement.* Toronto: University of Toronto Press.

Street, John (1997) *Politics and Popular Culture.* Cambridge: Polity Press.

Strelitz, Larry (2005) *Mixed Reception: South African Youth and their Experience of Global Media.* Pretoria: UNISA Press.

Stromer-Galley, Jennifer (2002) "New voices in the public sphere: A comparative analysis of interpersonal and online political talk." *Javnost/The Public* **9**(2): 23–42.

Sullivan, Andrew (2002) "The blogging revolution: Weblogs are to words what Napster was to music." *Wired Magazine,* issue 10.05. Available online: http://www.wired.com/wired/archive/10.05/mustread.hmtl?pg=2

Sunstein, Cass (2007) *Republic.com 2.0.* Princeton, NJ: Princeton University Press.

Sussman, Gerald (1997) *Communication, Technology and Politics in the Information Age.* London: Sage.

Tarrow, Sidney (2005). *The New Transnational Activism.* Cambridge: Cambridge University Press.

Taylor, Charles (1994) *Multiculturalism: Examining the Politics of Recognition.* Princeton, NJ: Princeton University Press.

Taylor, Gary and Steve Spencer, eds. (2004) *Social Identities: Multidisciplinary Approaches*. London: Routledge.

Taylor, Paul A. and Jan L. Harris (2005) *Digital Matters: The Theory and Culture of the Matrix*. London: Routledge.

Temple, Mick (2006) "Dumbing down is good for you." *British Politics* 1(2): 257–273.

Tester, Keith (2001) *Compassion, Morality and the Media*. Philadelphia: Open University Press.

Thompson, John B. (1995) *The Media and Modernity*. Cambridge: Polity Press.

Thompson, John B. (2000) *Political Scandal: Power and Visibility in the Media Age*. Cambridge: Polity Press.

Thompson, John B. (2005) "The new visibility." *Theory, Culture & Society* 22(6): 31–51.

Thussu, Daya Kishan (2006a) *International Communication: Continuity and Change*. London: Hodder Arnold.

Thussu, Daya Kishan, ed. (2006b) *Media on the Move: Global Flow and Contra-Flow*. London: Routledge.

Thussu, Daya Kishan (2007) *News as Entertainment: The Rise of Global Infotainment*. London: Sage.

Thussu, Daya Kishan and Des Freedman, eds. (2003) *War and the Media*. London: Sage.

Tilley, Charles (2007) *Democracy*. New York: Cambridge University Press.

Tocqueville, Alexis de (2004) *Democracy in America*. New York: Library of America.

Todd, Emmanuel (2003) *After the Empire: The Breakdown of the American Order*. New York: Columbia University Press.

Tomlinson, John (1999) *Globalisation and Culture*. Cambridge: Polity Press.

Tonkiss, Fran, Andrew Pasey, Nancy Fenton, and Leslie C. Hems, eds. (2000) *Trust and Civil Society*. London: Palgrave Macmillan.

Touraine, Alain (1988) *Return of the Actor: Social Theory in Postindustrial Society*. Minneapolis: University of Minnesota Press.

Touraine, Alain (2000) *Can We Live Together?: Equality and Difference*. Palo Alto, CA: Stanford University Press.

Touraine, Alain (2001) *Beyond Neoliberalism*. Cambridge: Polity Press.

Tracey, Michael (1998) *Decline and Fall of Public Service Broadcasting*. New York: Oxford University Press.

Trenz, Hans-Jörg and Klaus Eder (2004) "The democratizing dynamics of a European public sphere." *European Journal of Social Theory* 7(1): 5–25.

Tsaliki, Liza (2002) "Online forums and the enlargement of the public sphere: Research from a European project." *Javnost/The Public* 9(2): 95–112.

Turner, Stephen (2003) *Liberalism 3.0: Civil Society in an Age of Experts*. London: Sage

Turow, Joseph (2006) *Niche Envy: Marketing Discrimination in the Digital Age*. Cambridge, MA: MIT Press.

Tyler, Imogen (2007) "From 'The Me Decade' to 'The Me Millennium': The cultural history of narcissism." *International Journal of Cultural Studies* 10(3): 343–363.

Underwood, Doug (1995) *When MBAs Rule the Newsroom*. New York: Columbia University Press.

Villa, Dana R. (2001) "Theatricality in the public realm of Hannah Arendt." In M. Hénaff and T. B. Strong, eds. *Public Space and Democracy*. Minneapolis: University of Minnesota Press.

Vinken, Henk (2007) "Changing life courses, citizenship, and new media: The impact of reflexive biographization." In Peter Dahlgren, ed. *Young Citizens and New Media*. New York: Routledge.

Virilio, Paul (2000) *The Information Bomb*. London: Verso.

Virilio, Paul (2002) *Ground Zero*. London: Verso.

Voakes, Paul S. (2004) "A brief history of public journalism." *National Civic Review* **93**(3): 25–35.

Voet, Rian (1998) *Feminism and Citizenship*. London: Sage.

Voirol, Olivier, ed. (2005) "Visibilité/Invisibilité." Theme issue of *Reseaux*, no. 129–130.

Wall, Melissa (2005) "Blogs of war: Weblogs as news." *Journalism*: **6**(2): 153–172.

Walsh, Katherine Cramer (2003). *Talking About Politics: Informal Groups and Social Identity in American Life*. Chicago: University of Chicago Press.

Waltz, Mitzi (2005) *Alternative and Activist Media*. Edinburgh: University of Edinburgh Press.

Walzer, Michael (1983) *Spheres of Justice*. Oxford: Blackwell.

Warner, Michael (2002) *Publics and Counterpublics*. New York: Zone Books.

Warren, Mark E. (1996) "What should we expect from more democracy?" *Political Theory* **24**: 241–270.

Warren, Mark E., ed. (1999) *Democracy and Trust*. Cambridge, MA: MIT Press.

Warschauer, Mark (2003) *Technology and Social Inclusion*. Cambridge, MA: MIT Press.

Waterman, Peter (2005) "Between a political-institutional past and a communicational networked future? Reflections on the Third World Social Forum, 2003." In Wilma de Jong, Martin Shaw, and Neil Stammers, eds. *Global Activism, Global Media*. London: Pluto Press, pp. 68–83.

Watson, Don (2004) *Death Sentence: The Decay of Public Language*. New York: Vintage Books.

Webster, Frank, ed. (2001) *Culture and Politics in the Information Age: A New Politics?* London: Routledge.

Wellman, Barry and Caroline Haythornwaite, eds. (2002) *The Internet in Everyday Life*. London: Macmillan.

Wilhelm, Anthony G. (2000) *Democracy in the Digital Age*. London: Routledge.

Wimmer, Jeffrey (2005) "Counter-public spheres and the revival of the European public sphere." *Javnost/The Public* **12**(2): 93–110.

Witschge, Tamara (2004) "Digital delibertion: Engaging the public through online policy dialogues." In Peter M. Shane, ed. *Democracy Online: The Prospects for Politicial Renewal Through the Internet*. London: Routledge, pp. 109–122.

Witt, Leonard (2004) "Is public journalism morphing into the public's journalism?" *National Civic Review* **93**(3): 49–57.

Wolin, S. (1996) "Fugitive democracy." In S. Benhabib, ed. *Democracy and Difference: Contesting the Boundaries of the Political*. Princeton, NJ: Princeton University Press, pp. 31–45.

World Internet Usage Statistics. Available online: www.internetworldstats.com/stats.htm (accessed April 10, 2007).

REFERENCES

Wyatt, R., E. Katz, and J. Kim (2000) "Bridging the spheres: Political and personal conversation in public and private spaces." *Journal of Communication*, 71–92.

Yankelovitch, Daniel (1991) *Coming to Public Judgment: Making Democracy Work in a Complex World*. Syracuse, NY: Syracuse University Press.

Young, Iris Marion (1990) *Justice and the Politics of Difference*. Princeton, NJ: Princeton University Press.

Young, Iris Marion (1996) "Communication and the other: Beyond deliberative democracy." In S. Benhabib, ed. *Democracy and Difference: Contesting the Boundaries of the Political*. Princeton, NJ: Princeton University Press, pp. 120–135.

Young, Iris Marion (2000) *Inclusion and Democracy*. New York: Oxford University Press.

Young, Jock (2007) *The Vertigo of Late Modernity*. London: Sage.

Yuval-Davis, Nira, Kalpana Kannabiran, and Ulrike M. Vieten, eds. (2006) *The Situated Politics of Belonging*. London: Sage.

Zaremba, Maciej (2007) "Proletariets diktatur får konkurrens." *Dagens Nyheter*, Kultur, December 29, pp. 6–8.

Zelozer, Barbie (2004) *Taking Journalism Seriously*. London: Sage.

Zelizer, Barbie and Stuart Allan, eds. (2002) *Journalism After September 11*. London: Routledge.

Zimmer, Michael, ed. (2008) "Critical Persectives on Web 2.0." Theme issue of *First Monday*, **13**(3). Available online: www.uic.edu/htbin/cgiwrap/bin/ojs/index.php/fm/issue/view/263.

van Zoonen, Liesbet (2005) *Entertaining the Citizen: When Politics and Popular Culture Converge*. Lanham, MD: Rowman & Littlefield.

van Zoonen, Liesbet and Minna Aslama (2006) "Understanding Big Brother: An analysis of current research." *Javnost/The Public* **13**(2): 85–95.

Zukin, Cliff, Scott Keefer, Molly Andoliona, Krista Jenkins, and Michale X. Della Carpini (2006) *A New Engagement? Political Participation, Civic Life, and the Changing American Citizen*. New York: Oxford University Press.

Index

journalism
  citizen, 177
  declining audiences for, 45
  evolving with Internet, 172
  participatory, 177
  responses to its crisis, 42
  transformation of, 41

Kantola, Anu, 22
Katz, Elihu, 94
Kavada, Anastasia, 196
Keren, Michael, 180
Klang, Mathias, 150
Klinenberg, Eric, 174
knowledge
  and experts, 77
  and opinion, 76
knowledge and civic cultures, 108, 145
Kohn, Margaret, 90, 91, 92

Lembo, Ron, 146
Lewis, Justin et al., 21, 130, 131
Lievrouw, Leah and Sonia Livingstone,
  2006, 150
Lippmann, Walter, 13, 76
Livingstone, Sonia, 73, 75, 160

market populism, 22
Marquand, David, 21
Marshall, T. H., 17
Mayhew, Leon H., 91
McChesney, Robert, 35
McNair, Brian, 55
McQuail, Denis, 4
media
  concentration, 36
  deregulation, 37
  digitalization, 39
  globalization, 38
  proliferation, 35
media generations, 202
media logic, 52, 159
media matrix, 52, 54, 55, 92, 168
Milner, Henry, 25, 47
Mouffe, Chantal, 14, 63, 67, 71, 87, 99,
  100, 111, 112, 122, 135, 194, 197
Mutz, Diana, 97

networks, 29
Nieminen, Hannu, 158, 184
Nip, Joyce, 177
Norris, Pippa, 25, 32, 194
Nunes, Mark, 155, 156

participation, 80
  resons for avoiding, 16
passion
  and engagement, 83
  and political theory, 84
political communication
  as research tradition, 4
  forms of, 143
  pluralization of, 48
political socialization, 105
politics
  alternative, informal, 31
  and entertainment, 138
  and popular culture, 136, 142
  performative, 31
  vs. "the political," 100
popularization, of journalism, 46
practices, online, 195
practices and civic cultures, 116, 146
public connection, 47
public journalism, 42
public relations, 49, 181
public sphere, 34
  and private sphere, 75
  as interactional practices, 72
  as research tradition, 4
Putnam, Robert, 12, 69, 159

Quan-Haase, Anabel and Barry Wellman,
  154

Scheuer, Jeffrey, 134
Schlesinger, Philip, 184
Schudson, Michael, 13, 60
Sennett, Richard, 93
Simons, Jon, 136
Skopcol, Theda, 12
Slaata, Tore, 183
social capital, 107
social movement theory, 108
social skills and civic agency, 71, 98

Titles in the series (*continued from page iii*)